AN INTRODUCTION TO PROGRAMMING USING ALICE 2.2

SECOND EDITION

by Charles W. Herbert

COURSE TECHNOLOGY
CENGAGE Learning

Australia • Brazil • Japan • Korea • Mexico • Singapore • Spain • United Kingdom • United States

COURSE TECHNOLOGY
CENGAGE Learning™

**An Introduction to Programming
Using Alice 2.2, Second Edition**

Charles W. Herbert

Executive Editor: Marie Lee

Acquisitions Editor: Amy Jollymore

Senior Product Manager: Alyssa Pratt

Development Editor: Mary Pat Shaffer

Content Project Manager: Melissa Panagos

Copyeditor: Harold Johnson

Proofreader: Christine Smith

Indexer: Sharon Hilgenberg

QA Manuscript Reviewers: Chris Scriver and
   Serge Palladino

Print Buyer: Julio Esperas

Art Director: Marissa Falco

Cover Designer: Marissa Falco

Compositor: GEX Publishing Services

For product information and technology assistance, contact us at
Cengage Learning Customer & Sales Support, 1-800-354-9706

For permission to use material from this text or product, submit all requests online at **cengage.com/permissions**
Further permissions questions can be emailed to
permissionrequest@cengage.com

Library of Congress Control Number: 2010931093

ISBN-13: 978-0-538-47866-3

ISBN-10: 0-538-47866-7

Course Technology
20 Channel Center Street
Boston, Massachusetts 02210
USA

Cengage Learning is a leading provider of customized learning solutions with office locations around the globe, including Singapore, the United Kingdom, Australia, Mexico, Brazil, and Japan. Locate your local office at:
international.cengage.com/region

Cengage Learning products are represented in Canada by Nelson Education, Ltd.

For your lifelong learning solutions, visit **course.cengage.com**

Purchase any of our products at your local college store or at our preferred online store **www.cengagebrain.com**

Printed in the United States of America
1 2 3 4 5 6 7 14 13 12 11 10

Brief Contents

Table of Contents

Preface

Few subjects have changed as much in the past few decades as computer science. Yet, even in computer science, some things, perhaps the most important things, don't change. Our job as students and teachers in computer science is to develop a firm understanding of the important things that don't change—the immutable foundations of the discipline—while developing the ability to handle the things that do change. The second edition of this book is intended to provide students who are new to the discipline with knowledge of some of the foundational concepts in computer programming—such as Boolean logic, the structure of branching and looping routines, and the notion that you should plan something before you try build it—while exposing them to some of the newest and most popular areas of computing—virtual worlds, animated moviemaking, and video game development—in a fun and interesting way.

Three things have been changed in this new edition of the text:

- It is based on Alice 2.2, rather than Alice 2.0.
- Two new chapters have been added, one on moviemaking and one on video games.
- The language and examples in the chapters from the previous edition have been revised, taking into account feedback from instructors and students on what worked and what didn't work, and how they use the book.

Alice 2.2

The second edition of this book is based on Alice 2.2 because this is the best current version of Alice for learning introductory programming for most students. Some of the features that did not work well, or at all, in Alice 2.0 now work in Alice 2.2, such as the ability to export movie files. Alice 3.0 is still not yet ready for prime time, and when it is it may not be the best vehicle for a general introduction to programming. It is significantly more complicated and more difficult to use than Alice 2.2. Alice 3.0 will probably be a better vehicle for a course in which students wish to develop more sophisticated programming skills, or for students who wish to dive deeper into things like the nature of events or human computer interaction in second-level Java courses. Because it is not as easy to use as Alice 2.0 or Alice 2.2, Alice 3.0 could be a barrier to getting started with programming for many students. Therefore, this book, which is intended to introduce students to the nature of computer programming, is based on Alice 2.2.

New Chapters

The two new chapters on making animated movies and video game programming aren't included to displace any of the previous chapters, but rather to extend them. The chapters should provide students with a good foundation in each area. The animated movie chapter teaches students about things like camera angles, fades, and transitions so that they can use these in programming virtual worlds or in making movies. The video game chapter discusses careers in the video game industry and exposes students to the kinds of programming needed for video games.

These chapters aren't intended for courses in filmmaking or game development, but to introduce these areas to students learning programming because these are things that many modern professional programmers need to learn. Moviemaking and gaming are also areas of interest to most students, which could spark an interest in computer programming and related math and physics.

Many years ago, Galileo and others explored the most fundamental concepts in the universe—optics, heat, mechanics, and so on—as a foundation for understanding and developing the newest technologies of the day. And so it is with modern computer science. The more we understand things that don't change, the more we can explore and affect things that do change. Conversely, the more we wish to know about today's newest and hottest technologies, the more we find ourselves learning about the immutable foundations of the universe in which we live. Today's emerging technologies that motivate people to learn include personal moviemaking and interactive gaming. It may seem like they have been around forever, but moviemaking and video gaming are relatively new topics that are becoming increasingly important for computer programmers, are motivating for students, and are just beginning to appear in most introductory computer programming courses.

Revision in Existing Chapters

The chapters that were in the first edition have been revised for this new edition in response to feedback from instructors and students. More images are included, the language of the text has been clarified in places, and some of the examples and exercises have been changed. The fundamental goals and approach of the text remain the same.

Organization of the Text

Each lesson in this text is composed of two parts—lecture and lab. The lecture part of the lesson includes reading material for the student and lecture material for the teacher that parallels the reading material. For the most part, the reading material is relatively brief and is intended to establish a foundation for the lab component. The new chapter on video game development contains a bit more reading material than most chapters, providing students with an overview of video game development careers and the kinds of programming used in video games.

The lab component includes hands-on tutorials in Alice, and sometimes related work intended to help them explore the concepts of the lesson. The lab component consists of one or more hands-on step-by-step tutorials, followed by review questions and open-ended exercises the students should be able to complete on their own, either individually, or in groups, once they understand the step-by-step exercises. The exercises contain notes directing the students' attention to what they should be learning as they carry out the exercise. It is not enough to complete the steps in the exercise, each student should understand what was done, why it was done, and should be able to repeat the exercise without the directions.

This edition of the book is organized in ten chapters, with goals as follows:

- Chapter 1—*An Introduction to Alice and Object-Oriented Programming*

  Goal: The student will develop a basic understanding of the concept of object-oriented programming and become familiar with the Alice interface.

- Chapter 2—*Methods*

  Goal: The student will learn to create methods in Alice that demonstrate the application of good modular design.

- Chapter 3—*Events*

  Goal: The student will learn to create events in Alice that allow the user to manipulate objects in three-dimensional space and the Alice camera showing viewers those objects.

- Chapter 4—*Algorithms*

  Goal: The student will develop a basic understanding of the logical structure of algorithms.

- Chapter 5—*Boolean Logic in Programming*

  Goal: The student will develop a basic understanding of Boolean logic and its application in computer programming and algorithm development.

- Chapter 6—*Text and Sound*

  Goal: The student will learn to use text, graphic images showing text, and sound as objects in Alice programs.

- Chapter 7—*Recursive Algorithms*

  Goal: The student will develop a basic understanding of recursion in computer programming, and learn to create and manipulate recursive algorithms in Alice.

- Chapter 8—*Lists and Arrays in Alice*

  Goal: The student will develop an understanding of the concept of a data structure and learn to implement the simple data structure known as a list in Alice.

- Chapter 9—*Making Animated Movies with Alice*

  Goal: The student will develop a basic understanding of moviemaking concepts, and will be able to produce short animated movies using Alice.

■ Chapter 10—*Video Game Programming*

> Goal: The student will develop a basic understanding of careers in video game development, the nature of video games, and the role of programming in video game development, and will be able to create simple video games using Alice.

The notion of objects is introduced in the first chapter. Understanding the nature of an object as a collection of properties and methods that can manipulate those properties is critical in modern computer programming. The text mentions but does not explore more sophisticated concepts of object-oriented programming, such as inheritance and polymorphism. In that sense, like Alice, it is not truly object-oriented, but might better be described as object-based. I have found that attempts to introduce students to a complete understanding of objects upon their first exposure to programming is counterproductive. Students can learn more about inheritance and polymorphism after they have some experience with objects and programming. This approach actually enables students to develop a better grasp of important fundamental concepts, like Boolean logic and the nature of algorithms, and to more deeply explore in a second course how inheritance—with public, private, and protected properties, subclasses, super-classes, and so on—really works.

Chapter 3 on event-driven programming precedes the chapters introducing algorithmic structures and Boolean logic for three reasons: first, because of the increasing importance of events in modern computer software; second, because students seem to enjoy working with events more than branching and looping; and third, because Alice handles events in such a simple, easy-to-use way. In practice, Chapters 4 and 5 could easily be covered before chapter three.

Chapters 7 and 8 present topics that are not covered by everyone in an introductory programming course. They are intended to provide students with a first exposure to recursion and to data structures. Some preliminary work with developmental math and English students has shown that the chapters work in making this material accessible to them.

The text can be used for:

> ■ An introduction to the concepts of object-oriented programming during the first several weeks of a semester in which Java or a similar "real" programming language is used for the remainder of the semester. This is the way Alice is being used in many places, with most teachers reporting that at the end of the semester they had actually covered more Java material than if they had not used Alice.
>
> ■ A semester-long course in programming and problem solving for the general student population. Such a course has been shown to be remarkably successful in helping "borderline" students succeed academically. It is especially helpful for students in developmental mathematics and English.

- A programming component for a general computer literacy or applications course. The National Research Council and other groups have suggested that all college graduates should be exposed to computer programming, yet currently less than ten percent of college students are required to take a course in programming. Not much can be done with Java or C++ in three weeks, but Alice and the material in the first few chapters of this book can be used to provide a basic understanding of objects and algorithms.

- A programming course or component of a programming course at the front of a multimedia development curriculum or a game development curriculum.

Lesson plans, course outlines, and additional instructional materials for all three approaches, as well as a complete proposal for a course based on Alice, can be found on the Web site for the text.

Acknowledgements

May people are responsible for the production of this book, and I am grateful to them all.

Mary Pat Shaffer was the Development Editor, who worked most closely with me in creating the book's second edition. I appreciate her hard work, and thank her for her patience and guidance in working with me. This is a much better book because of her efforts.

The book's copy editor was Harold Johnson. Copy editors are the unsung heroes of the publishing world; guardians of language and thought who painstakingly sift through material with a fresh eye, finding things that others miss. Chris Scriver and Serge Palladino served as quality assurance testers, checking each of the tutorials and exercises in the manuscript to make sure that the final text, the student data files, and the solutions for instructors are correct. Course Technology stands out among publishers in part because of their attention to such details.

I am grateful to Alyssa Pratt, Senior Product Manager and Amy Jollymore, Acquisitions Editor for Computer Science & Programming, two key people at Course Technology who helped make this edition of the book possible. Thanks also to Melissa Panagos, Content Product Manager, who guided this book through the production process, and to Marissa Falco, Art Director, who led the efforts to create the new cover and update the interior design for this edition.

The original manuscript for the second edition of this book was reviewed by:

Carol Buser, Owens Community College, Findlay Area Campus
Linda Cohen, Forsyth Tech
Norma Hall, Manor College
Stanley Leja, Del Mar College
Brian Snyder, Northampton Community College

I am grateful for their time and the influential insights they offered. Many improvements were made because of their efforts.

I'd like to thank Walt Johnson, one of my colleagues at Community College of Philadelphia, who provided the IBM flowchart template shown in chapter 4. Walt is retired now, but for years I had the opportunity to teach with him and learn much about programming from him. Early in his career, Walt worked with some now-primitive IBM equipment, like the 1401 and 360 series, and became a master at improvising and inventing new techniques to get a programming job done. Many things change rapidly in the world of computing, but one thing that will never change is the need for people like Walt, filled with intelligence, enthusiasm, and the ability to work well with computers and with the people who use them.

This book is dedicated to my father, George William Herbert, Jr., who passed away during the week when the first edition of the book went to press. He was the athletic director for the Maplewood School District in Colonie, NY for more than 30 years, but spent most of his summers driving our family around the country to visit as many of America's national parks as possible. There are many heroes in the world, but few as important as a good father.

Read This Before You Begin

The Alice software can be found at *www.Alice.org*, the official Alice Web site.

Each chapter of this book has clearly stated objectives, one or more readings related to those objectives, and several hands-on tutorials. A chapter summary, review questions, and further exercises are included at the end of each chapter. Note that Appendix A of this text contains technical information about the Alice software, which is easy to install and use.

Note that the text was quality assurance tested using Alice v. 2.2 on Windows 7 Ultimate.

Student Data Files These are provided on the Course Technology Web site at *www.cengage.com/coursetechnology*. The student data files contain all of the Alice worlds, image files, and so on that are needed within the tutorials.

Solution Files Solutions to the review questions and exercises found in the book are provided for instructors on the text's Companion Site at *www.cengage.com/coursetechnology*. The solutions are password protected. The solution files contain the completed Alice worlds that are the final product of each tutorial.

Foreword to the First Edition

Note from the author: I asked Randy Pausch, Dennis Cosgrove, and Caitlin Kelleher to tell us about the development of Alice, the current state of affairs regarding Alice, and where things seem to be headed in the future. The sections that follow are what they wrote in reply. We've also included their individual bios at the end of this foreword.

All About Alice

So far there have been three distinct phases in the development of Alice, the *Goggles and Gloves* phase, the *"rapid prototyping 3D graphics* phase," and the *Teaching Introductory Programming* phase.

The *Goggles and Gloves* phase started in the early 1990's at the University of Virginia, where Randy was on the faculty, heading a 20-person User Interface Group investigating the boundary where people and technology interact. We were trying to make virtual reality more accessible by developing improved interfaces and lower-cost human computer interaction hardware and software. The paper *Virtual Reality on Five Dollars a Day*, which was published in the April 1991 edition of the ACM SIGCHI's journal *Human Factors in Computing Systems,* describes some of our work. It's available online through *www.alice.org*, where we provide links to publications related to our work on Alice.

We call that first phase the *Goggles and Gloves* phase because we really were focusing on the development of virtual reality systems in which the participant (the term *user* really doesn't seem to capture the sense of it; Disney Imagineering uses the term "guest") enters a virtual world by putting on a VR helmet and gloves. One mantra was "If it doesn't have a glove, it's not VR." At the time, virtual reality was in its infancy. So, in addition to developing VR interfaces, we were working on software systems to test the interfaces. One of our early reseach projects was SUIT, the *Simple User Interface Toolkit*, to which Matt Conway and Rob DeLine contributed heavily. Matt was instrumental in recognizing that vocabulary matters—that the choice of names for behaviors is critically important in a system for novices. His work was very influential in shaping the direction of the development work that led to the Alice system we have today. His doctoral dissertation, *Alice: Easy-to-Learn 3D Scripting for Novices* should be required reading for people interested in how to design systems for novices. It's available on the Web at *www.alice.org*.

The language for programming VR systems required one to think in terms of X,Y,Z coordinates, and to use terms like *translate, scale,* and *rotate* to describe things happening in a virtual world. On the early Silicon Graphics machines, angles were measured in integers representing tenths of a degree, so commands like *rotate -3600* were common. A person needed fairly advanced mathematics skills to program graphical objects in a 3D system.

Engineers and physicists had the keys to get in, but many other intelligent, talented and creative people, such as artists, and filmmakers, did not. Matt saw that the language of VR was a part of the problem and that if we could change the language, then VR systems would be easier to use, and thus more accessible for novices and more powerful for experts at the same time. In his dissertation he wrote that "the tradeoff between power and simplicity is often a false one." He led us in discovering that using more everyday terms terms like *move*, *turn*, and *resize* instead of technically-oriented terms like *translate*, *rotate*, and *scale* could go a long way toward achieving the powerful simplicity that would become one of the hallmarks of Alice. *Turn left 1 revolution* makes sense to a lot more people than *rotate X -3600*.

The first version of Alice emerged as an easy-to-use scripting system for building virtual worlds. The system itself was a combination of C and Python code, with which one could rapidly create virtual worlds by iterating Python scripts. Over the years, the programming features of Python have been replaced with dragging and dropping code elements.

It's important to note that even early versions of Alice could not have been created without the efforts of a dedicated team of people. In particular, PhD student Rich Gossweiler, was responsible for the implementation of the very early versions of Alice, and its co-system DIVER. Tommy Burnette was also responsible for a great deal of the early Alice software implementation. A complete listing of people who have contributed to the Alice project over the years is available at *www.alice.org* .

At about this time (the mid 1990's) our work was funded by a variety of sources, including the National Science Foundation (NSF) and the Defense Advanced Research Projects Agency (DARPA). These are two of the most amazing agencies in the federal government, when it comes to return on investment of public money. A while back, NSF and DARPA asked for funding to explore using computers as tools for communication among educators, scientists, and engineers, and the result is the Internet. We believe that any time they ask for money, Congress should jump at the chance to spend public funds so wisely. One day one of the people from the Department of Defense who was overseeing our project said that we should forget about the virtual reality hardware and concentrate on the software we were building. He argued that our most important contribution was the way in which our software could be used as a rapid development system for 3D graphics prototyping.

During the summer and fall of 1995, Randy spent a sabbatical at Walt Disney Imagineering's Virtual Reality Studio working on the "Aladdin" project which was featured at EPCOT Center and, later, at DisneyQuest. The experience working with the Imagineering team helped to make it clear that we were moving into a realm of work that would require both artists and engineers. In the spirit of bringing artists and engineers together, Randy created a course called "Building Virtual Worlds" in which teams of artists and engineers work together to create interactive virtual worlds. In the Spring of 1997, the research group moved to Carnegie Mellon University, in order to take advantage of the fairly unique cross-disciplinary focus at CMU. However, no story of the Alice system would be complete without acknowledging how gracious the University of Virginia was in allowing us to continue work on Alice seamlessly, by allowing us to transfer our funding and research to another university, and we are very grateful for their support. We have fond memories of the University of Virginia and highly recommend it to students looking for a great place to go to school.

Over the next few years we gradually moved into the third phase of our work as we developed better ways to build virtual worlds. Alice became a workhorse for the "Building Virtual Worlds" course, which was then being taught at Carnegie Mellon, for several years, finally realizing our dream of allowing "a 1,000 creative flowers to bloom." However, with respect to making 3D graphics programming easier, we slowly began to realize that we had the problem inside-out. Instead of thinking about how to improve programming to make 3D graphics more accesible, it started to become clear that 3D graphics could make programming more accesible. A seminal event occured one day when Randy was on a family trip to DisneyWorld. His ten year old nephew Christopher spent the day working with Alice on a laptop as they drove. Chris programmed 3D graphics for eight hours straight, never really having trouble with the 3D part, but constantly asking for help about "where the commas and semicolons had to go." In Randy's words: "I immediately realized that this was a problem we could solve." Some work had already been done on the drop and drag interface, but now the creation of a drag and drop interface for creating Alice programs became a priority.

Wanda Dann and Steve Cooper both became important contributors to the future of Alice at about this time. Wanda, who teaches Computer Science at Ithaca College, and Steve, who teaches at St. Joseph's University, have long been interested in how visualization can be used to teach object-oriented programming concepts. They began to work with us to shape Alice as a better tool to teach introductory programming. We were all beginning to recognize that Alice works well for teaching introductory programming for three primary reasons: minimization of the problems of syntax, the ability to see the results of object-oriented programming in a live virtual world, and the motivation provided by working in such an exciting environment. Since 1999 Steve and Wanda's efforts developing educational materials based on Alice, testing Alice in the classroom, and providing feedback to Dennis and company as the software was refined have been instrumental in shaping the current look and feel of Alice.

In addition to helping students with the technical hurdles, Alice is allowing us to begin changing the ways in which we introduce students to computer programming. The way we teach computer programming hasn't changed much in the past 50 years, despite the fact that the way we use computers has. The first computers that appeared in the middle of the 20th century were literally used to help bombs hit their targets. The early high-level programming language, FORTRAN, was designed to help scientists and engineers with their number crunching. Today, how many high school students are excited about writing code to generate the first 10 Fibonacci numbers? Using Alice, students learn the basics of programming while creating animated stories and games. Wanda Dann has been a strong proponent for using Alice to introduce programming through storytelling at the college-level, and Caitlin has been studying using the activity of storytelling in Alice to interest middle-school girls in learning to program. In addition to being more motivating than assignments like sorting a list of numbers, creating animated stories helps to make computer programming seem less foreign. Not many people are familiar with the concept of mathematical algorithms, but everyone is familiar with storytelling. By using Alice to tell story in a virtual world, young people become engaged in linear sequencing, modular development, and planning before implementation—three of the most important skills for early success in computer programming.

One highly desirable side effect of using Alice to introduce programming through storytelling is that more young women are attracted to the discipline. It's no secret that Computer Science, unlike Law and Medicine, has failed to attract women in significant numbers. Currently, women constitute less than one-third of all Computer Science majors in the US, and less than one-fourth of those earning Ph.Ds in Computer Science. According to Caitlin's research (her dissertation, when completed, will be available at *www.alice.org*), Alice has the power to begin to change that; thereby changing the culture of the Computer Science classroom and workplace.

So where do things stand now? Well, Chuck Herbert's programming textbook is only the second book to use Alice as a tool to teach programming. The Dann, Cooper and Pausch book was the first. Course Technology's Alice CourseCard is the first widely available reference material for Alice 2.0. More material is sure to follow as the number and type of schools using Alice increases. Last year we knew of approximately 30 colleges and universities using Alice. This year we are aware of about 60 colleges and universities and at least that many high schools, as well—and there are probably more folks using Alice that we don't know about.

Currently most people who use Alice seem to be doing so to teach introductory programming, although it is starting to be used in other disciplines. The most widespread educational model for the use of Alice is to use Alice for the first half of an introductory programming course, followed by the use of Java or a similar commercial programming language in the second half of the semester. That model seems to be working remarkably well in places like Duke University, the University of Mississippi, Haverford College, and here at Carnegie Mellon.

Within the past three years other models for the use of Alice have emerged, particularly in the community colleges, and in courses other than computer programming. Here are just a few of the efforts we know about:

- Bill Taylor is leading a group of faculty members at Camden County College in New Jersey who are studying the use of Alice in problem solving and programming courses for students in developmental Mathematics and English courses. Their preliminary work has shown that Alice is an effective tool for improving the overall academic performance of developmental students.

- Chuck Herbert is leading a team of 40 faculty members at Community College of Philadelphia exploring the use of Alice for a programming module in computer literacy and applications courses. Their preliminary work shows that the use of Alice in such courses is attracting new students to computer-related disciplines.

- Sharon Wavle at Tompkins Cortland County College in New York is offering an online programming course using Alice.

- For each of the past two Fall semesters, 1,300 freshman engineering students at Virginia Tech have used Alice as a tool to explore programming and problem solving in their introductory engineering course.

- ITESM, a 33-campus, 80,000 student high-end University in Mexico has been using Alice,and reports very similar results to the American experience, giving us hope that the storytelling approach works in a fairly culture-independent way.

The most common question people ask us these days is about the future of Alice. Right now, the 04/05/2005 Version of Alice 2.0 is reasonably stable and reliable, and runs on Windows and the Macintosh. There are no plans develop it further. Instead, work is beginning on Alice 3.0. How will Alice 3.0 be different? Well, to start with, one thing about it will be the same— it will continue to be provided free of charge to the public from Carnegie Mellon University. The University has been very gracious in supporting us, and we are committed to maintaining Alice as an open source, non-commercial, piece of software. This "purity" is important; many students have worked hard over the years to contribute to the Alice effort, and we believe it must continue to be "for the people." All of Randy Pausch's royalties from the Dann, Cooper and Pausch book are donated by him to Carnegie Mellon, to help support the software development. We are glad to hear that Chuck Herbert has also pledged a portion of his royalties from this book to the Alice effort. We had various corporate sponsors over the years, most notably Intel and Microsoft, and we are pleased to say that Electronic Arts (EA) is a major sponsor of Alice version 3.0.

We expect that Alice 3.0 will be a pure Java implementation, and that you will be able to dump the Java code for an Alice 3.0 world and then work with it in Java. That's a big change from Alice 2.0, which does not create Java code, but works more like an interpreter that directly executes Alice methods. This should serve several purposes, including helping to make the transition form Alice to Java smoother in introductory programming courses.

You can expect the new version of Alice to be more truly object-oriented than the current version. Alice 2.0 is a good tool to introduce the concept of an object as a collection of properties and methods, but it does not provide the ability to create true class-level methods, true inheritance, or the overriding necessary for polymorphism. Alice 3.0 should have some, if not all, of these features.

Caitlin's work has shown that users, especially young people, can do more and learn more with objects that have higher order primitive methods, such as walk, sit, and touch instead of just move, turn, and so on. There will probably be more methods that manipulate objects and their sub-parts together, and the gallery of available objects will probably be richer that the current Alice gallery.

The overall look and feel of Alice will also probably be less toy-like. Anyone who has used Alice for more than a few minutes knows it's not a toy, but it *looks* like a toy. The new version should still be easy to use, but people probably won't think "Fisher Price" when they first see it.

The team that started working on virtual reality interfaces years ago at the University of Virginia had no idea that our work would lead to Alice and that it would become such an important tool in Computer Science education. As is the case with many NSF funded projects, the taxpayers have gotten more than their money's worth, but just not in the way one would have thought reading the original proposals. Such is the path of science and exploration. Now that we know where we are headed, our goal is to make Alice the vehicle of choice for someone's first exposure to computer programming, for everyone—worldwide—from 5th grade through college.

Randy Pausch
Dennis Cosgrove
Caitlin Kelleher
Carnegie Melon University,
December 2005

Randy Pausch was a Professor of Computer Science, Human-Computer Interaction, and Design at Carnegie Mellon University, where he co-founded the university's Entertainment Technology Center (etc.cmu.edu). He led the research group at CMU responsible for the development of Alice. This groups' mission is "to explore and develop the mechanisms by which humans can more effectively and enjoyably interact with technology, and to have fun while doing so." Randy Pausch died as a result of pancreatic cancer on July 25, 2008. He was 47 years old and will be missed by many people in the world of computing.

Dennis Cosgrove is a Human Computer Interaction Project Scientist (formerly Senior Research programmer) at Carnegie Mellon University, where he has spent the last several years as the primary software architect and implementer for Alice 2.0, 2.2, and 3.0. He was one of the principal developers of the earlier PC/Windows 95 Alice implementation at the University of Virginia. In addition to his work on Alice, he has contributed to the development of an eye-tracking system that allows quadriplegics to interact with a computer.

Caitlin Kelleher is an assistant professor of Computer Science and Engineering at Washington University in St. Louis. As a Graduate Research Assistant at Carnegie Mellon University she developed Story Telling Alice as part of her Ph.D. thesis work, which focused on creating a programming system that is attractive to middle school girls by focusing on storytelling. She developed the online, stencil-based tutorials that are part of the current Alice software.

An Introduction to Alice and Object-Oriented Programming

After finishing this chapter, you should be able to:

- [ ] Provide a brief definition of the following terms: algorithm, computer program, object, property, method, state of an object, object-oriented programming (OOP), computer programming language, Integrated Development Environment (IDE), function, event, class, instance, instantiation, and method parameter

- [ ] Run the Alice software and locate and describe the following components of the Alice interface: World window, Object tree, Details area, Editor area, Events area, menu bar, Trash can icon, Clipboard icon, Play button, Undo button, and Redo button

- [ ] Load and play an existing Alice world

- [ ] Create a new Alice world by adding objects to a blank world, positioning them, and using simple methods to animate those objects

- [ ] Print the code for Alice methods and events

- [ ] Save an Alice world as a QuickTime movie file (*.mov)

OBJECT-ORIENTED PROGRAMMING AND ALICE

An **algorithm** is a step-by-step process. A computer program is a set of instructions telling a computer how to perform a specific task. As such, every **computer program** is an algorithm. Early computers were far less complex than computers today—their memories were smaller and their programs were much simpler. To help manage the growing complexity of computers, computer scientists developed the notion of objects and object-oriented programming. Anything that is manipulated by a computer program is an object. It is possible for modern computers to manipulate many objects at the same time.

An object can be something in the physical world or just an abstract idea. An airplane, for example, is a physical object that can be manipulated by an autopilot—a computer that can fly the plane. To the computer, the airplane is an object.

Most objects that computers manipulate are not physical objects. A bank transaction is an example of an object that is not physical. There is usually a paper record of a transaction; however, the transaction itself is simply a concept. It is an object, but not a physical object.

Whether an object exists in the physical world doesn't matter much in terms of what happens inside a computer. To a computer, an object is simply something that can be represented by data in the computer's memory and manipulated by computer programs. The data that represents the object is organized into a set of **properties**. Each property describes the object in some way. For example, the weight of an airplane, its location, the direction in which it is facing, and so on are all properties of the airplane. A computer manipulates an object by changing some of its properties or some of the properties of parts of the object. For instance, the autopilot might change the angle of a wing flap, which in turn affects the entire airplane.

Sometimes the hardware in a computer translates these changes in properties into actions that affect the physical world—as an airplane's autopilot does—and sometimes the changes in an object only affect information in the computer's memory and have no direct effect on the physical world. For example, when a bank deposit is recorded on a computer, the amount of money in the bank balance property of the bank account object is changed, but there is no other immediate effect on the physical world.

The programs that manipulate the properties of an object are called the object's **methods**. An **object** is a collection of properties along with the methods that are used to manipulate those properties. The values stored in the properties of an object at any given time are collectively called the **state of an object**. This modern approach to computer programming is known as **object-oriented programming**, or **OOP** for short.

A **computer programming language** is an instruction set for programming a computer, along with the grammar and syntax for using those instructions. Most modern computer programming languages are object-oriented languages, in which programs are organized as sets of methods that manipulate the properties of objects.

Learning to program a computer is often a difficult task because it requires learning about programming concepts and the language of programming at the same time. It's also difficult because people find it hard to visualize all of the changes that are occurring as a computer program runs. Alice can make it easier to learn to program a computer by helping with both of these problems.

Alice uses an object-oriented style of programming. The objects in Alice exist in a three-dimensional virtual world, much like a modern video game. In fact, the virtual world itself is an object in Alice—it has properties and methods that can be used to manipulate those properties. Alice is similar to other modern object-oriented programming languages, such as Java, C++, or Visual Basic. However, as you will see, Alice is constructed so that you don't need to memorize the grammar and syntax of the language to write computer programs. As you are learning Alice, you can concentrate on learning about the ideas of computer programming, such as the logic of your algorithms, instead of having to worry about the spelling and grammar of a new language at the same time.

The virtual world of Alice is one that you can see. Like the real world, it has three-dimensional space (and time), and each object has properties just like physical objects have properties; these include color, size, position, the direction in which the object is facing, and so on. Alice has a camera that allows you to see its virtual world on a computer screen, just as you might view a movie or a video game. This ability to see what happens to objects in your virtual world makes it easier to learn computer programming with Alice than with almost any other system of programming. For instance, if you try to program a white rabbit to run around in a circle, and instead he simply stays in one spot and spins, you can see that happening on the screen. You can get instant feedback from viewing the way Alice runs the programs you have created. Not every programming system is so easy to use.

NOTE □ □ □ | For more information on computer programming languages, see Appendix C of this book.

In summary, there are three things about Alice that make it a more effective tool for learning programming than almost any other system of programming:

- Minimal memorization of syntax—Alice is constructed so that you do not need to learn the grammar and syntax of a strange new language and can instead focus your attention on the concepts of computer programming.

- Visualization—Alice allows you to see the effects of your programs and any changes you make to them.

- Rapid feedback—Alice provides rapid feedback, which you may get at any time by simply starting your virtual world and watching what happens.

You will also find that Alice is fun and interesting to use, which never hurts when one is trying to learn something new.

TUTORIAL 1A—EXPLORING THE ALICE INTERFACE

In this tutorial, you will explore the Alice 2.2 interface, and then load and play an Alice world. Before starting, you should have a computer system with the Alice software properly installed. Fortunately, installing Alice is easy. The software is available freely from Carnegie Mellon University via their Web site at *www.alice.org*. See Appendix A for further instructions on acquiring, installing, and starting the Alice software.

Anyone attempting this exercise should have experience using a computer. You certainly don't need to be an expert, but you should have some experience with things like word processing and accessing the Internet so that you are familiar with Windows, a mouse, a keyboard, and a printer.

1. Start the Alice software. You will see the Welcome to Alice! dialog box open in front of the Alice Integrated Development Environment (IDE), as shown in Figure 1-1. If Alice opens without showing you the Welcome to Alice! dialog box, click **File**, and then click **New World** to open this window. An **Integrated Development Environment (IDE)** is a computer program that is used to write other computer programs. Most modern programming languages have IDEs with everything you need to create and run computer programs. Alice is no exception, but its IDE is simpler than most. The Alice IDE is often called the Alice interface.

 The *Show this dialog at start* check box appears in the lower-left corner of the Welcome to Alice! dialog box. It should be checked so that the Welcome to Alice! dialog box will appear when Alice starts.

FIGURE 1-1: The Alice interface with the Welcome to Alice! dialog box

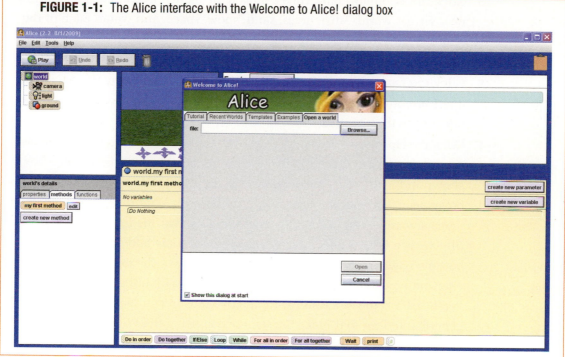

2. Notice that the Welcome to Alice! dialog box has five tabs: Tutorial, Recent Worlds, Templates, Examples, and Open a world. You can return to this dialog box at any time while using Alice by clicking **File** on the menu bar, and then clicking **New World** or **Open World**. Let's look at each of these tabs before continuing.

3. Click the **Tutorial** tab and you will see four Alice tutorials. You won't use the tutorials now, but you may want to come back to them later as an exercise on your own. When you are ready to use the tutorials, either click the tutorial you would like to run, or click the large **Start the Tutorial** button to follow them in order. They are quite easy to follow.

NOTE □ □ □   Dr. Caitlin Kelleher from Washington University in St. Louis created the original version of these tutorials while she was a graduate student at Carnegie Mellon University.

4. Click the **Recent Worlds** tab. You will see thumbnail sketches of the most recently saved Alice worlds. If no worlds have been saved since the Alice software was installed on your system, this tab will say *No recent worlds*.

5. Click the **Templates** tab. Alice comes with six blank templates for starting a new virtual world—dirt, grass, sand, snow, space, and water. Each of the templates includes a texture for the surface, which is called the ground in Alice, and a background color for the sky.

6. Click the **Examples** tab. Several example worlds created by the Alice developers are provided with the Alice software. We'll return to the Examples tab later in this tutorial.

7. Click the **Open a world** tab. This tab is used to access Alice worlds saved on your computer. Click the **Browse** button to open the Open dialog box, as shown in Figure 1-2. This dialog box is very similar to the Open File dialog boxes seen in other programs, such as Microsoft Windows, with navigation icons across the top, a list of folders and Alice worlds from the current directory in the middle, and some controls to view and open files at the bottom. Notice that the Alice world files end with the extension *.a2w*. This extension indicates that the files were created with either version 2.0 or version 2.2 of the Alice software, the two most recent versions. Alice uses a generic interface that looks the same when using the Windows, Apple, or UNIX operating systems. Click the Cancel button to return to the Open a world tab when you are ready to move on.

FIGURE 1-2: The Open dialog box

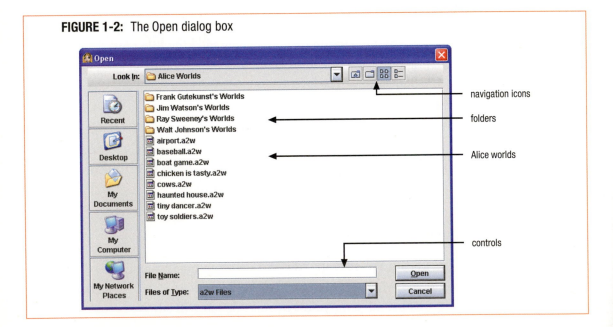

8. Next, you will look at the Alice interface with an Alice world open. Click the **Examples** tab, click the **lakeSkater** thumbnail, and then click the **Open** button to open the **lakeSkater** Alice world. It will take a few seconds for Alice to load all of the elements of the world. The name of each element will briefly appear in a small window in the center of the screen while this happens. When Alice is finished loading the world, your screen should resemble Figure 1-3.

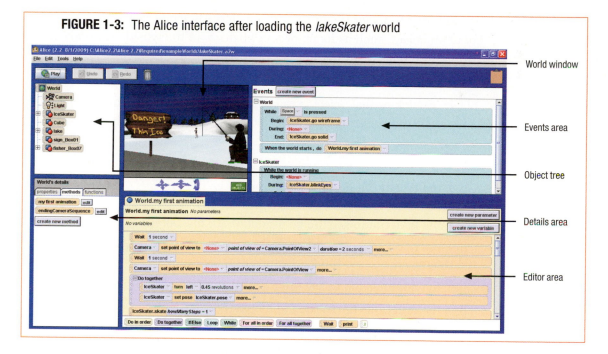

FIGURE 1-3: The Alice interface after loading the *lakeSkater* world

The Main Work Areas of the Alice Interface

The Alice interface has five main work areas, as shown in Figure 1-3: the World window, the Object tree, the Details area, the Editor area, and the Events area. There are also several elements across the top of the interface—a menu bar, three control buttons, a Trash can icon, and a Clipboard icon. Let's look at each of these before playing the *lakeSkater* world.

The World Window

The World window contains a view of the *lakeSkater* virtual world. The set of blue arrows below the window controls the Alice camera, which provides you with the view in the window. Next to the arrows is a large green *ADD OBJECTS* button, which you will use in Tutorial 1C when you create your first Alice world.

The Object Tree

The Object tree appears to the left of the World window. It shows the objects in the current Alice world organized as a tree of tiles, with a tile for each object. The plus sign next to an object shows that it has sub parts, which may be seen by clicking the plus sign. Click the *plus sign* to see the parts of the IceSkater object, and then click the *minus sign* to hide its parts.

The Details Area

The Details area of the Alice interface is located below the Object tree. It has tabs to show properties, methods, and functions for the currently selected Alice object. Properties contain information about an object, such as its color and position in the world. Methods are programs that manipulate an object. A **function** is a method that returns a value, such as the distance between two objects.

You may select an object by clicking that object in the World window or by clicking its tile in the Object tree. Information about the currently selected object will be displayed in the Details area.

Try each of the following:

- Click the **World** tile in the Object tree to see the World's details in the Details area.
- Click the **lake** tile to see the lake's details in the Details area.
- Click the **IceSkater** tile in the Object tree and then the properties tab in the Details area to see the IceSkater's properties.
- Click the **methods** tab to see the IceSkater's methods.
- Click the **functions** tab to see the IceSkater's functions.

The Editor Area

The largest area of the Alice interface is the Editor area, which appears to the right of the Details area. Here, you assemble and edit methods by clicking and dragging tiles from other parts of the interface. The bottom of the Editor area has a row of logic and control tiles that can be used to put branching, looping, and other logical structures into the algorithms that will make up an object's methods. Most of the time that you spend working with Alice will be spent using the Editor area.

The Events Area

The Events area in Alice is above the Editor area. The Events area shows existing events and is used to create new events. An **event** consists of a condition, called an event trigger, and a method, called an event handler. Whenever the event trigger occurs, the event handler is called into action. For example, you might want the sound of a splash to occur if an ice skater falls through the ice. Falling through the ice would be the event trigger, and the method that makes the splash sound would be the event handler.

Some events, such as causing a method to run when a key is pressed, provide user interaction for an Alice world. The flight simulator world that can be accessed through the Examples tab is an interactive world that you might want to take a look at after finishing this chapter. Events are very important for interactive simulations and gaming and are covered in detail in Chapter 3.

Other Elements of the Alice Interface

In addition to the main work areas that you have just explored, the Alice interface also has two icons, three buttons, and a menu bar near the top of the screen.

Buttons and Icons

The Trash can icon and the Clipboard icon are used for editing Alice worlds.

You can delete an item in an Alice world, such as an object or instruction tile, by dragging and dropping it in the Alice Trash can. You can also right-click an object or tile, and select *delete* from the menu that appears.

You can copy any object, event, or method in the Editor area by dragging and dropping its tile onto the Clipboard icon in the top-right corner of the interface, and then dragging it from the Clipboard icon to a new location. You can also duplicate a method tile by right-clicking it and selecting *make copy* from the menu that appears; however, this does not work with Alice objects or events.

The *Undo* and *Redo* buttons near the top-left corner of the interface are also useful for editing an Alice world. You can undo the last change you made by clicking the *Undo* button. The effects of the *Undo* button can be reversed by using the *Redo* button. Alice can remember the last several dozen changes that you made. The Ctrl+Z and Alt+U shortcut keys can be used for Undo. The Ctrl+Y and Alt+R shortcut keys can be used for Redo. There are no shortcut keys for cut, copy, and paste.

The *Play* button is used to play an Alice world.

Menus

The Alice interface has a menu bar at the top of the screen with four menus: File, Edit, Tools, and Help. The menus in Alice are used much less frequently than in many other computer programs. For now, you will look at only a few of the items on these menus. All of the features on the Alice menus are listed in Appendix B.

File Menu The Alice File menu has commands for opening and saving Alice worlds, and for exiting Alice. It also has several other items that you will explore later, including options for exporting an Alice world as a Web page or as a video, and exporting code from an Alice world for printing. You will use these options in later tutorials throughout this book.

Edit Menu Currently the only option on the Alice Edit menu is Preferences, which is used to change settings for the Alice software. Appendix B of this book lists and describes these settings. The most important thing to know for now is that the Alice Edit menu is not used to edit Alice methods in the same way that an Edit menu might be used in other software. Instead, Alice emphasizes the use of a drag-and-drop interface, which uses the editing icons and buttons described throughout this book.

Tools Menu The Alice Tools menu contains three options: Text Output, Error Console, and World Statistics. The Text Output option allows you to see system messages generated as you play Alice worlds, and the Error Console can be used to look at detailed Alice error messages. Both of these are rather sophisticated, and are not very useful for novice programmers. The World Statistics option allows you to see statistics, such as the number of objects in a world, the time the world has been open, and many other useful items. Only some of the information here will be meaningful to you until you learn more about Alice and computer graphics.

Help Menu The Help menu does not contain an option to look up the features of Alice as you might expect. By not providing a way to look up features, the developers of Alice were hoping to encourage people to learn about Alice by experimenting with it.

The Help menu does have three options: Tutorials, Example Worlds, and About Alice. Example Worlds and Tutorials will both take you back to the Welcome to Alice! dialog box. The About Alice option provides general information about Alice and the Alice Web site, *www.alice.org*.

NOTE □ □ □ From time to time you may encounter errors while using the Alice software. The Alice error message box contains a button to copy the error message to the clipboard. You can then paste the message into programs such as Word or Notepad, although they are often too sophisticated for novice programers to read. You may submit bugs and suggestions about Alice through the Alice Web site. The Alice team wants to hear from the users of Alice.

TUTORIAL 1B—PLAYING AN ALICE WORLD

In this tutorial, you will experiment with playing an Alice world. Alice worlds fit into one of two different categories—some Alice worlds are interactive in the way a video game is; others are simply run and viewed like a movie. In either case, experienced Alice users refer to "playing" an Alice world the way most software developers talk about "running" a computer program.

The Alice world you will play in this tutorial is the *lakeSkater* world discussed in Tutorial 1A. It is not an interactive world; rather, it is more like watching a movie of an ice-skater's performance. If you have just finished Tutorial 1A and still have the *lakeSkater* world open, then continue with the steps that follow. If not, you will need to run the Alice software and open the *lakeSkater* world before starting this tutorial.

1. There are three buttons near the top of the Alice interface, labeled *Play*, *Undo*, and *Redo*. *Undo* and *Redo* are used for editing, as described in Tutorial 1A. The *Play* button is used to play the current Alice world. When this button is clicked, the world will play in a larger version of the World window, with player controls at the top of the window, as shown in Figure 1-4. Click the **Play** button now and watch the show unfold. Let the world play through to the end at least once before proceeding.

FIGURE 1-4: The World window with the *lakeSkater* world running

2. Notice that the new window has a speed slider control and five buttons across the top of the window in which the Alice world plays. The buttons are labeled *Pause*, *Play*, *Restart*, *Stop*, and *Take Picture*.

3. The *Restart* button is used to begin playing the current world again from the beginning. The *Pause* and *Play* buttons work like the pause and play buttons on a DVD player. Click the **Restart** button now to restart the *lakeSkater* world, and then experiment with the *Pause* and *Play* buttons.

4. The speed slider is used to change the speed of the world while it is playing. Restart the world, and experiment with the speed slider control.

5. The *Take Picture* button captures an image of the currently playing world and saves it in a data file. Restart the world and click the **Take Picture** button to take a picture of the world. An Image captured and stored dialog box will appear, showing you the full path name of the file that was saved. The stored image file can be viewed and used as any other computer image file can be. By default, the images are saved as JPEG files to the desktop. Appendix B has more information on changing the settings for Alice's screen capture feature. Click **OK** to close the dialog box.

6. The *Stop* button stops the world that is currently playing and returns you to the standard Alice interface. Once the *Stop* button is pressed, you will need to click the standard interface's *Play* button to replay the world. Try this now. After you have finished experimenting, click the **Stop** button one last time to return to the standard Alice interface.

Alice is a graphics-intensive program that can use a lot of a computer's memory, so you should exit the Alice program when it is not in use. Now that you are finished with this tutorial, you should exit the Alice program.

1. Click **File** on the menu bar, and then click **Exit**.

2. If you have made any changes to the current world since it was last changed, a Save World? dialog box will appear, asking you if you want to save the world first. If this happens when you attempt to exit Alice after viewing the *lakeSkater* world, click **No** so that you do not change the saved example world.

NOTE □ □ □ While you are viewing or editing an Alice world, a dialog box will appear every 15 minutes, warning you that you have not saved your Alice world. If this happens while you are playing an Alice world, such as in Tutorial 1B, then it's probably safe to ignore the warning. If it happens while you are creating or editing your own Alice world, then you should save your world.

TUTORIAL 1C—CREATING YOUR FIRST ALICE WORLD

In this tutorial, you will create, play, and save a new Alice world. You should finish Tutorials 1A and 1B before starting this tutorial. You will create an Alice world in which a bunny will move from the right side of the screen to the center, turn to face the camera, and then say "Hello, World!" This is an Alice equivalent of the Hello, World! program that students traditionally write as their first program in a new programming language.

NOTE □ □ □ This tutorial begins with the Alice software closed. If you have an Alice world open, then exit Alice before continuing.

1. Start the Alice software.

2. In the Welcome to Alice! dialog box, click the **Templates** tab. If the Welcome to Alice! dialog box does not open automatically, click **File** on the menu bar, and then click **New World**. You should now see the Templates tab of the Welcome to Alice! dialog box, as shown in Figure 1-5.

FIGURE 1-5: The Templates tab with six templates for new Alice worlds

(screenshot of the Welcome to Alice! dialog box showing the Templates tab with six thumbnails: dirt, grass, sand, snow, space, water, and the Open, Cancel buttons, with "Show this dialog at start" checked)

---

3. Thumbnail sketches for the six new world templates are now available— dirt, grass, sand, snow, space, and water. The templates appear to be very simple, but looks can be deceiving. There is actually a great deal of computer programming behind a new Alice world, with a camera, ambient light, and other elements already in place. Click the **grass** thumbnail, and then click the **Open** button.

A new Alice world based on the grass template is now open, and you can see the standard Alice interface that you used earlier in the chapter. Notice that the Object tree in the upper-left part of the interface contains the four tiles that appear in every new Alice world: *world*, *camera*, *light*, and *ground*, as shown in Figure 1-6. You can see from the way the tree is organized that the other objects are subobjects of the world object.

FIGURE 1-6: The Object tree after starting a new world

The new world also has the default event—When the world starts, do world.my first method—in the Events area, and a blank default method—world.my first method—in the Editor area.

Adding Objects to an Alice World

The next several steps will introduce you to the Alice object galleries and the process of adding objects to an Alice world. Many people get carried away with creating big worlds with many objects when they first start to use Alice. In this tutorial, you will start with a very small Alice world with a minimum number of objects. Objects are added to an Alice world in Scene Editor mode.

1. Click the large green **ADD OBJECTS** button in the bottom-right corner of the World window to enter Alice's Scene Editor mode, which is used to add objects and position them in an Alice world.

2. Note that the Alice interface now looks different, as shown in Figure 1-7. The Object tree and the Details area are still visible on the left, but there is a new area on the right side of the screen. This new area is called the Scene Editor.

FIGURE 1-7: The Alice interface in Scene Editor mode

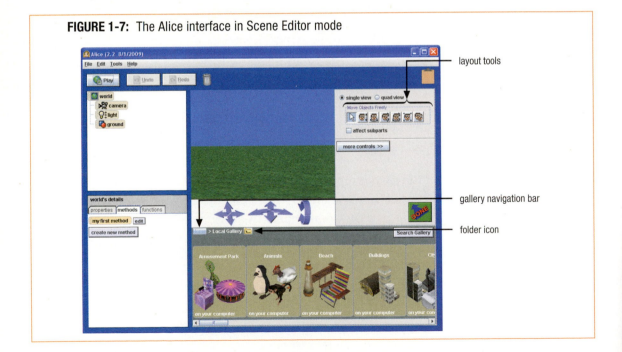

The Scene Editor has new controls, a larger World window, and object galleries on the bottom. The Scene Editor replaces the Events area and the Editor area when you are in Scene Editor mode.

There are two Alice object galleries: a Local Gallery provided with the Alice software, and a Web Gallery maintained by Carnegie Mellon University. (You need an active Internet connection to use the Web Gallery.) The Local Gallery is visible at the bottom of the screen in Scene Editor mode, as shown in Figure 1-7. The galleries are organized as a tree of folders containing related objects. You can navigate the tree of galleries by clicking a gallery folder to enter that gallery, or by using the gallery navigation bar, which is just above the galleries. You will explore the galleries a bit before preparing to add objects to your new world.

1. Click the **folder** icon on the gallery navigation bar to move up one level in the tree of galleries, so that you can see the top level in the tree, as shown in Figure 1-8. Two icons are visible: one for the Local Gallery and one for the Web Gallery.

FIGURE 1-8: The top level in the tree of object galleries

2. Click the **Local Gallery** icon to go back to the Local Gallery. Scroll left and right through the Local Gallery using the scroll bar below the gallery folders, and you will see some of the many categories of objects available in Alice.
3. Find and click the **Animals folder** icon to open the folder. Scroll left and right through this gallery to see some of the animal objects available in Alice.

Object Classes and Instances in Alice

Each of the tiles in the Animals folder represents a class of objects. A **class** is a group of objects with the same properties and the same methods. Objects in the same class are virtually identical to each other, except that the values stored in some of their properties may be different. For example, you could have an Alice world with two Penguin objects. They would both have the same methods and the same properties, but the values of some of those properties, such as location or color, might be different.

Each copy of an object from a particular class is called an **instance** of the object. As you use Alice, you will notice that the object class tiles in the object galleries have the word *class* in their title and each begins with a capital letter, such as *Class Bunny* or *Class Chicken*, but once an instance of an object is placed in a particular Alice world, its name begins with a lowercase letter. Of course, it is possible to rename objects, so this distinction is not always maintained.

The act of adding an instance of an object class to an Alice world is called **instantiation**. The same terminology—classes, instances, and instantiation—is used in most object–oriented programming languages.

You are going to add an instance of an object from the Animals folder in the Local Gallery to your new Alice world. You are going to instantiate a Bunny class object.

1. Click the **Class Bunny** icon. A window with information about Bunny class objects, like the one in Figure 1-9, should appear.

FIGURE 1-9: The Bunny class information window

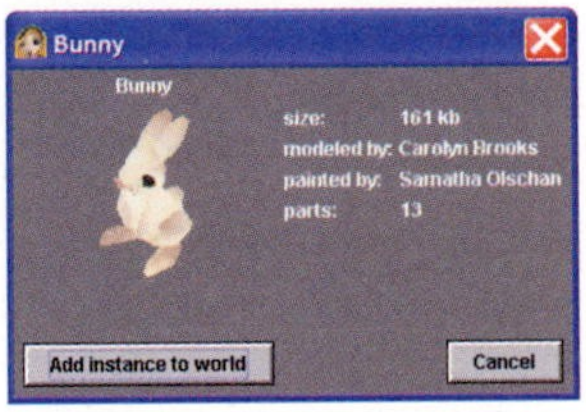

2. Click the **Add instance to world** button to put a bunny into the world. This is sometimes called dropping an object into the world. You should see a bunny appear in the center of the World window.

3. You can also add an object to an Alice world by clicking an object class tile and dragging it into place in the World window. Try this now: drag and drop a **chicken** tile into your Alice world. This approach lets you place the new object wherever you would like on the ground in the World window; however, it does not show you the object's information window first.

4. You should now have an Alice world with two objects—a bunny and a chicken. Notice that tiles for the new objects have also been added to the Object tree. You really don't need the chicken for the rest of this exercise.

To delete the chicken, right-click the object or the object's tile in the Object tree and select **delete** from the menu that appears.

Positioning Objects

The **layout tools** to the right of the World window in Scene Editor mode can be used to manipulate objects. This area contains the seven standard tools listed in Table 1-1.

TABLE 1-1: The seven Scene Editor layout tools

Button	Name	Function
	Pointer tool	Selects an object and moves the object parallel to the ground
	Vertical tool	Moves an object up or down
	Turn tool	Turns an object along its X-Y plane parallel to the ground
	Rotate tool	Rotates an object forward or backward (Z-axis rotate)
	Tumble tool	Freely turns and rotates an object in any direction
	Resize tool	Changes the size of an object
	Duplicate tool	Creates a new instance of the same object

1. The Pointer tool is already selected, so experiment a bit by using the pointer to click the bunny and move it around the screen. Notice that you can move the bunny on the ground with the pointer, but you cannot use the pointer to turn the bunny, rotate it, or move it up and down.

2. Click the **Rotate** tool and try turning the bunny a few times. You may be tempted to use the other tools, but please wait—for now they'll only confuse things. You can come back and experiment with them after you've finished this chapter.

3. Before exiting Scene Editor mode, you need to properly position the bunny in its starting position for the new Alice world you are creating. Remember, in this world, the bunny will move from the right side of the screen to the center, turn to face the camera, and then say "Hello, World!" Position the bunny using the pointer and then the rotate tool, so that it is near the right side of the window, facing toward the viewer's left, as shown in Figure 1-10.

FIGURE 1-10: The bunny in position

4. After the bunny is in position, click the large green **DONE** button to close the Scene Editor and go back to the standard Alice interface.

Adding Some Action

The next step is to add some motion to your world. You can start with something simple—making the bunny move across the screen—and then add a little more action. To make things happen in your world, you need to use methods for the objects. In the Editor area, you already have the default method, which is `world.my first method`. The full name of every method has two parts: the name of the object associated with the method (which comes before the period) and the name of the method itself (which comes after the period).

1. Click the **World** tile in the Object tree in the upper-left corner of the interface.

2. Click the **methods** tab in the Details area. You will see that the name of the method in the Details area is simply `my first method`, but in the Editor, you see the full name, `world.my first method`.

   The default event can be seen in the Events area on the top-right side of the interface. In Figure 1-11, you can see the tile for the default event, which shows that the event trigger is `When the world starts`, and the event handler is `world. my first method`. Any instructions you add to `world.my first method` will be executed when the world starts to play.

FIGURE 1-11: The default event

When the world starts, do | world.my first method

3. Click the **bunny** tile in the Object tree. Now you can see information about the bunny in the Details area. You should be able to see the bunny's methods in the Details area. You create new code for Alice objects by dragging tiles for objects, other methods, and control structures into the method you are currently editing. You get object tiles from the Object tree, method tiles from the methods tab in the Details area, and logic and control tiles from the bottom of the Editor area.

4. Make sure that the methods tab is selected in the Details area, and then find and drag the **bunny move** tile into the middle of `world.my first method` in the Editor area.

5. A short menu will appear asking you to choose the direction and amount you want the bunny to move. Select **forward** for the direction, and then **1 meter** for the amount.

NOTE □ □ □ Information that you must give to a method whenever you use the method is called a **method parameter**. Direction and amount are two parameters for the move method.

6. To test your world, click the **Play** button near the upper-left corner of the Alice interface. You will see the bunny move. It's not much, but it's a start. Click the **Restart** button to play the world again, and then click the **Stop** button to return to the standard Alice interface.

7. To change the amount the bunny moves, click the **1 meter** parameter in the *move* tile in your new method, and then choose one of the values in the drop-down menu. You can also click **other** and then enter a number on the calculator-style keypad that appears. Try changing the amount a few times and then playing the world after each change until you can make the bunny move to approximately the middle of the screen.

8. Let's add a few more instructions. First, find the *bunny turn to face* method tile. It's in the Details area about 11 or 12 tiles below the *bunny move* tile that you just used. You will probably need to scroll down to see it. The parameter for this tile will be the object you want the bunny to face. Click and drag the **bunny turn to face** tile into the Editor area and drop it below the *bunny move* tile, and then choose **camera** as the object you want the bunny to face.

9. Next, you are going to add two tiles to make the bunny speak, and then you will save the world. First, find and drag the **bunny say** tile into the Editor area and drop it below your other two instructions. The parameter for this method is the phrase you want the bunny to say. This parameter is a string parameter, which contains a string of characters from the keyboard. When the parameter menu appears, click **other**, and then type **Hello, World!** in the *Enter a string* input box that appears, and then click **OK**.

Why "Hello, World!"? One of the most useful and popular programming languages ever created was the C programming language developed at AT&T labs in the 1970s. The Hello, World! program first appeared in a C language book written by two AT&T software developers, Brian Kernighan and Dennis Ritchie. Dr. Kernighan, who later became a professor at Princeton University, actually wrote the first Hello, World! program for a tutorial on an earlier programming language. Ever since then, it has been the custom for someone programming in a new language to write a version of the Hello, World! program as his or her first program. Congratulations, you've just done that in a new language! Let's add one more instruction before saving the program.

To add another instruction and save your world:

1. Add another *bunny say* tile to make the bunny say "Hello, Dr. Kernighan!"
2. Now play your world again (several times if you'd like), and when you are finished, click the **Stop** button to return to the Alice interface.
3. To save the world you created, click the **File** menu and then click **Save World**. Notice that Alice has File menu options to Save World and to Save World As. The first time you try to save a new world, you will see the Save World As dialog box, as shown in Figure 1-12. This dialog box looks similar to Save As dialog boxes in Windows programs, such as Microsoft Word; the dialog box contains a navigation bar and other controls. Whenever you want to make a copy of an Alice world, particularly if you have made changes to it and want to keep the old world, use the Save World As feature, and give the new copy a different name.

FIGURE 1-12: The Save World As dialog box

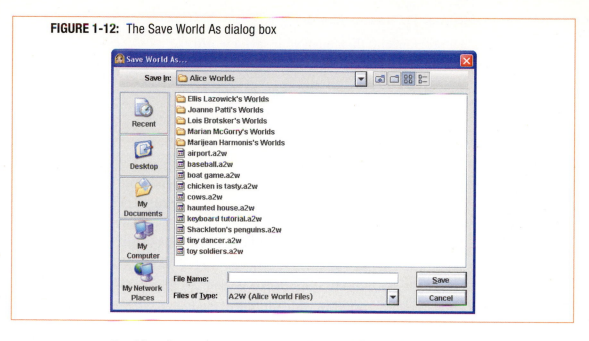

4. Decide where you want to save the world, and then navigate to the correct folder.

NOTE □ □ □   You may save Alice worlds wherever you wish. If you are in a course using Alice, please find out where your instructor would like you to save your files, because this may depend on how your classroom computers are configured. If you are working on your own, you should save them someplace where they will be easy to find; remember (or write down) where you saved each file. Appendix B contains more information about changing the default settings for the save command.

5. Type the name **hello world**, with no punctuation, in the File name box. Notice that the file type shown below the File Name box is A2W (Alice World Files). This indicates that the file you save will end in the extension *.a2w.* You should not change this. Click the **Save** button to save your world.

NOTE □ □ □   Whenever you want to make a copy of an Alice world, particularly if you have made changes to it and want to keep the old world, use the Save World As feature, and give the new copy a different name.

Closing and Reloading a Saved World

Next, close the Alice program and then open your saved world.

1. Click **File** on the menu bar, and then click **Exit**. The Alice program will close.

2. Reopen the Alice software. Click the **Recent Worlds** tab in the Welcome to Alice! dialog box, and then open the **hello world** world that you created. If the name of a world you want to open does not appear on the *Recent Worlds* tab, you can click the **Open a world** tab and look for your world in the tree of folders.

TUTORIAL 1D—PRINTING CODE FROM AN ALICE WORLD

The code from methods and events in an Alice world can be saved on an HTML Web page, which you may then print, send as an e-mail attachment, or view like any other Web page. You can also cut and paste items from the resulting Web page to other programs, such as Microsoft Word or PowerPoint.

The steps in this tutorial show you how to save the code from your Hello, World! project as an HTML file in the root directory on the C: disk drive. If you are a student in a course using Alice, it is best to ask your instructor whether you should use the C: disk drive or another location.

1. Click **File** on the menu bar. Notice that there are menu options to export an Alice world as a Web page and to export code from an Alice world for printing. You are going to use *Export Code For Printing*, which will put the code from your Alice world as text on a Web page, rather than putting the Alice world itself on a Web page as a Java Applet. These options on the file menu are discussed in more detail in Appendix B. Click the **Export Code For Printing** option. The Export to HTML dialog box, as shown in Figure 1-13, should appear.

FIGURE 1-13: The Export to HTML dialog box

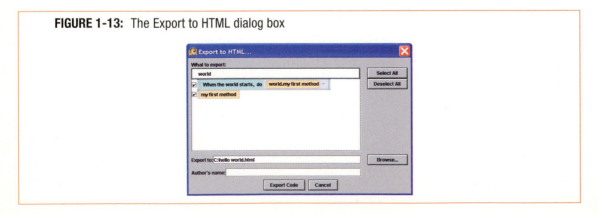

2. Notice that you need to tell the computer what to print. In Figure 1-13, you can see that you have only two items in your world that you can print. The first is the default event, `when the world starts, do world.my first method`, and the second is the default method, `my first method`. The code for an Alice world consists of the code for all of its events, and for all of its methods, but Alice lets you decide what parts of that code you want to print. In this exercise, you will print everything because you only have a small amount of code, but with large Alice worlds you may choose to print just a few items at a time. Make sure that the boxes in front of both items are checked, as shown in Figure 1-13.

3. You now need to tell Alice where you want to save the HTML file. This is the tricky part. Use the Browse button to select the folder where the HTML file will be saved, or enter the file name of the new HTML page in the *Export to*: input box, as shown in Figure 1-13. Use the full path name, such as "C:\hello world.html" (or another name, if directed to do so by your instructor).

4. You also need to add your name as the author of the code. Type your name in the *Author's name* input box.

5. Click the **Export Code** button to create the new HTML document. Now you can find the document where you saved it and open it in a Web browser to look at your code. You can print the HTML page to print your code, cut and paste from the page into Word or PowerPoint, copy the HTML page to another location, send it as an e-mail attachment, or do anything with it that you can do with any other HTML page.

TUTORIAL 1E—SAVING AN ALICE WORLD AS A MOVIE FILE

Alice 2.2 allows you to record the view in the World window while an Alice world is playing as a QuickTime Movie file (**.mov*). You can view QuickTime movies on a computer with QuickTime-compatible video player software, or via a Web browser equipped with a QuickTime plug-in. Many computers and most Web browsers are equipped with such facilities. QuickTime movies can also be e-mailed, burned on a CD or DVD, and posted to Web sites, such as YouTube. You can convert QuickTime movies to other formats and edit them with video-editing software, such as Adobe Premiere or Apple's iMovie. Chapter 7 of this book discusses this further.

In this tutorial, you will record as a movie file the *hello world* Alice world that you created in Tutorial 1C.

1. Start Alice, and open the **hello world** Alice world that you created in Tutorial 1C.

2. Click the **Play** button and watch the world as it plays so that you are more familiar with how long it takes to play. This world should take about three seconds to play, so the movie you save will be short.

3. Click the **Restart** button if you wish to view the world again. Then, click the **Stop** button to return to the standard Alice interface.

4. Click **File** on the Menu bar, and then click the **Export Video** option. You may be surprised to see that the Save World As dialog box appears. This is because you must save the world again as a part of the process of recording a video. Type the the name of your world in the File Name box.

5. Click the **Save** button to save the world. When Alice finishes saving your world, the video recording window will appear, as shown in Figure 1-14.

FIGURE 1-14: The video recording window

6. You will only use a few of the items in the video recording window to record this video. The rest are discussed in Chapter 7. Begin by typing the name of your movie file in the File name box. It does not need to be the same as the name of the Alice world.

7. Now you will actually record the video. You will click the **Record** button to start recording. The world will start playing *and* recording when you press the *Record* button. You will need to press the **Stop Recording** button to

finish recording; the recording does not stop automatically when the world finishes playing. Do this now—click the **Record** button to start recording and then click the **Stop Recording** button to finish recording. You will need to pay attention and be quick; this movie is only about three seconds long.

8. Next, you will export the recorded video to a file. The file will be saved in the same folder as the Alice world file (*.a2w*) for this world. Click the **Export Video** button. If the button is dimmed, then wait—Alice is not yet finished rendering the video.

9. When you click the **Export Video** button, Alice will first encode the video and then the audio. Next, Alice will merge the sound and video. Information boxes will appear telling you that this is happening, as shown in Figure 1-15. Alice renders and saves the movie file frame by frame. This process takes a few seconds for a short video and much longer for long videos, so be patient. When the information boxes stop appearing, then the video has been saved.

FIGURE 1-15: A message box appears as Alice saves a recorded video

10. Click the **Stop** button to close the window, and then close the Alice software. Your video file should be in the same folder as the Alice world you recorded.

Chapter Summary

This chapter consisted of an introduction followed by five hands-on tutorials. The introduction discussed the following:

- ☐ An algorithm is a step-by-step process; computer programs are algorithms.

- ☐ Most modern computer programming languages are object-oriented languages in which programs are organized as sets of methods that manipulate the properties of objects stored in a computer.

- ☐ An object is a collection of properties and methods that can be used to manipulate those properties.

- ☐ The values stored in the properties of the object at any given time are called the state of the object.

- ☐ A class of objects is a collection of all objects that have the same properties and methods.

- ☐ Each individual object in a class is called an instance of that class.

- ☐ Alice uses an object-oriented style of programming; in Alice, objects exist in a three-dimensional virtual world, which can be seen on a computer screen.

- ☐ Alice makes it easier to learn programming because it requires minimal memorization of syntax and it provides visualization and rapid feedback.

In Tutorial 1A, you explored the Alice interface, which has five main work areas—the World window, the Object tree, the Details area, the Editor area, and the Events area, as well as a menu bar, a *Play* button, an *Undo* button, a *Redo* button, a Trash can icon, and a Clipboard icon.

In Tutorial 1B, you learned to load and play an Alice world, and to use the speed slider control and the *Pause*, *Play*, *Restart*, *Stop*, and *Take Picture* buttons that appear when a world is playing.

In Tutorial 1C, you learned to create your own simple Alice world. You learned how to add objects from the object gallery, position them in the virtual world with the Scene Editor layout tools, and add instructions to the default method that is initiated by the default event.

In Tutorial 1D, you learned that Alice code may be exported to an HTML Web page and then viewed or printed from the Web page.

In Tutorial IE, you learned how to export a playing Alice world as a QuickTime movie file.

Review Questions

1. Define the following terms:

☐ algorithm	☐ function	☐ object
☐ class	☐ IDE	☐ OOP
☐ computer program	☐ instance	☐ property
☐ computer programming language	☐ instantiation	☐ state of an object
☐ event	☐ method	
	☐ method parameter	

2. List and describe the five tabs in the Welcome to Alice! dialog box, which appears when the Alice software is first started.

3. Describe the role of each of the five main areas of the Alice interface: the World window, the Object tree, the Details area, the Editor area, and the Events area.

4. What is the difference between a method and a function?

5. Briefly describe how to do each of the following:
   a. Add an object to an Alice world.
   b. Delete an object from an Alice world.
   c. Change the value of a method parameter.
   d. Capture and store an image of an Alice world while it is playing.
   e. Save an Alice world.
   f. Print the code from an Alice world.
   g. Save an Alice world as a movie file.

6. What is the difference between the *Pause* and *Stop* buttons in the window for a playing Alice world?

7. What is the function of the speed slider control in Alice?

8. What is the difference between the standard Alice interface and Scene Editor mode?

9. List and describe the function of the following Scene Editor layout tools: the Pointer tool, the Vertical tool, the Turn tool, the Rotate tool, and the Tumble tool.

10. Alice methods have full method names, such as `robot.dance.` Describe the meaning of the two different parts of the full method name.

Exercises

1. It can be very difficult for people to write clear and complete algorithms, such as a set of directions. People often take things for granted when writing directions; however, individuals are usually able to interpret poorly written directions. For example, directions often contain phrases like "turn left at the third red light." But, what if one of the lights is green? Does it count? Would a person even ask this question, or would he or she just make an assumption about what the writer meant? How would a computerized robot handle such a problem? Try writing a detailed set of directions for a simple everyday process, such as making a pot of coffee, and then exchange your directions with another student. Critique each other's directions to see if they are clear and complete. Did the writer make assumptions that caused steps to be left out of the algorithm?

2. Comments can appear in the code for Alice methods to identify the author and purpose of the method, and to describe any parameters or special techniques used in the method. You can add comments to a method by dragging the *comment* tile, shown in Figure 1-16, and dropping it into the method where you want the comment to appear. You can edit the *comment* tile by clicking it, and then editing the text.

Open the **hello world** Alice world that you saved as part of Tutorial 1C, and add two comments at the beginning of the method, as shown in Figure 1-16.

Comments will be discussed in more detail in Chapter 2.

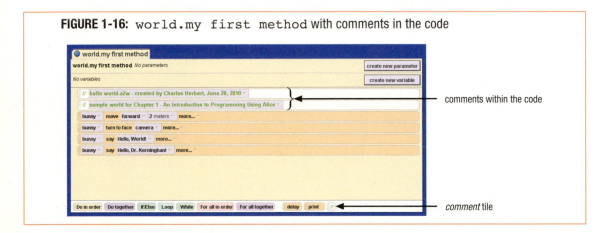

FIGURE 1-16: `world.my first method` with comments in the code

3. Open the **hello world** Alice world that you saved as part of Tutorial 1C, and add some additional animation to the world. You may want to experiment with the methods to make the bunny move, turn, and roll. See if you can do the following:

    a. Make the bunny jump up and down.
    b. Make the bunny jump up, turn one revolution, and then land.
    c. Make the bunny jump up, roll one revolution, and then land.
    d. Make the bunny move and turn several times to go around in a full circle (or polygon).

    What is the difference between turn and roll? What difference does it make if you change the order of instructions in a particular world? When you are finished, click Tools on the menu bar, and then click World Statistics to see how long your Alice world has been open.

4. The methods available for the Bunny class of objects are called *primitive methods* and are available for all Alice objects. Certain classes of objects, such as the Penguin class, have additional methods available. Try starting a new world with a penguin and experiment with some of its user-created methods. These methods include `wing_flap, glide, jump, jumping, walk, and walking`.

5. Try creating, playing, and saving another Alice world on your own. While doing so, follow these two pieces of advice:

    a. Follow McGinley's Rule for New Programmers: K.I.S.S.—Keep it Small and Simple. You should experiment, but be careful about getting in over your head. Try a few simple things with only a few objects to get started.
    b. Try to plan what you will do in the world before you start working on it. Keep in mind the Rule of the Six P's: Proper Prior Planning Prevents Poor Performance. Many developers of Alice worlds like to outline or storyboard their work first. They draw a series of a few simple sketches of what they would like to try to make the objects in the world do. Professional programmers also use pseudocode and flowcharts, which you will learn about in later chapters, to design the algorithms that methods will follow.

6. Try planning and creating a simple Alice world as part of a team of students. How does this experience differ from working on your own?

7. In Alice, tool tips appear if you place the mouse pointer on one of the tools, buttons, or tabs on the Alice interface and leave it still for more than two seconds. Table 1-1 in Tutorial 1C shows how the Scene Editor tools can be used to manipulate objects, but the table doesn't tell you everything. The tool tip for the pointer tool in the Scene Editor mode lists several additional ways to use the Alice pointer. See if you can find out what they are.

8. There are many Web sites that contain useful information about computer technology. Here are two for you to try: *www.webopedia.com* and *www.wikipedia.com*. Both are free online encyclopedias. Webopedia focuses on computer technology and provides a brief definition of terms and links to other sites. Wikipedia is more general. Wikipedia is a free Web-based encyclopedia written collaboratively by volunteers. Pick a few of the terms from this lesson, such as algorithm, object-oriented programming, or IDE, and see what you can find out. You can also look up people, such as Brian Kernighan. The Wikipedia page at *http://en.wikibooks.org/wiki/Computer_programming/Hello_world* has the Hello, World! program in dozens of different computer languages.

9. A class is often called "a blueprint for instances of an object." What does this mean with regard to object-oriented programming?

10. Alice lacks some of the features of a true object-oriented programming system, such as polymorphism and true inheritance. See if you can find out what the terms *inheritance* and *polymorphism* mean with regard to object-oriented programming, and describe them in your own words.

Methods

After finishing this chapter, you should be able to:

☐ Provide brief definitions of the following terms: top-down design, module, modular development, reusable code, software development cycle, test for correctness, unit test, integration test, testing shell, primitive methods, user-defined methods, encapsulation, off-camera, CamelCase, method header, variable, and parameter

☐ Describe the processes known as top-down design and modular development, and discuss why they are often used together, how organizational charts are used in these processes, and some of the advantages of modular development of new software

☐ List and describe the steps in the software development cycle

☐ Describe the difference between primitive methods and user-created methods in Alice, and demonstrate how to run primitive methods to directly position objects and manipulate the camera in an Alice world

☐ Create new methods in Alice in a manner that demonstrates good top-down design and modular development

☐ Create and demonstrate the use of methods in Alice that contain method parameters

TOP-DOWN DESIGN AND MODULAR DEVELOPMENT

Engineers are the people who design and build things, and just as civil engineers design and build roads and bridges, software engineers design and build computer software. Computer programming is part of the software engineering process, which usually involves newer object-oriented design, combined with more traditional methods of algorithm development.

Object-oriented software engineering starts with understanding what the new software must do. Software engineers decide what objects will be needed for the program, and then use existing objects and build new ones to create the software. You will use Alice to develop new software—in this case, small virtual worlds—using objects from Alice's galleries of objects. You will focus on creating methods and events for the objects in your virtual worlds. Since each method is an algorithm, a step-by-step process, this chapter focuses on the design of algorithms. You will learn some techniques for designing and building methods so that you can begin to design and build your own computer programs.

The language of problem solving is often used in engineering. Working to complete a task that is part of an engineering project is seen as building a solution to a problem. The process starts with problem specification. Once you have a clear understanding of the problem, you can start to solve it.

It's easier to solve smaller problems than it is to solve big ones, so good engineers often start solving a problem by trying to break it into more manageable parts. This process of decomposition is sometimes referred to as a divide-and-conquer approach to problem solving. In this approach, a problem is broken into parts, those parts are solved individually, and then the smaller solutions are assembled into a big solution. Computer programmers and software engineers do the same thing when developing new software.

NOTE□ □□ According to projections by the United States Department of Labor, software engineering will be one of the fastest growing career fields over the next decade. For more information about software engineering as a career, view the Department of Labor's Occupational Outlook Handbook online at *www.bls.gov/oco/ocos267.htm*.

This process, also known as **top-down design** or **top-down development**, starts at the top with one concept or big idea, which is then broken down into several parts. If those parts can be further broken down, then the process continues. The end result is a collection of small solutions, called **modules**, which collectively contain the overall solution to the original problem.

Here is an example of top-down development from the world of business. Imagine that you want to write a computer program to process the payroll for a large company. Your big idea is named "Payroll." What would you need to do if you were going to process a payroll? Generally, you would need to get some data, perform some calculations, and output some results. Figure 2-1 shows Payroll broken down into these three modules.

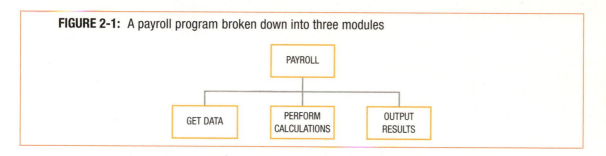

FIGURE 2-1: A payroll program broken down into three modules

You can go further in breaking down the problem. There are two different sets of data—old data, such as a list of employees, and new data, such as the number of hours each person worked during a specific week. The old data will probably come from a database, while the new data will be entered into the system for the first time. Therefore, the Get Data module can be broken down further into Get Old Data and Get New Data. If the Perform Calculations and Output Results modules are broken down in a similar manner, and then the submodules of those modules are broken down, and so on, then the final design might look something like the one in Figure 2-2. Such a diagram is called an organizational chart.

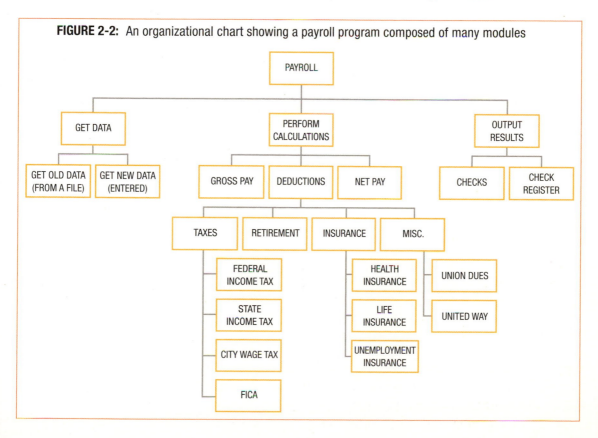

FIGURE 2-2: An organizational chart showing a payroll program composed of many modules

Organizational charts show how separate units are organized to form a single complex entity. The upper levels are broken down into the parts at the lower levels, and the parts at the lower levels are layered together to form the upper levels. In Figure 2-2, you can see how the specific modules are combined to form the overall payroll program. A programmer, or a team of programmers working together, can create each of the modules as software methods, and then put them together to build the entire payroll program.

The process of top-down design leads to **modular development**, in which parts, or modules, are developed individually and then combined to form a complete solution to a problem. Modular development of computer software has the following advantages, especially for larger projects:

- Modular development makes a large project more manageable. Smaller and less complex tasks are easier to understand than larger ones and are each less demanding of resources.

- Modular development is faster for large projects. Different people can work on different modules, and then put their work together. This means that different modules can be developed at the same time, which speeds up the overall project.

- Modular development leads to a higher-quality product. Programmers with knowledge and skills in a specific area, such as graphics, accounting, or data communications, can be assigned to the parts of the project that require those skills.

- Modular development makes it easier to find and correct errors in computer software. Often, the hardest part of correcting an error in computer software is finding out exactly what is causing the error. Modular development makes it easier to isolate the part of the software that is causing trouble.

- Most important, modular development increases the reusability of your solutions. Solutions to smaller problems are more likely to be useful elsewhere than solutions to bigger problems.

The last point in this list is one of the most important concepts in all of computer programming. **Reusable code** makes programming easier because you need to develop the solution to a problem only once; then you can use that code whenever you need it. You can also save the modules you have developed and reuse them later in other projects, modifying them if necessary to fit new situations. Over time, you can build libraries of software modules for different tasks. All computer programs, from the lowest levels of an operating system that directly control hardware to the most complex user applications, are made up of layers of short programming modules that are constantly reused in different situations.

Object-oriented programming, by its very nature, encourages the development of reusable code. Objects created for one project can be reused as needed for other projects.

Figure 2-3 shows a portion of the methods tab for the iceSkater from the *lakeSkater* world seen in Chapter 1. Methods to perform simple tasks, such as `spin`, `blinkEyes`, and `jump`, are reused as necessary to form the overall routine in this Alice world. The entire skater object can be reused in other worlds where different routines might be assembled from these simple methods. As you create Alice worlds, you should keep this concept in mind and try to write small reusable methods as often as possible. This approach to programming will serve you well in any language you use and is one of the driving principles behind much of the modern object-oriented approach to programming. Good computer software is filled with reusable code, and Alice is no exception.

FIGURE 2-3: The methods tab for the iceSkater from the *lakeSkater* world

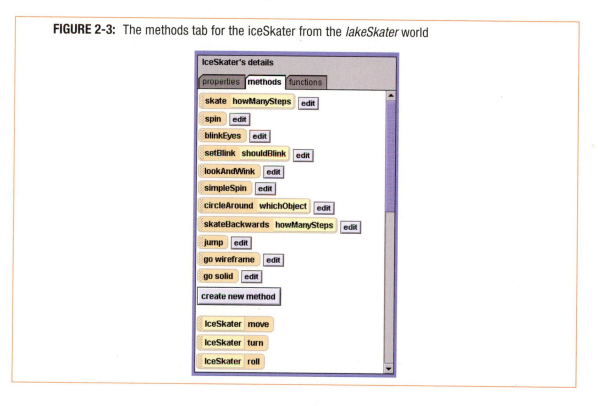

THE SOFTWARE DEVELOPMENT CYCLE

Computer programming and software engineering generally follow a four-step process known as the **software development cycle**, in which developers design, code, test, and debug software, as shown in Figure 2-4. Individual developers may use variations of the cycle, but they all basically follow a process similar to this one for overall software projects, as well as for the individual methods that make up each project.

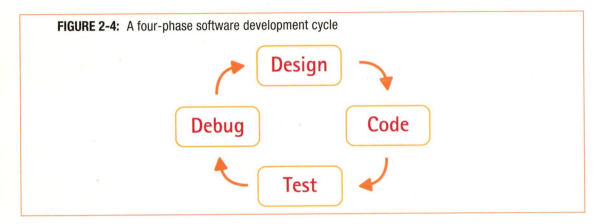

FIGURE 2-4: A four-phase software development cycle

Designing Methods

Software design begins by writing clear specifications for what the software is supposed to do. Before you can design something, you must have a clear understanding of what it is supposed to do. Top-down development and modular design are used from the beginning of the design process and help designers break a complex problem into parts that can be more easily understood. The parts can then be coded and tested as individual methods, each with its own specifications for completing a single task.

Techniques for describing the design of software methods, such as the use of flowcharts, pseudocode, and storyboards, will be discussed in subsequent chapters. In this chapter, to begin, you simply list or outline what your new software is supposed to do, and then break down your design into smaller parts that can be developed as individual methods performing single tasks.

The software design process does not depend on a particular programming language, although it does help to know what language will be used to implement the software. That way, your design can take advantage of the features of that language. This is difficult for new programmers, who are trying to learn about software design and a new language at the same time. In this chapter, you will gain some more experience using Alice, which will help you become a better designer of Alice software.

Coding Methods in Alice

One of the unique features of Alice is its drag-and-drop interface, in which tiles containing existing instructions or logic and control structures can be dragged into place to create a new method. Recall from Chapter 1 that tiles for existing methods can be found on the methods tabs for various objects, while logic and control tiles can be found at the bottom of the Editor area, as shown in Figure 2-5. Logic and control tiles will be discussed in Chapter 3.

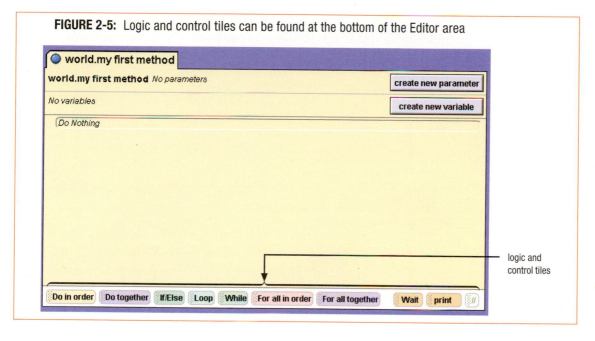

FIGURE 2-5: Logic and control tiles can be found at the bottom of the Editor area

In more traditional programming languages, such as Java, C++, or Visual Basic, the coding phase of software development includes carefully translating a software design into a particular language, and then entering that language into the computer. Dragging Alice's language tiles into place to create new methods, however, is a little different. Alice programmers are able to focus their attention on the logic of how new methods will operate rather than on the syntax of the language.

Testing and Debugging Alice Methods

Software testing is a specialized branch of software engineering. The techniques that professional software developers use to test newly developed methods are varied and can be complex, but generally they involve answering a few simple questions, such as the following:

- Does the new method do what it is supposed to do? This is known as a **test for correctness**. Tests for correctness measure whether the program meets the original specifications.

■ Is the method reasonably efficient? How much time does it take for the method to complete its task, and how much storage space does it use? If a program takes two hours to sort a list that another program can sort in two seconds, then it is not a very time-efficient program. Similarly, one program might use more or less storage space than another program. Typically, time efficiency is more critical than space efficiency as computer memory chips and disk drives become larger and less expensive.

■ Does the method have any undesirable side effects? For example, if a method to print a long document also erases the hard disk drive, then the method has an undesirable side effect. Side effects can be related to how methods change stored data, how one method affects another method, or even how two instructions in the same method affect each other. For example, Alice methods to move and turn an object at the same time can produce unexpected results if the programmer failed to consider that the object's direction was changing as it turned.

Software testers must develop a testing plan that examines new software under all possible circumstances. If the program will perform operations on data sets, such as sorting a list or performing a numerical analysis of the data, the software testers need to develop sample data sets that test the program under all possible scenarios.

Software developers perform two general types of tests: unit tests and integration tests. A **unit test** checks to see if the method works as expected all by itself. An **integration test** checks to see if the method works when it is placed into a larger program in combination with other methods.

Sometimes a unit test can be performed by running a newly developed method all by itself, and sometimes it is necessary to create another method, called a **testing shell**. A testing shell is a short method that simulates the environment in which a newly developed method will be used.

In the *lakeSkater* demonstration that you have already seen, the iceSkater's spin method could be tested without a testing shell. The method could be run all by itself, and the tester could observe the action to see if the method performs according to specifications.

Once a method has been unit tested and debugged, it can be integration tested. That is, it can then be put in position in the overall program, which is then be run to see if it works with the new method in place.

This chapter only scratches the surface of testing and debugging, which can be quite complicated and detailed. For now, just try to keep the following questions in mind:

■ Does the method do what it supposed to do according to the specifications? Does it work by itself? Does it work as a part of a larger program?

- Is it reasonably efficient? Is there any indication that something is taking too long or using up too much memory?

- Is anything unexpected happening when the program runs?

- Has the program been tested under all possible circumstances? This is especially important if the program has numeric input. For example, what happens if you tell a method to move forward a negative amount? What happens if you tell a method to turn a negative number of revolutions?

If any problems are discovered when the software is tested, then the cause of the problem needs to be isolated. Here unit tests are most helpful, especially if the software has been developed as many smaller modules, rather than as a few larger modules. Once you know what is causing the error, you can develop a plan to fix the problem, modify the necessary method or methods, and then test again.

TUTORIAL 2A—WORKING WITH PRIMITIVE METHODS IN ALICE

Alice objects have two kinds of methods—primitive methods and user-defined methods. **Primitive methods** are built-in, predefined methods that are part of each Alice object. They provide simple basic behaviors, such as move, turn, and roll. **User-defined methods** are written by people who use Alice. Some of the objects in the Alice object galleries already include user-defined methods in addition to the standard set of primitive methods. For example, the Penguin class has a `wing_flap` method. You can use primitive methods and user-defined methods to write new methods of your own.

Primitive methods are also encapsulated methods. **Encapsulation** means that the details of a method are hidden from the user; the user cannot see or edit the details of the method. All primitive methods are encapsulated. In Alice, user-defined methods are not encapsulated.

To examine the methods for Penguin class objects:

1. Start Alice, click the **Templates** tab when the Welcome to Alice! dialog box appears, and begin an Alice world using the snow template.
2. Once the new world is open, click the large green **ADD OBJECTS** button in the lower-right corner of the World window to enter Scene Editor mode.
3. Now you can see the object galleries at the bottom of the screen. Click the **Animals gallery**, and then find and click the **Class Penguin** tile.

You should see the Information window for the Penguin class of objects, as shown in Figure 2-6. It contains information about the designers who modeled and painted the Penguin class, specifies how much memory is required for an instance of the object, and lists user-created methods that the designers included to give the penguin additional behaviors, such as flapping its wings, turning its head, and walking.

FIGURE 2-6: The Information window for the Penguin class of objects

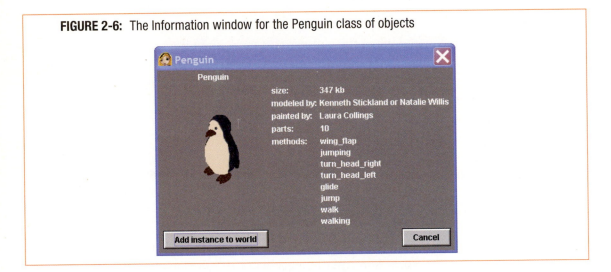

Let's add the penguin to the new world and then look at its methods tab.

1. Click the **Add instance to world** button, and then click the **DONE** button. This will return you to the standard Alice interface.

2. Click the **penguin** tile in the Object tree and the **methods** tab in the Details area. You can now see the methods tab for your instance of the Penguin class of objects, which is shown in Figure 2-7.

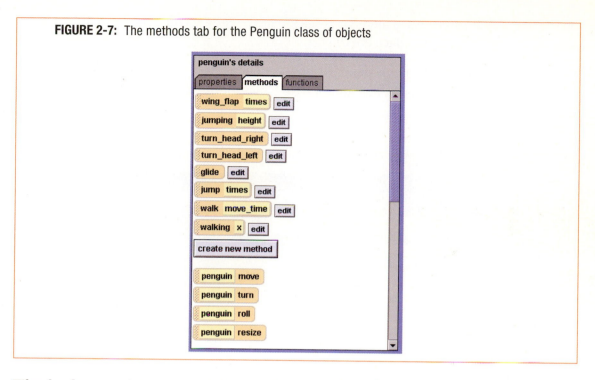

FIGURE 2-7: The methods tab for the Penguin class of objects

Tiles for the penguin's user-created methods appear above the *create new method* button and are each followed by an *edit* button. Notice that this set of methods matches the list in the Penguin's Information window. The tiles below the *create new method* button are the primitive methods that come with each Alice object. They have no *edit* button because they are encapsulated.

Running Primitive Methods Directly

Primitive methods may be used to build more complex methods, or they may be run directly. You can run a primitive method directly by right-clicking an object or an object tile in the Object tree, and then selecting the method you want to run from the list that appears.

One of the penguin's primitive methods is the `turn to face` method. Let's run this method directly to make the penguin face the camera.

1. Right-click the **penguin** tile in the Object tree, and then select **methods** on the small menu that appears. Now you should see a list of the penguin's primitive methods, as shown in Figure 2-8.

FIGURE 2-8: A menu showing the penguin's primitive methods

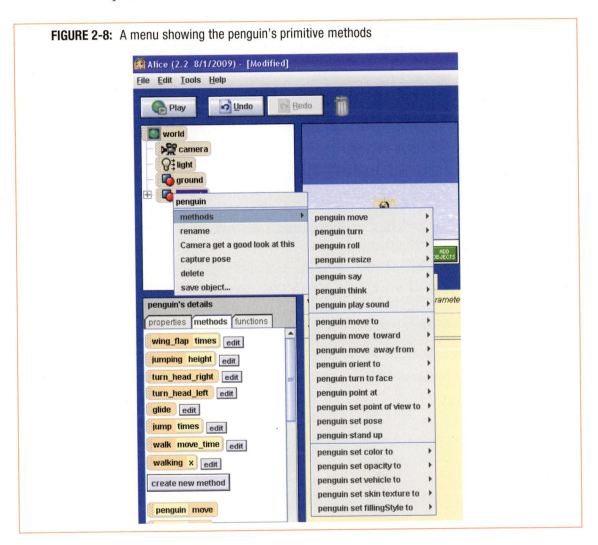

2. One of the methods in the list is `penguin turn to face`. It's about halfway down the menu. Point to **penguin turn to face**, and then click **camera** from the submenu that appears. On the screen you should see the penguin turn to face the camera.

This is an example of how you can run primitive methods directly, without saving them as part of a program in the Alice world. This is a good technique to use to manipulate objects when setting the scene for an Alice world, or simply to learn how certain methods work.

Using Primitive Camera Methods to Find a Lost Object

Sometimes in Alice, an object is off-camera, and you may not be sure exactly where the object is. **Off-camera** means that an object cannot be seen on the screen with the camera in its current position. Often it can be difficult to find an off-camera object by manually manipulating the camera. There are several primitive methods that you can run directly to help find the lost object.

1. First, using the blue arrow controls at the bottom of the World window, manipulate the camera so that you cannot see the penguin anymore. Now the penguin is off-camera.

2. Now you can find the penguin. Right-click the **camera** tile in the Object tree, select **methods** on the menu that appears, and then select **camera point at**. On the target menu that appears, select **penguin**, and then select **the entire penguin**, as shown in Figure 2-9. On your screen you will see that the camera is now pointing at the penguin. Can you see how this might be a useful method to run directly?

FIGURE 2-9: A menu showing the camera's primitive methods with the `camera point at` method selected

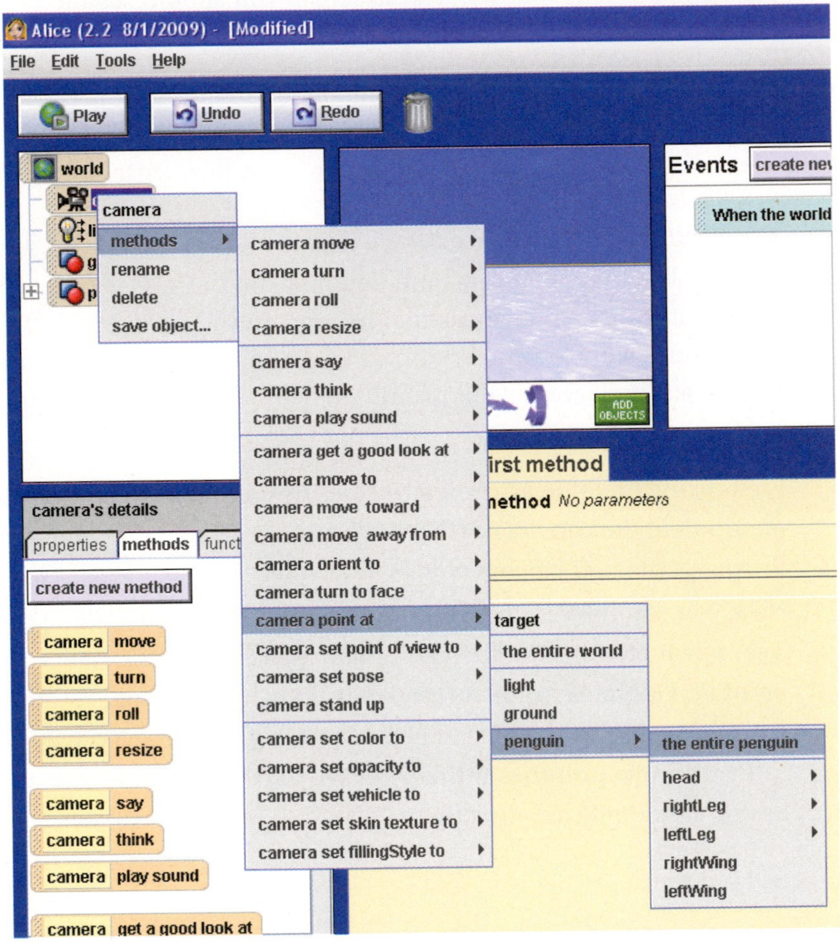

3. Using the blue arrows, again move the camera so that the penguin is off-camera.

4. This time, run the `camera get a good look at` method on **the entire penguin**. Do you see how this is a little different than the `camera point at` method?

5. Try experimenting by running a few more of the penguin's methods directly before moving on to the next tutorial. For example, determine the difference between the `turn` and `roll` methods by running them directly.

Some of the methods, such as `resize`, provide more control in manipulating objects than the object manipulation tools in the Scene Editor. If you run into trouble, you can recover with the *Undo* button, which is located near the upper-left corner of your screen.

6. There is no need to save this experimental world, so when you are finished, close the Alice software before continuing. You will open Alice again in the next tutorial, but it is a good idea to close Alice and reopen it between worlds. It isn't always necessary, but it can help avoid side effects, such as memory overflows, which can sometimes happen when loading one large Alice world after another.

TUTORIAL 2B—CREATING NEW METHODS IN ALICE

In this tutorial, you will practice some of the techniques discussed earlier in the chapter to create an Alice world with several new methods. You will create a world with three objects from Lewis Carroll's *Alice's Adventures in Wonderland*—the Cheshire Cat, the White Rabbit, and Alice, and you will write methods to make them jump up and down. The Alice software really has no connection to Lewis Carroll's story except for the name *Alice*, but it might be more interesting to use these characters in this exercise.

It's easy to find objects for Alice and the Cheshire Cat in the object galleries, but you need to be careful with the White Rabbit—there are classes for Bunnies, Rabbits, and Hares, in addition to the WhiteRabbit class. You want the White Rabbit with the waistcoat and pocket watch on a chain, as described by Lewis Carroll in *Alice's Adventure's in Wonderland*.

Alice started to her feet, for it flashed across her mind that she had never before seen a rabbit with either a waistcoast-pocket, or a watch to take out of it, and burning with curiosity, she ran across the field after it …

—Alice's Adventures in Wonderland
by Lewis Carroll, 1865

Setting the Scene

The first step in creating a new world is to set the scene by opening a template, adding necessary objects, and positioning things. In long programs, a naming convention is needed to make it easier to read the names of the many objects, methods, and variables used within the program. As you work with Alice, you will notice that the names of classes and objects in Alice follow a pattern called the CamelCase naming convention, which is used with most programming languages and is recommended by many software developers, such as Microsoft.

CamelCase is the practice of writing compound names without using blank spaces, but capitalizing the first letter of each name that forms the compound name, like the name *CamelCase* itself. In *Alice in Wonderland,* the proper name of the character is *Cheshire Cat*, while the name of the class of characters in the Alice object gallery is CheshireCat. You will also notice that the very first letter of object class names begin with capital letters, whereas the names of instances of a class begin with lowercase letters. The class name is CheshireCat, with a capital *C* at the beginning; the first instance of the class is named cheshireCat with a lowercase *c*.

1. Start the Alice software, select the **grass** template from the Templates tab, and then click the **Open** button. Next, click the **ADD OBJECTS** button to enter Scene Editor mode.

2. You need to add the three characters to this Alice world and position them so they appear as shown in Figure 2-10. Start with the Cheshire Cat. Click **Local Gallery**, and then click **Animals**. Click the **CheshireCat** tile, and then click the **Add instance to world** button. A cheshireCat should appear near the center of the world window, and a *cheshireCat* tile should appear in the Object tree.

FIGURE 2-10: A world with three objects from *Alice's Adventures in Wonderland*

3. Drag the **cheshireCat** over to the left side of the World window, as seen by the camera.

4. Next, you will make the cat turn to face the camera. Right-click the **cheshireCat** tile in the Object tree, and then point to methods from the small menu that appears. You should see a list of the cheshireCat's primitive methods, similar to Figure 2-11.

FIGURE 2-11: cheshireCat's primitive methods

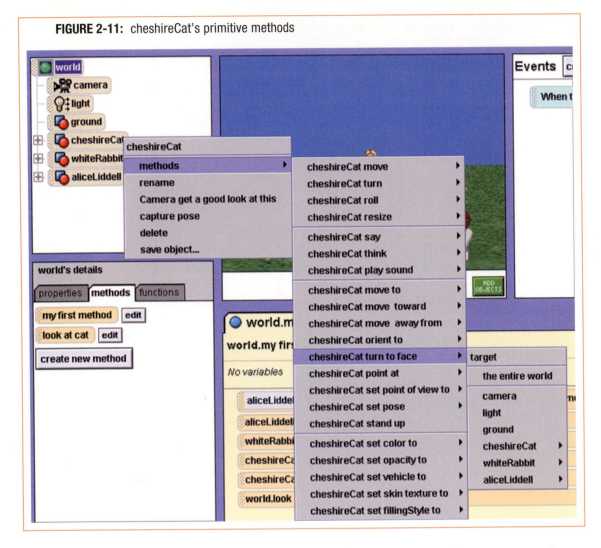

5. About halfway down the list, find and point to the **cheshireCat turn to face** method, and then click **camera** as the target object. On the screen you should see the cheshireCat turn to face the camera.

6. The WhiteRabbit class is in the same animal gallery as the CheshireCat class. Note that you will have to scroll to the far right in the Animals gallery to see it. Add an instance of the WhiteRabbit class to your world.

7. After you have added an instance of the WhiteRabbit class to the world, you will need to position it on the right side of the world window, facing the camera, just as you positioned the cheshireCat on the left. To do this,

drag the **whiteRabbit** over to the right, and then run the method to make it face the camera as you did with the cheshireCat.

8. Finally, add an instance of the AliceLiddell class to your world. The aliceLiddell object can be found in the People gallery. Alice Liddell was the young daughter of a friend of Lewis Carroll's for whom the story *Alice's Adventures in Wonderland* was named. Leave Alice in the center of the scene, and make her turn to face the camera, as you did with the other two objects. You are finished setting the scene, so exit the Scene Editor Mode by clicking the large green **DONE** button.

Designing a Method

The design of a new method begins with specifications. In the simple case in this tutorial, the specifications are given: the three characters will first appear on a grass background, and then they will jump. The White Rabbit jumps, the Cheshire Cat jumps, and then Alice Liddell jumps. Alice's programming language has no primitive instruction to make an object jump up and down, so you will need to use the move up and move down methods to make each character jump. Figure 2-12 contains the organizational chart for the program.

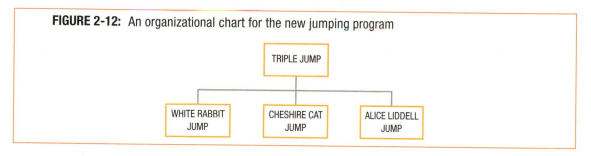

FIGURE 2-12: An organizational chart for the new jumping program

The outline for the program would resemble Figure 2-13.

FIGURE 2-13: A first outline for the jumping program

```
Triple Jump Program
1. whiteRabbit jump
2. cheshireCat jump
3. aliceLiddell jump
```

And finally, an expanded outline for the program would resemble Figure 2-14.

FIGURE 2-14: An expanded outline for the jumping program showing more detail

```
Triple Jump Program
1. whiteRabbit jump
        a. whiteRabbit move up
        b. whiteRabbit move down
2. cheshireCat jump
        a. cheshireCat move up
        b. cheshireCat move down
3. aliceLiddell jump
        a. aliceLiddell move up
        b. aliceLiddell move down
```

Top-down design and modular development suggest that separate jump methods should be written for each object rather than placing all of the code into a single method. By using proper programming techniques as you begin to write short programs like this one, you will develop good habits that will help you when you write larger programs, whether in Alice, Java, Visual Basic, or another language.

Coding the Jump Methods

To make an object jump, you will simply move the character up one meter and then move the character down one meter.

1. Start by creating a `jump` method for the whiteRabbit. Click the **whiteRabbit** tile in the Object tree, and then click the **methods** tab in the Details area.

2. Click the **create new method** button, and a small New Method dialog box will appear asking you to name the method. Type **jump** as the name for the new method, and then click the **OK** button. In the Editor area, a new tab appears for a blank method with the name `whiteRabbit.jump`, as seen in Figure 2-15.

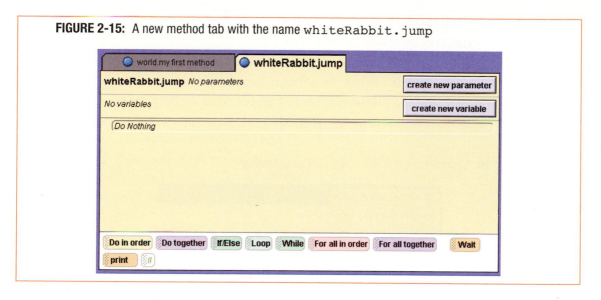

FIGURE 2-15: A new method tab with the name `whiteRabbit.jump`

The new blank method in the Editor area has several components. The name of the method appears on a tab at the top of the method and again on the method's first line of text, followed by the phrase *No parameters.* To the right of this is a *create new parameter* button. On the next line of text is the phrase *No variables,* with a *create new variable* button on the right. Your method will not have any variables or parameters, so for the moment, you can ignore these buttons. (You will learn more about variables and parameters later in this chapter.) The lines of text at the top of the method can be considered a **method header**, which gives us information about how the method works. From the header information, you can see that you can run this method without any parameters, and that there are no variables in the method.

You can see a box with rounded corners containing the phrase *Do Nothing* below the header for the method. This part of your method is sometimes called the instruction zone. Right now there are no instructions in the method, so the zone has the text *Do Nothing.*

You now want to add an instruction to your method to make the whiteRabbit move up one meter, followed by an instruction to make the whiteRabbit move down one meter, as shown by the specifications in Figure 2-14.

1. Drag the **whiteRabbit move** tile from the left side of the screen and drop it on the *Do Nothing* phrase. The tile will be surrounded by a red border as you drag it. The border will turn green when you reach the right place.

2. When you drop the tile into the instruction zone, a menu will appear asking you the direction in which you want to move the object. Select **up** for the direction, and then select **1 meter** for the amount. *Direction* and *amount* are

two parameters, or pieces of information, that you must give a method whenever you want to use the method.

3. Next, drag another copy of the **whiteRabbit move** tile from the left into the instruction zone below your first instruction. This time set the direction to **down**, and the distance again to **1 meter**. Your whiteRabbit.jump method should now look like Figure 2-16.

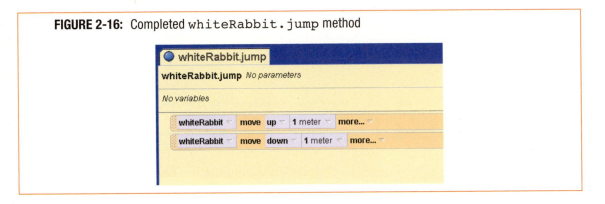

FIGURE 2-16: Completed whiteRabbit.jump method

You are finished with the whiteRabbit.jump method. Now you need to create a jump method for the cheshireCat, just as you did for the whiteRabbit.

1. Select the **cheshireCat** tile in the Object tree, and then click the **methods** tab in the Details area.
2. Click the **create new method** button, and then name the method **jump**.
3. Add an instruction to make the cheshireCat move up **1** meter.
4. Add an instruction to make the cheshireCat move down **1** meter.
5. Create a jump method for aliceLiddell in a similar manner.

Creating the Main Method

Next, you need a method that calls all three jump methods in the order in which you want the characters to jump. This method will be your main method, at the top of the organizational chart. World.my first method is often used as this top-level method, and you will use that here. This is a world-level method, associated with the world itself rather than with any particular object in the Alice world.

1. Start by clicking the **world** tile in the Object tree, and then click the **methods** tab, to view the methods in the Details area. Things look a little different here than when you looked at an object's methods. There are no primitive methods listed below the *create new method* button, but my first method already exists as a user-created method.

2. Click the **edit** button. This will open up the method for editing in the Editor area. It begins as a blank method with no parameters, variables, or instructions. Your plan calls for the whiteRabbit to jump, followed by the cheshireCat, and then by aliceLiddell.

3. First, you want the whiteRabbit to jump. Click the **whiteRabbit** tile in the Object tree, and then click the **methods** tab in the Details area. Notice that there is a tile for the jump method above the *create new method* button because this is a user-created method that can be edited.

4. Click the **jump** tile and drag a copy of it into the instruction zone of world.my first method.

5. Next, you need to add a cheshireCat.jump method. Click the **cheshireCat** in the Object tree and drag and drop the cheshireCat's **jump** method into world.my first method. Make sure that you drop it just below the whiteRabbit.jump instructions in the desired sequence.

6. Finally, you need to add the aliceLiddell.jump method by clicking **aliceLiddell** in the Object tree and then dragging and dropping its **jump** method below the cheshireCat.jump instruction. Your screen should resemble Figure 2-17.

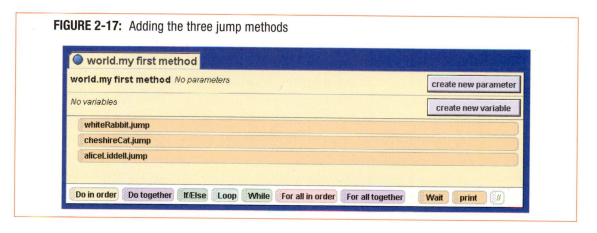

FIGURE 2-17: Adding the three jump methods

Testing (and Debugging) Your Finished Software

If you have done everything correctly, then your Alice world should be ready for testing.

1. Click the **Play** button to play the Alice world.

2. Watch what happens. Did it perform according to your original specifications? Did the whiteRabbit, then the cheshireCat, and then the aliceLiddell

each jump up and down? If not, then you need to look at each of your methods, find the error, and fix it.

3. Before you move on to the next tutorial, you should save your Alice world as **triple jump**. (You can do this through the File menu, just as you do with most Windows programs.) Remember to pay attention to where the file is saved; you will need this file for the next tutorial.

You can think of each method as a module that performs a single task. If an object is doing something wrong, then you should ask which method performs that task. If you have an error, then it could be in either the main method or one of the jump methods. If the three objects are jumping in the wrong order, then the error is probably in the main method. If one of the objects is not jumping properly, then that object's jump method probably contains the error. Writing small methods for each individual task is good modular development. It is much easier to debug software that is written as small modules, each performing an individual task.

TUTORIAL 2C—METHODS WITH PARAMETERS

In the previous tutorial, you created an Alice world with methods to make each of your three objects jump up and down 1 meter. But, what if you want an object to jump a different height? You created a `whiteRabbit.jump` method, a `cheshireCat.jump` method, and an `aliceLiddell.jump` method. In this tutorial, you will create a jump method that will work with any height.

Your new method will have a variable parameter. A **variable** is a name for a memory location that temporarily stores a value while a method is running. Variables are a lot like the properties of objects. They have data types, just like properties, and they are stored in the memory of the computer, just like properties. However, properties are associated with an object, and their values are maintained as long as the object exists, whereas variables are associated with a particular method, and their values exist only inside the method. Once the method stops running, their values are gone, unless you had saved them somewhere else while the method was running.

A **parameter** is a variable whose value is passed from one method to another—just like a baton is passed from one runner to another in a relay race. A variable is a value that can change inside a method, and a parameter is a variable whose value is passed from one method to another. In the last tutorial, you had to tell the `whiteRabbit.move` method the direction and amount you wanted the whiteRabbit to move in your jump method. These values are parameters for the primitive `whiteRabbit.move` method. In this tutorial, you will add a *height* parameter to the `whiteRabbit.jump` method.

Creating a Parameter

You need to give your parameter a name, and declare what data type the parameter will be. Remember that the computer stores different data types in different formats, so you need to tell the system what data type to use for this new parameter. The data type can be an Alice object, a number, a Boolean value (true or false), or any one of more than a dozen types built into Alice, such as a string of text, a color, a sound file, a direction, and so on.

1. First, open the **triple jump** Alice world from the previous tutorial.

2. Save the world with the new name **triple jump with parameters** before you begin editing. This will ensure that you do not change the original *triple jump* world.

3. Next, select the **whiteRabbit** tile in the Object tree, and then click the **methods** tab in the Details area. Click the **edit** button, and the `whiteRabbit.jump` method will appear in the Editor area.

4. Click the **create new parameter** button on the right side of the `jump` method's header information, and a Create New Parameter dialog box appears, as seen in Figure 2-18.

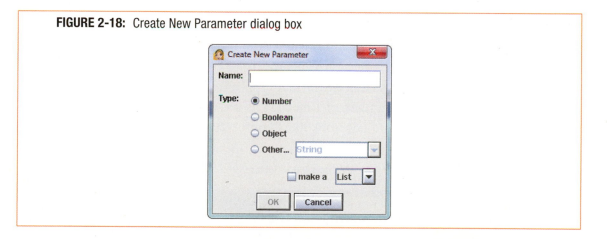

FIGURE 2-18: Create New Parameter dialog box

5. Type **height** as the name of your new parameter and select **Number** as the data type. Make sure that the make a List box is not checked, and then click the **OK** button. Now you should see a tile appear after the name of the method showing you that this method has a number parameter, as shown in Figure 2-19. The *height* parameter may now be used like a variable within the method, and its value must be specified whenever this method is called from another method.

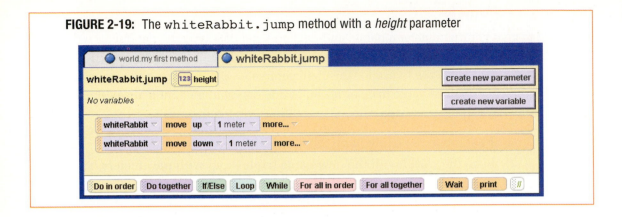

FIGURE 2-19: The whiteRabbit.jump method with a *height* parameter

Using a Parameter

Notice in Figure 2-19 that the *whiteRabbit.move* instruction tiles in the whiteRabbit.jump method in the Editor area each say *up 1 meter* and *down 1 meter*. These are the values passed to the primitive whiteRabbit.move method as it is called from the whiteRabbit.jump method. You are going to replace *1 meter* in each of these instructions with the new *height* parameter that you just created. Then, whenever the whiteRabbit.jump method is used, the programmer will be able to specify how high the whiteRabbit should jump.

1. Drag the **height** parameter tile and drop it in the **whiteRabbit move up** instruction tile in place of **1 meter**.

2. Drag the **height** parameter tile and drop it in the **whiteRabbit move down** instruction tile in place of **1 meter**. The whiteRabbit.jump method in the Editor area should now look like Figure 2-20.

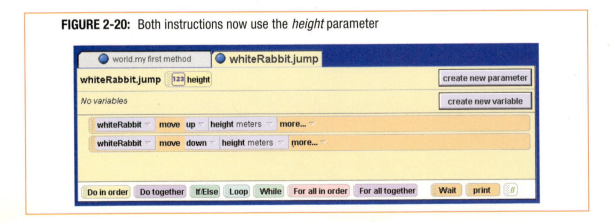

FIGURE 2-20: Both instructions now use the *height* parameter

3. Now click the **world.my first method** tab in the Editor area to see that method. Notice that the *whiteRabbit.jump* tile now uses the *height* parameter and that its value is set to *1*. The jump method tiles for the *cheshireCat* and *aliceLiddell* do not yet have this parameter.

4. Click the **height** parameter tile in the *whiteRabbit.jump* tile and a menu should appear as shown in Figure 2-21. Select **2** from the menu.

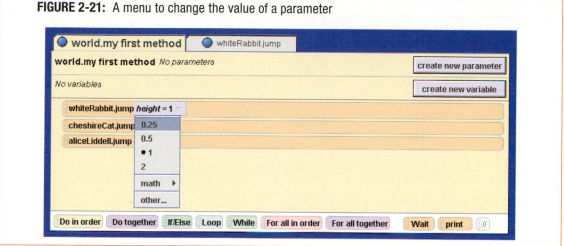

FIGURE 2-21: A menu to change the value of a parameter

5. Now play the world and watch how the height that the whiteRabbit jumps is higher than the height that the cheshireCat and aliceLiddell jump.

6. Change the value of the **height** parameter several times and try the world again. Remember to save the world and exit Alice when you are done.

The set of parameters that appear in the method header at the top of a method is called the **formal parameter list**. The values that are used when the method is called from another method are called the **actual parameters**. Actual parameters are very much like arguments of a function in mathematics, such as the value *45 degrees* in the expression *X = SIN(45 degrees)*.

Chapter Summary

This chapter consisted of discussions of top-down development, modular design, and a simple software development cycle, followed by three hands-on tutorials involving Alice methods. The section on top-down design and modular development discussed the following important points:

☐ Computer programming is part of the software engineering process, which usually involves newer methods of object-oriented design, combined with more traditional methods of algorithm development.

☐ Good engineers often break a large problem into more manageable parts. This process, also known as top-down design or top-down development, starts at the top with one concept or big idea, which is then broken down into several parts.

☐ The process of top-down design leads to modular development. In modular development, parts, or modules, are developed individually and then combined to form a complete solution to a problem.

☐ Modular development makes a large project more manageable, is faster for large projects, leads to a higher-quality product, makes it easier to find and correct errors, and increases the reusability of your solutions.

☐ Saving solutions to small problems so that they can be applied elsewhere creates reusable code. Object-oriented programming encourages the development of reusable code.

The discussion of a software development cycle included the following:

☐ Programmers follow a software development cycle, in which they design, code, test, and debug methods.

☐ Software testers need to be able to develop a testing plan that examines new software under all possible circumstances. They examine the correctness of a method, its time and space efficiency, and whether or not it has any undesirable side effects.

☐ Unit tests check to see if methods work as expected individually. Sometimes a testing shell is used in unit testing to simulate the environment in which a method will operate.

☐ Integration tests check to see if larger methods work after newer methods are incorporated into them.

In Tutorial 2A, you explored the primitive methods that come with every Alice object. Sometimes it is desirable to run primitive methods directly, such as when you need to position objects to set up a scene or find a lost object. You also saw that some methods come with user-created methods to provide them with additional behaviors, such as the walk method in the Penguin class.

In Tutorial 2B, you applied some of the methods discussed earlier in the chapter to create an Alice world with a top-level method and separate sublevel methods to make three characters from *Alice's Adventures in Wonderland* jump up and down on the screen.

In Tutorial 2C, you learned to create and use a parameter for a method. You learned that a parameter can be used to pass a value to a method when the method is called.

Review Questions

1. Define the following terms:

   ☐ CamelCase   ☐ off-camera   ☐ testing shell

   ☐ encapsulation   ☐ parameter   ☐ top-down design

   ☐ integration test   ☐ primitive methods   ☐ unit test

   ☐ method header   ☐ reusable code   ☐ user-defined methods

   ☐ module   ☐ software development cycle ☐ variable

   ☐ modular development   ☐ test for correctness

2. Describe the processes known as top-down design and modular development, and explain how they are used together.

3. How do organizational charts help with top-down design and modular development?

4. List and describe the advantages of using modular development.

5. How does the practice of object-oriented programming encourage the development of reusable code?

6. List and describe the steps in a simple software development cycle.

7. What is the difference between a unit test and an integration test? Why are they both used in software development?

8. What are the differences between primitive methods and user-defined methods in Alice? Which of these are encapsulated methods, and what does that mean?

9. Describe two different primitive methods that can be used to find objects that are off-camera. What are the differences between using these methods?

10. Describe what parameters are, and how they are used in Alice methods.

Exercises

1. Create an organizational chart showing a top-down, modular design for each of the following:

   a. Baking a cake
   b. Traveling from your house to Buckingham Palace in London
   c. Sorting a list of names alphabetically by last name
   d. The plot of your favorite film or television show episode
   e. The solution to your favorite math problem

2. Modify the *triple jump with parameters* world from Tutorial 2C, by adding height parameters in the jump methods for the cheshireCat and aliceLiddell just as you did for the whiteRabbit. Run the world a few times using different values for the parameters.

3.   Create an Alice world with a bunny in it. Create a **hop** method for the bunny that has the object move forward while jumping up and down. (*Hint:* Use the *do together* logic and control tile.) Create and test a generic hop method that has three parameters—*who, how high,* and *how far.*

4.   Modify the *triple jump* world from Tutorial 2B, so that it functions as follows:

   a. The three characters appear on the screen in the same position as before.
   b. Alice says, "Simon says, Jump!"
   c. Alice jumps.
   d. The White Rabbit jumps.
   e. The Cheshire Cat jumps.
   f. The Cheshire Cat disappears, but his smile stays visible. (*Hint:* There is a property named *opacity.* Dragging a property into a method will create an instruction to set the property to a new value. The cat should disappear, but his smile should not, so you may have to program a part of the object. Clicking the plus sign next to an object's tile in the Object tree will give you access to the object's parts.)
   g. Alice and the White Rabbit both turn their heads to look at the Cheshire Cat.

   Save your new world with a different name so that the *triple jump* world is preserved. You might also try printing the code from the methods in your world, or saving the world as a movie file.

5.   Clicking **more**. . . on a method tile in the Editor area will reveal additional parameters for a method. Open the **triple jump with parameters** world from Tutorial 2C, and then click the **whiteRabbit** in the Object tree and the **edit** button for the `whiteRabbit.jump` method in the Details area. The method will open in the Editor area. Find and change the *duration* parameter to make the rabbit jump more quickly or more slowly.

6.   Some Alice method names do not follow the CamelCase naming convention. How should `world. my first method` be renamed so that it is in CamelCase? What about the names of user-created methods that are supplied with the Penguin class of objects?

7.   Examine the code in the ***lakeSkater*** world that is provided with the Alice software as an example world and that was used in Chapter 1.

   a. Describe how the organization of the iceSkater's object-level methods are related to the concept of reusable code.
   b. While the world exhibits good modular design in many of its methods, the method `world.my first animation` could be improved. Create an organizational chart showing an improved design for `world.my first animation` that exhibits better modular design.

8.   The American Film Institute's list of *The 100 Greatest Movie Quotes Of All Time* appears on the Web at *http://connect.afi.com/site/DocServer/quotes100.pdf*. Pick one of the quotes and create a short Alice world in which one of the characters uses the quote. Make sure that your world exhibits good modular design.

9. Every method for an object is an algorithm. On the surface of the moon there is a crater, named al-Khwarizmi. It was named after Abu Ja'far Muhammad ibn Musa al-Khwarizmi, who lived in the ninth century. See if you can find out why he is important enough in the history of mathematics to have a crater on the moon named after him. What does his work have to do with computer programming and developing software methods?

10. Select one of the themed folders in the Alice galleries, such as the Japan, Egypt, or Old West folders. Select several objects from the folder and develop an outline for a short story using those objects. Create an organizational chart that shows the modules in the story, and develop a list of the Alice methods that you would need to write to implement your story as an Alice world. Which of these methods do you think would be reusable for other stories? If you have high-speed Internet access, you can to look in the Web Gallery, which is more extensive than the Local Gallery.

3

Events

After finishing this chapter, you should be able to:

☐ Provide a brief definition of each the following terms: Graphical User Interface (GUI), command-driven interface, event-driven software, event listener, event trigger, event handler, dimension, quantification, orientation, point of view, absolute direction, object-relative direction, object-relative position, Cartesian coordinates, ordered pair, Euclidean 3-space, BDE event format, side effects, tilt, zoom, pan, and framing

☐ Describe what is meant by event-driven programming, including how event listeners, event triggers, and event handlers work together to make events function

☐ Describe what is meant by an object's point of view, and list and describe the six object-relative directions and six object-relative positions in Euclidean 3-space

☐ Describe basic camera operations, including move, pan, tilt, and zoom, and how to implement these in Alice

☐ Create Alice events to allow the user to manipulate objects moving in three-dimensional space

 There are two topics in this chapter. The first topic is relatively short, describing event-driven programming. The second, which is a bit longer, discusses the nature of three-dimensional space. They are combined in this chapter because events in Alice often are used to manipulate objects in three-dimensional space.

EVENT-DRIVEN SOFTWARE

One of the most important places in the history of computer technology is the Xerox Palo Alto Research Center (Xerox PARC) in California. Xerox PARC was established as a research lab where some of the world's best computer scientists and designers could work to improve modern computer technology. We see their innovations almost every time we use a modern computer. Local area networks, the laser printer, and the **Graphical User Interface (GUI)** were all developed or refined at Xerox PARC.

NOTE □ □ □ | For more information on XEROX PARC, see *www.parc.com*.

A GUI has icons on the computer screen and a mouse to control a pointer that can be used to operate the computer. Most modern software, such as word-processing and spreadsheet programs, Internet browsers, and computer games, depends on the use of a GUI. Before GUIs existed, people had to control a computer by typing commands into what was called a **command-driven interface**. Often it was necessary to write or run a computer program to complete tasks that involved more than a few steps, such as formatting the output for a document.

It's no coincidence that the use of personal computers really took off after the introduction of the Graphical User Interface. The Apple Macintosh approach to computing and the Microsoft Windows operating system both incorporate a GUI based directly on developments at Xerox PARC.

The use of a GUI on a computer system requires event-driven software. **Event-driven software** is software in which the flow of the program depends on the occurrence of events outside the software, such as a user pressing a key or clicking a mouse button. An event occurs whenever an event listener detects an event trigger and responds by running a method called an event handler. An **event listener** is a combination of hardware and software that repeatedly checks the computer system for an event trigger. Modern operating systems contain facilities to let programmers set up event listeners in their software. An **event trigger** can be any activity or condition selected by the programmer, such as a user clicking a mouse button or pressing the Enter key or a bank account balance going below zero. An **event handler** is a method that is activated when the event trigger occurs. Almost any method can serve as an event handler. When the event listener detects an event trigger, an event handler is called into action. Everything from word-processing software to computer games depends on event-driven programming, because events allow for keyboard and mouse controls for interactive software.

There are nine different event types in Alice, as described in Appendix B. In this chapter, you will use some of those events to manipulate objects moving in three-dimensional space. Before we begin, let's look at the nature of three-dimensional space.

THREE-DIMENSIONAL SPACE

A **dimension** is a way of measuring something. The word dimension is derived from the ancient Latin word *demetiri*, meaning to measure out. It is an abstract idea, a concept invented by people to help us understand something. We create a dimension whenever we assign a value on a continuous scale to some property. This process is called **quantification**. For example, a survey might contain the question, "On a scale of 1 to 10, how much do you like chocolate ice cream?" Someone has created a scale to quantify the popularity of chocolate ice cream, making popularity a dimension of the chocolate ice cream.

If you want to measure the location of a point on a straight line, then you only need one number. You could mark a starting point on the line, and then measure distance—how far a point is from the starting point. By using negative and positive numbers, you could also indicate which direction the distance spans. Figure 3-1 shows a line marked with a scale to help us quantify the location of each point on the line.

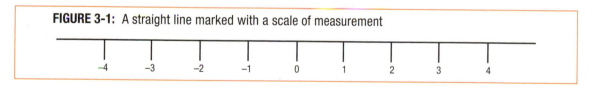

FIGURE 3-1: A straight line marked with a scale of measurement

In addition to the concepts of distance and direction, we also have the concept of **orientation**, which means the direction an object is facing. If an object is facing the positive direction on the line, toward higher numbers, its orientation would be forward. An object facing the negative direction, toward lower numbers, would be facing backward.

Location and orientation together are known as the **point of view** of an object. Figure 3-2 shows three people in a straight line with the point of view for each of them.

FIGURE 3-2: Three people in a straight line with the one-dimensional point of view for each person

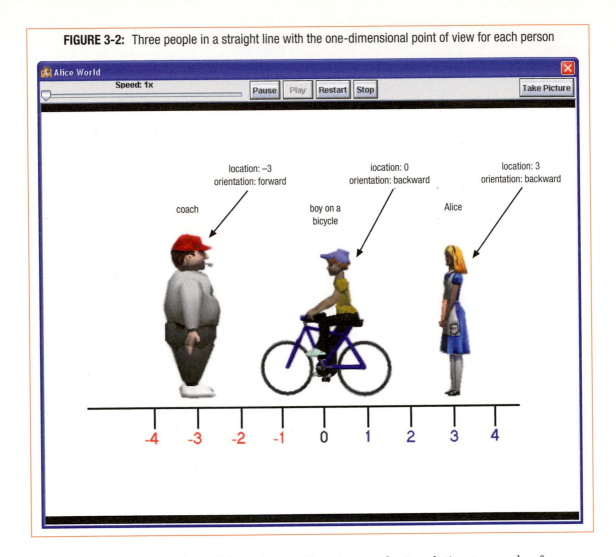

Actually, there are two ideas of direction. A direction can be in relation to a scale of measurement, called **absolute direction,** or from the point of view of another object, called **object-relative direction**. In Figure 3-2, the absolute direction of the boy on the bicycle is backward, but the direction he is facing in relation to Alice is forward. **Object-relative position** can also be considered. From the coach's point of view, Alice is behind the boy, while the coach is in front of the boy. In front of and behind are two object-relative positions.

On a flat surface, like a sheet of paper, you need two values to specify an object's position. That is, you need two scales of measurement, each called an axis. The first would measure the object's position along a straight line, and the second how far away that object is from that straight line along a second straight line. A flat surface is two-dimensional. Such a flat two-dimensional surface is called a plane.

The French mathematician René Descartes developed a system of quantification for two dimensions called **Cartesian coordinates**. Cartesian coordinates have an X-axis and a Y-axis. The location of each point is referenced by an ordered pair of the form (x, y), in which x represents the point's location along the X-axis, and y represents its location along the Y-axis. An **ordered pair** is any pair in which one dimension is always listed first, and another dimension is always listed second. For example, a set of numbers showing the temperature at various times throughout the day might be given in the form of ordered pairs with the format (time, temperature). The data set would look something like this: (8:00 am, 54°), (9:00 am, 56°), (10:00 am, 59°), (11:00 am, 61°), and so on. In Cartesian coordinates, the X-axis value is always listed first. Figure 3-3 shows several points marked on a Cartesian plane.

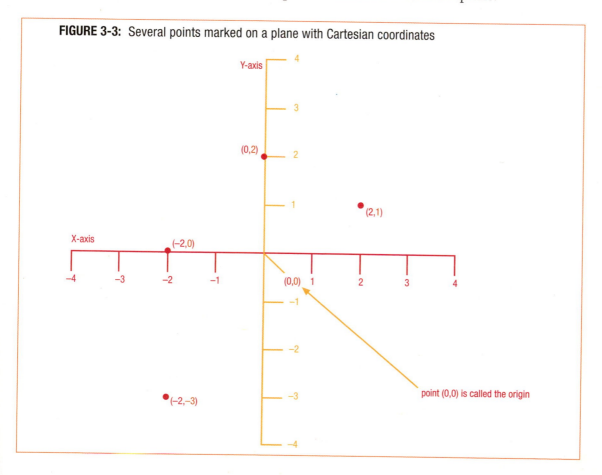

FIGURE 3-3: Several points marked on a plane with Cartesian coordinates

Moving up or down off a flat plane requires a third axis and a third number to indicate how far a point is above or below the plane. In other words, a third dimension is needed. So, instead of an ordered pair to indicate location, an ordered triplet is used, with three values. Each point has x, y, and z coordinates. Figure 3-4 shows three buildings with an x-axis, a y-axis, and a z-axis for orientation in three-dimensional space. You can think of the x-axis as running east and west, the y-axis as running north and south, and the z-axis as running up and down.

The physical world around us is a three-dimensional space. Mathematicians sometimes call such a space a **Euclidean 3-space** after the ancient Greek mathematician, Euclid. Around the year 300 B.C., Euclid wrote *The Elements*, one of the most popular textbooks of all time, about geometry on flat surfaces and in a corresponding three-dimensional space. Today we also have non-Euclidean geometries, such as hyperbolic geometry and parabolic geometry, to describe location, distance, etc., on curved surfaces, but the virtual world of Alice is a simple Euclidean 3-space.

FIGURE 3-4: These buildings sit on a plane with an X-axis (east-west), a Y-axis (north-south); and a Z-axis (up-down); unlike the curved surface of the Earth, the X-Y plane in Euclidean 3-space is flat

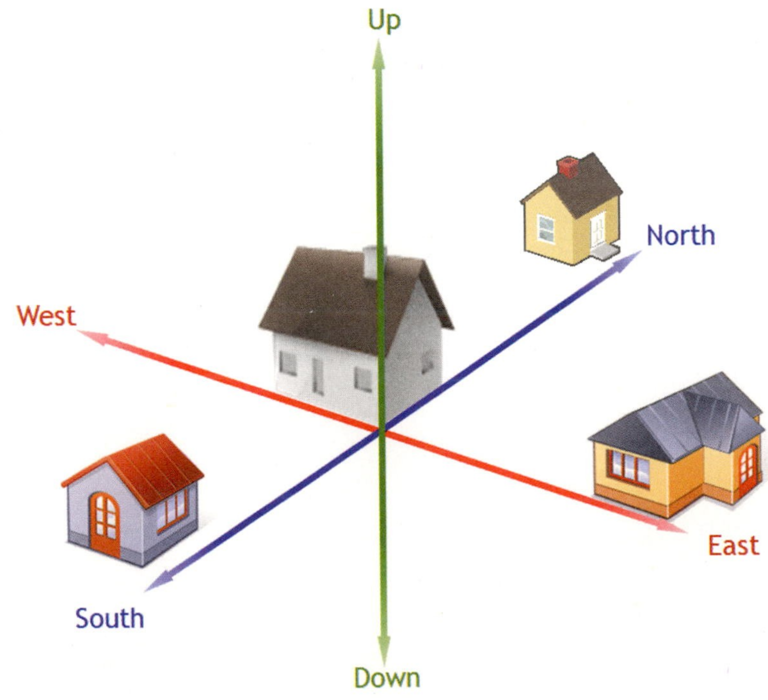

You saw that on a straight line, an object can be facing forward or backward, either absolutely or in relation to another object. You also saw that on a straight line, there were the two object-relative positions: in front of and behind. In Alice's Euclidean 3-space, there are six object-relative directions, one opposing pair of directions for each axis. There are also six object-relative positions. Figure 3-5a shows the six object-relative directions—forward and backward, left and right, and up and down. Figure 3-5b shows the six object-relative positions—in front of and behind, to the left of and to the right of, and above and below.

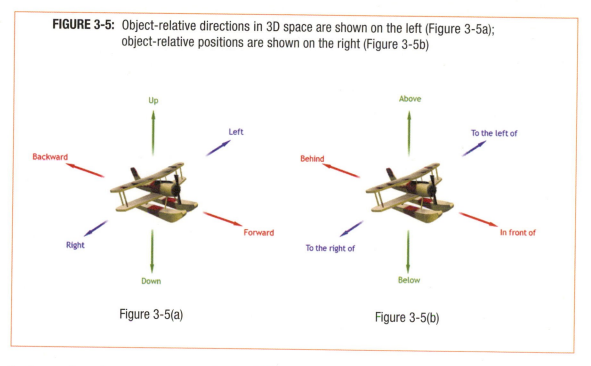

FIGURE 3-5: Object-relative directions in 3D space are shown on the left (Figure 3-5a); object-relative positions are shown on the right (Figure 3-5b)

Figure 3-5(a)

Figure 3-5(b)

Is there a four-dimensional space? Albert Einstein pointed out that time is a dimension, and suggested what he called a four-dimensional space-time continuum. Many important developments in the field of physics during the past 100 years have been based on Einstein's work. So, you see, the simple idea of quantification, of applying a system of measurement to something such as the location of a point in space, can lead to some very sophisticated results. In fact, almost all of modern science is based on dimensioning—quantifying the properties of objects, and then studying how those quantities change and affect one another.

The goal of this chapter is to learn about events and computer programming in the three-dimensional space of Alice. Even though the text refers to direction and movement, we will try to do so without getting too caught up in the mathematics of it all.

TUTORIAL 3A—EVENTS IN ALICE

In this tutorial, you will explore events in Alice and create several simple events. Before starting, you should understand the nature of event-driven programming, as discussed earlier, especially the terms event trigger and event handler. You should also have an understanding of methods, as discussed in Chapter 2.

Exploring Events

In this tutorial, you will explore event types in Alice.

1. Start the Alice software and open the **amusementPark** example world. In the Events area of the Alice interface, you see seven event tiles, as shown in Figure 3-6.

   The first tile contains an event to let the user move the camera with the four arrow keys on the keyboard. The other six event tiles are of the form *When the world starts, do <event handler>*. These events run methods to animate the amusement park rides when the world starts.

FIGURE 3-6: The seven event tiles in the *amusementPark* example world

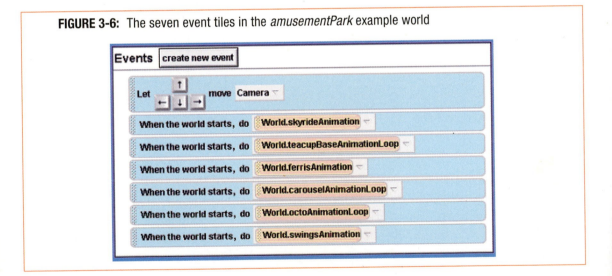

 If you cannot see all seven events at once, then you might need to adjust the size of the areas in your Alice interface. You can do this by clicking the background space between areas and dragging the pointer to resize the areas. To lengthen the Events area, click between the Events area and the Editor area and drag the pointer down the screen.

2. Play the world and use the arrow keys to move the camera around to look at the various parts of the amusement park. You can see the effects of the six events that animate the amusement park rides. Also notice that the camera moves down slightly when it moves forward, and up slightly when it moves backward. This is because the original camera position was tilted slightly downward. Take a few minutes to look around the amusement park before continuing. If you restart the world, the camera will move back to its original position.

Creating a Sample World for Event Exploration

You are going to start a new Alice world with two objects—a blue ballerina and a pink ballerina—to explore the different Alice event types.

1. Exit Alice and restart the Alice software with a blank world using the **grass** template. The *amusementPark* world uses a lot of memory, and exiting and restarting Alice is a good way to be sure that it is cleared from the memory before continuing.

2. You are going to build a world with two objects, a blueBallerina and a pinkBallerina. Click the green **ADD OBJECTS** button and add a **blueBallerina** and a **pinkBallerina** to the world from the People folder in the Local Gallery.

3. Move the ballerinas apart from each other and turn them to face the camera, as seen in Figure 3-7. When you are finished setting up this simple world, click the **DONE** button to exit Scene Editor mode and return to the standard Alice interface.

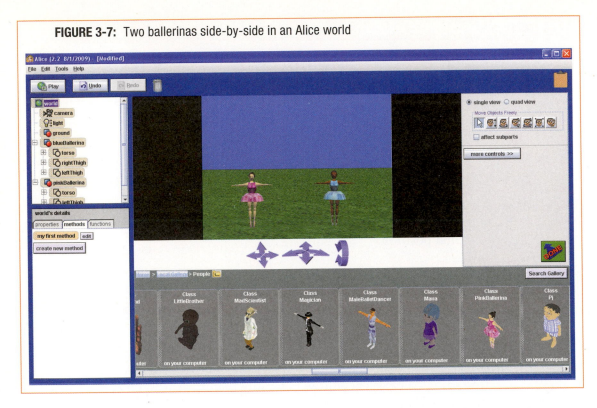

FIGURE 3-7: Two ballerinas side-by-side in an Alice world

4. Next, you are going to create a world-level method to make both ballerinas spin at the same time. Click the **world** tile in the Object tree, and then click the **methods** tab in the Details area. Now click the **create new method** button, and when the dialog box appears, name the method **bothSpin**, and then click **OK**.

5. You now need to add instructions to the `bothSpin` method to make the two ballerinas spin. The code in the Editor area in Figure 3-8 shows what this will look like when you are finished. First click and drag a **Do together** tile from the bottom of the Editor area into the instruction zone to replace the phrase *Do Nothing* in the `world.both spin` method.

FIGURE 3-8: The `world.bothSpin` method

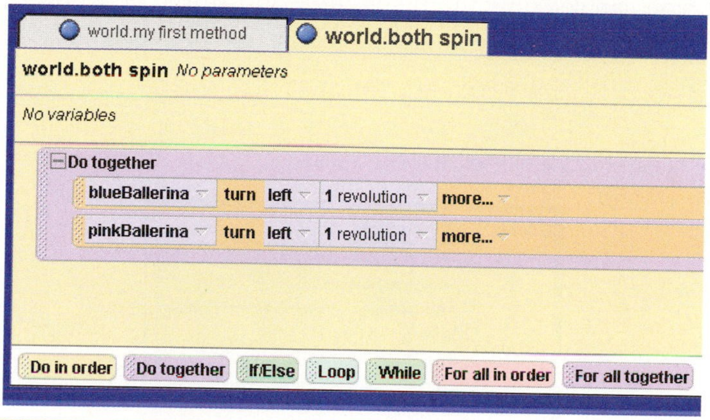

6. Click the **blueBallerina** tile in the Object tree and then the **methods** tab in the Details area. Drag and drop a **blueBallerina turn** method tile from the Details area into the *do together* tile in the `world.both spin` method. Choose **left** and **1 revolution** as values for the direction and amount parameters.

7. Click the **pinkBallerina** tile in the Object tree and drag and drop a **pinkBallerina turn** tile into the `world.bothSpin` method below the *blueBallerina turn* tile. Choose the same values, **left** and **1 revolution**, for the direction and amount parameters.

8. You are finished creating your new method; now you need to add it to the default event tile as the event handler. Make sure that **world** is selected in the Object tree and that the **methods** tab is selected in the Details area. Drag the **bothSpin** tile from the methods tab into the Events area and drop it in place of *world.my first method* in the default event.

9. You no longer need *world.my first method*, so drag the **world.my first method** tile from the methods tab and drop it in the trash can; the method is removed from the world.

10. Now play the world; you should see both ballerinas spin together. Before proceeding, save the world using the name **two ballerinas**. If you want to save a copy of the world during the rest of this tutorial, save it with a different name, so that your basic ballerina world is saved.

Alice Event Types

In the Events area, you can see only the *When the world starts, do world.bothSpin* default event. Whenever the *create new event* button is clicked, a list of the nine event types in Alice appears, as shown in Figure 3-9.

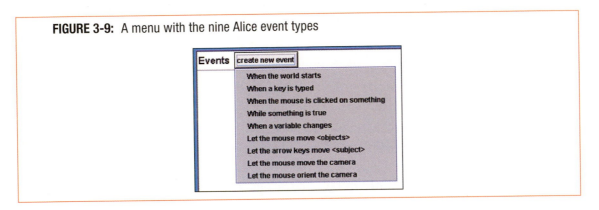

FIGURE 3-9: A menu with the nine Alice event types

Next, you will experiment with a few of the event types. Figure 3-10 shows what the Event area will look like when you are finished. Remember, your goal is to learn something about events and building object controls with events, not to learn everything there is to know about events in Alice. A discussion of the nine event types in Alice is included in Appendix B.

FIGURE 3-10: The Event area with the events to be added in this tutorial

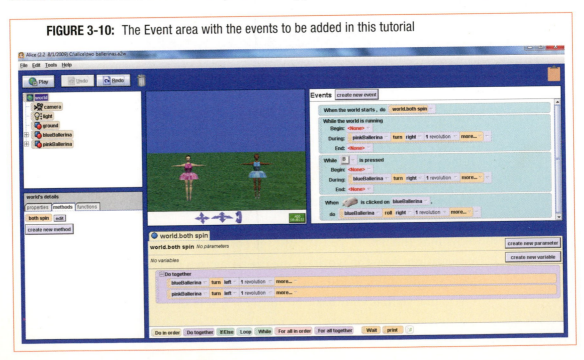

You'll begin with *When the world starts.*

1. Click the **create new event** button, and then click **When the world starts**. A new event tile of that form will appear in the Events area, as shown in Figure 3-11.

FIGURE 3-11: *When the world starts* event tile

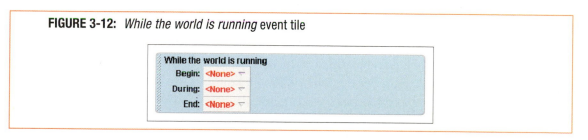

2. This event functions the same as the default event. It will cause a method to run whenever the world starts. You can change the form of the *When the world starts* event to make a method run continuously while the world is playing. To do so, right-click the new event tile. (Make sure you click the blue background of the tile itself, and not a parameter within the tile.) On the menu, three items will appear: *delete*, *change to*, and *disable*. The *delete* option will remove an event from your world. The *disable* option will keep the event, but it will not function until you again right-click the event and enable it. You need to change the form of the event, so click **change to**, and then click **While the world is running**. Now you can see a more sophisticated version of an event handler, as shown in Figure 3-12.

FIGURE 3-12: *While the world is running* event tile

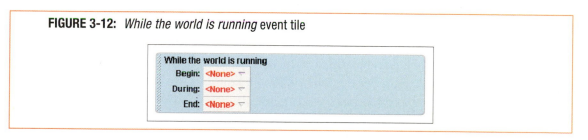

3. The *While the world is running* event now has places for three different event handlers. You can tell the world what methods to run when the world *begins* to run, *during* the time that the world is running, and when the world *ends* running. This format for an event in Alice is called the **BDE**

event format, for **Before**, **During**, and **End**. There are BDE formats for several different events. What you see in Figure 3-11 is only one of several event types with the BDE format. You are going to make the pink ballerina spin to her right while the world is running.

4. Click the **pinkBallerina** tile in the Object tree, drag a **pinkBallerina turn** tile from the methods tab, and drop it into the event tile in place of *None* following the phrase *During*. Choose the values **left** and **1 revolution** for the direction and amount parameters.

5. Now play the world again. Notice two things—first, the pink ballerina continues to spin while the world is running, and second, when the world starts, she spins more quickly. Restart the world, and you will see this happen. Why does she spin more quickly when the world starts? The default event handler causes the pink ballerina to spin left. Combined with the spin from the new event you just added, she spins twice as fast the first time around. This is an example of a **side effect**, an unintended result caused by two methods running at the same time.

6. Change the direction of the spin to **right** in the `while the world is running` method and then run the world again. Now what happens? The pink ballerina doesn't spin at all the first time, because the two methods triggered by the two events cancel out each other. After the first method stops, she spins to her right. This is another example of a side effect. Professionals who test computer software routinely check for such side effects.

The *When a Key is Typed* Event

Alice has a *When a key is typed* event that will cause a method to run whenever a particular key is pressed. The event trigger will be the press of a key, and the event handler can be almost anything that can be coded in an Alice method.

1. Click the **create new event** button again, and this time click **When a key is typed** from the menu that appears. This event takes two parameters: the first is the key that will trigger the event, and the second is the method that will serve as the event handler. The event tile is shown in Figure 3-13.

FIGURE 3-13: *When a key is typed* event tile with the *any key* menu

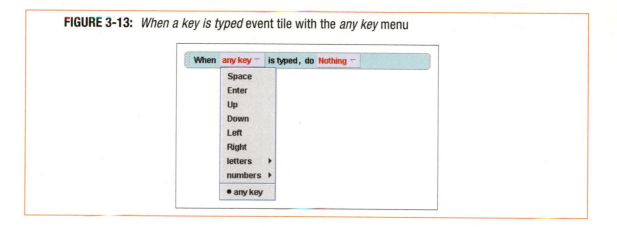

The default menu choice in the *When a key is typed* event tile is *any key*, which can be changed to a specific key.

2. Let's set up an event and give it a try. Click the **any key** box and you will be allowed to select a key from a drop-down menu, as shown in Figure 3-13. The small arrowheads show us menu items that lead to submenus, with the various letter and number keys listed on the submenus.

3. Select **letters** from the menu and then the letter **B** for blue as the trigger key for this event. Click the **blueBallerina** tile in the Object tree and then click the **methods** tab in the Details area. Drag a **blueBallerina turn** method tile from the Details area and drop it into the event tile in place of *Nothing*; choose **right** and **1 revolution** as values for the *direction* and *amount* parameters. This is one of the events shown in Figure 3-10.

4. Now play the Alice world. Wait at least one second until the opening move is complete, and then try the **B** key a few times. Each time you press it, the blue ballerina spins to her right. If you hold down the **B** key, notice that she will *not* continue to spin. Note that Alice event triggers are not case sensitive—this event will be triggered by an uppercase *B* or a lowercase *b*. Stop the world when you are finished experimenting.

The *While a Key Is Pressed* Event

You can change the form of the *When a key is typed* event to make a method run continuously as long as the triggering key is held down.

1. Right-click the **When B is pressed** event tile's blue background, select **change to**, and then click **While a key is pressed**. Now you can see a more sophisticated version of an event handler, as shown in Figure 3-14.

FIGURE 3-14: *While a key is pressed* event tile

While B ▽   is pressed
   Begin: <None> ▽
  During: <None> ▽
     End: <None> ▽

---

2. Notice that the B key is still in place as the trigger, but that the three event handlers are now all empty. Drag and drop a **blueBallerina turn** tile into place after *During*, as you did before, with the values **right** and **1 revolution** as parameters.

3. Now play the world again. After the opening move is complete, try pressing and holding down the **B** key a few times for different durations. Notice that even though the method calls for the ballerina to turn one complete revolution; when you let go of the key, the method stops, even if the ballerina is in midturn.

The *When the Mouse Is Clicked on Anything* Event

Alice has an event type that will cause a method to run whenever the mouse is clicked on an object. Let's experiment with it.

1. Click the **create new event** button, and select **When the mouse is clicked on something** from the menu that appears. A new tile of this type will be added to the Events area. New events are added to the bottom of the Events area, so it might be necessary to scroll down in the Events area to find the new event.

2. You're going to create an event to make the blueBallerina roll one revolution whenever the mouse is clicked on her. First, click the word **anything** in the new event tile, and a menu of the objects in this Alice world will appear, as shown in Figure 3-15. Select **blueBallerina, the entire blueBallerina** as the target object. Next, make sure that the **blueBallerina** is selected in the Object tree, and that the **methods** tab is selected in the Details area. Drag the **blueBallerina roll** tile from the methods tab and drop it to replace *Nothing* in the event tile. Choose the values **right** and **1 revolution** for the direction and amount parameters.

FIGURE 3-15: The *When the mouse is clicked on anything* event tile with a menu of objects

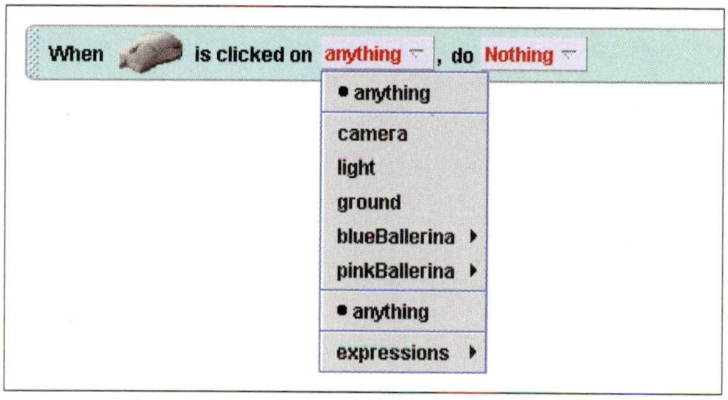

3. Now play the world and try the new method. After the opening move, click the **blue ballerina** and watch her roll. The B key event is still active, so you can try that also. Experiment a little. What happens if you click the blue ballerina while holding down the B key to make her turn? The two methods combine to cause unexpected results. If things get really messed up, you can restart the world and try again.

Additional Notes About Mouse Events

Sometimes it is very difficult to click an object while it is moving, so it is best to choose a stationary object as the target object. For example, you could put a tree into the world and make the ballerina spin while the mouse is pressed on the tree.

You can change the *When the mouse is clicked on anything* event to be *While the mouse is pressed on anything*, with the BDE format. This change will be similar to what you did with the *When a key is typed* and *While a key is pressed* event types.

Alice also has an event type to let users change the position of an object while a world is running. This event type is *Let the mouse move <objects>*. However, this event type requires the use of a data structure called a list, which isn't covered until Chapter 9, so we'll look at it when we get there.

TUTORIAL 3B—BUILDING CAMERA CONTROLS WITH EVENTS

In this tutorial, you are going to build controls to allow the user to manipulate the camera while a world is running. The tutorial will be brief because Alice has several event types with built-in event handlers for camera control.

Open an Existing World

You are going to add some camera controls to the *lakeSkaterDemoStart* world that is included with the Alice software.

1. First, start the Alice software. If it is already open, then close it and open it again to make sure that the old Alice world has been cleared from the computer's memory. When the Welcome to Alice! dialog box appears, open the **lakeSkaterDemoStart** world from the Examples tab. This is not the same *lakeSkater* world that you saw in Chapter 1, but a similar world named *lakeSkaterDemoStart*. The *lakeSkaterDemoStart* is a nice world to use for experimenting with camera controls because it contains some interesting winter scenery with a frozen lake, hills, and trees.

2. Note that once the world loads, you can see the world window with three sets of blue arrows below it to manipulate the camera, as shown in Figure 3-16.

FIGURE 3-16: The *lakeSkaterDemoStart* world window with the camera controls at the bottom

The curved arrow on the right is the camera's **tilt** control. It is used to tilt the camera up or down, just as you might tilt your head up or down. The center control is a mixed control, to **zoom** and **pan** the camera. A camera can zoom in and zoom out, and pan left and pan right. Zooming in means the camera moves in closer to get a tighter shot of something, so that it fills more of the screen. Zooming out means the camera moves out farther to get a longer shot of something, so that it becomes smaller on the screen. Panning means turning the camera left or right without moving the position of the camera, although it is possible to pan and move at the same time.

Most cameras have a lens that will allow the photographer to zoom in and zoom out without moving the camera. In Alice, you zoom in and zoom out by actually moving the camera forward and backward.

Remember, an object in 3D space can move in six different directions: forward, backward, left, right, up, and down. The left set of arrows at the bottom of the world window is the move control, which provides controls to move the camera left and right, and up and down, while the vertical arrows in the center set move the camera forward and backward.

Take a few minutes to experiment with the camera controls and explore the landscape in this Alice world. Try to see if you understand the concepts of tilt, zoom, pan, and move. Pick an object, such as a particular tree, and see if you can frame it in the world window. To **frame** an object means to position the camera so that the object fills the screen. You could frame an individual object, a group of objects, or a particular scene.

The blue arrows can be used to control the Alice camera before a world starts, but they don't work once a world is running. There are three Alice events designed to let us manipulate the camera once a world is running:

- *Let the mouse orient the camera*

- *Let the mouse move the camera*

- *Let the arrow keys move the camera*

We'll look at each one individually.

The *Let the Mouse Orient the Camera* Event

1. Click the **create new event** button, and you will see the list of the nine event types in Alice, as shown earlier in Figure 3-9. Select **Let the mouse orient the camera,** the last item in the list. You should see a new event of this type appear in the Events area, as shown in Figure 3-17.

FIGURE 3-17: *Let the mouse orient the camera* event tile

Let   orient the camera

2. This event calls a special hidden event handler that will let the user pan the camera with the mouse when an Alice world is running. You cannot tilt or zoom the camera with this event; you can only pan left and right.

3. Play the world and try panning left and right by dragging the mouse. After you are finished experimenting, stop the Alice world.

The *Let the Mouse Move the Camera* Event

Alice has an event to allow the user to move the camera by clicking and dragging the mouse around the window for the playing world.

1. Click the **create new event** button, and this time click the second-to-last item in the list, **Let the mouse move the camera**. As before, you should see a new event of this type appear in the Events area, as shown in Figure 3-18.

FIGURE 3-18: *Let the mouse move the camera* event tile

2. Note that this event is only slightly different from the *Let the mouse orient the camera* event. It allows the user to pan the camera left and right (not move the camera as the name implies), and move the camera backward and forward.

3. Play the world and then test the new event by dragging the mouse. Do you see how this is different from *Let the mouse orient the camera*? When you are finished, stop the world before continuing.

The *Let the Arrow Keys Move the Camera* Event

A separate event in Alice allows the user to move the camera by using the arrow keys, as shown in Figure 3-19.

FIGURE 3-19: The *let the arrow keys move the camera* event tile

Let's take a look at this event.

1. Click the **create new event** button, and look at the list that appears.

2. Notice that there is no method named *Let the arrow keys move the camera*. However, the third item up from the bottom of the list says *Let the arrow keys move <subject>*. Select this item, and a new event of this type appears in the Events area. The last two events you saw had no parameters, but this one does. The default value for the **subject** parameter is the camera, so it's easy to use this event to move the camera with the arrow keys.

3. Like the last event, it only allows you to move the camera forward and backward, and to pan left and right. This was the event used to let the user control the camera in the *amusementPark* world in Tutorial 3A. Try it now in this world, and then you are finished with this tutorial. It is not necessary to save your work.

TUTORIAL 3C—BUILDING A FLYING MACHINE IN ALICE

In this tutorial, you will create a flying machine—an object that can move around in three-dimensional space under the control of a user. The purpose of the exercise is to learn to build user controls for moving objects.

Software Specifications

Let's start with some specifications for the flying machine. The first step in creating software is to make sure that you as the programmer know what the program is supposed to do. Software specifications provide that information. The specifications usually come from the client—the person requesting that the software be written. The specifications then need to be refined by the programmer to more specifically reflect the features of a particular programming language or development system.

In this part of the tutorial, you will review and refine the specifications but not actually create the code. The development of clear specifications is part of the first step in the the program development cycle discussed in the last chapter—design, code, test, and debug.

In this case, use the following specification as a starting point for the flying machine world:

1. It should contain a flying machine in a somewhat realistic environment.
2. The flying machine should be able to move in three-dimensional space.
3. There should be user controls to turn the object up, down, left, and right while the flying machine is in motion.
4. The user should be able to find the flying machine if it moves off camera.

Refining Specifications

Let's refine each of these specifications by adding more precise details. First, you need to find objects in the Alice object galleries that could serve as a flying machine and then select one.

1. Start the Alice software and open a blank world with the **grass** template. Next, click the **ADD OBJECTS** button to look at the Alice galleries. The Vehicles folder seems like a good place to start, so let's look there. Scroll through it, and you will see object class tiles for a Biplane, a Blimp, a Helicopter, a Jet, a NavyJet, and a Seaplane, as shown in Figure 3-20. Don't add anything to the world, yet; you are just looking through the galleries for ideas to help refine the specifications.

FIGURE 3-20: Some of the object class tiles from the Vehicles folder in the Local Gallery

2. So far, you have worked with the grass template, so for this world, let's pick the **seaplane**, and use the **water** template. Right now you're just putting together the specifications, so close the object gallery and note the revision to the first specification, as follows:

   1. Create a water world with a seaplane in it.

3. The specifications call for the world to look somewhat realistic, so let's add a few items to the water world to make it look better. The Vehicle Gallery contains a sailboat, and the Environment Gallery contains two different islands. You can use these. The revised first specification looks like this:

   1. Create a water world with a seaplane in it:
      a. Select the water template.
      b. Add a seaplane to the world.
      c. Add a few more items—such as an island or two, and a sailboat.

4. Our second specification says that the object should be able to move in three-dimensional space. To do this, you will create an event to keep the seaplane moving while the world is playing. The primitive move method has parameters for distance and amount. Our refined specifications will call for the seaplane to move forward one meter. This event will keep happening while the world is running—as soon as the seaplane finishes moving forward one meter, it will move forward another meter, and so on, for as long as the world runs. Our revised second specification is:

   2. Create an event—while the world is running: do seaplane move forward one meter.

5. The primitive move method has additional parameters that are not often used. We can get to them by clicking the word **more** in the turn method and then selecting **style** from the list that appears. Four styles are available, as seen in Figure 3-21: *gently, begin gently, end gently,* and *abruptly.* Gently means that our movement will begin and end gently. Abruptly means that the movement will be at a constant speed. If we choose abruptly, then the motion of our seaplane will look more even.

FIGURE 3-21: The move and turn events have four style parameters

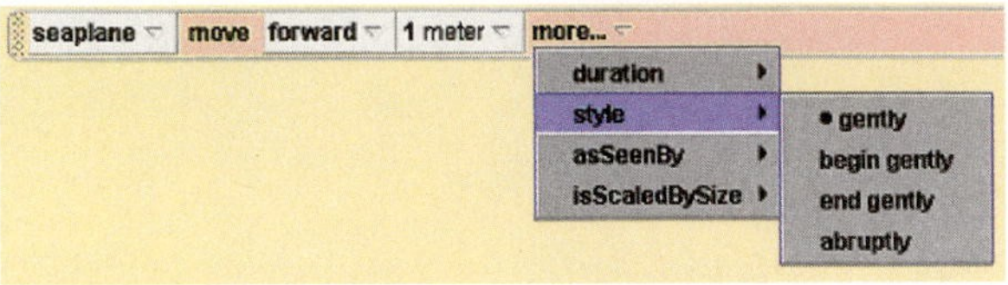

Now our specification should say:

2. *Create an event: While the world is running do: seaplane move forward one meter, style = abruptly.*

The specifications don't call for us to be able to modify the seaplane's speed, so we will assume the speed to be constant. When we set up and then test the world, we can change the speed by changing the distance parameter for each move from one meter to a larger or smaller amount.

6. We need user controls to make the seaplane turn up, down, left, and right. The built-in method for controlling an object with the keyboard lets us move objects, but not turn them. We need to build those controls—left arrow to turn left, right arrow to turn right, down arrow to turn down, and up arrow to turn up. The `turn` method has two commonly used parameters— direction and amount.

Left and right are easy, but the `turn` method does not have parameters up and down; it has parameters forward and backward. Is turning up the same as turning forward or backward? Try this: stand or sit facing straight ahead. Tilt your head backward. Did your face move up or down? We can see that turning backward makes an object's orientation turn up, and, conversely, turning forward makes an object's orientation turn down.

We also need to decide how much the seaplane will turn each time we press one of the arrow keys. Try one-eighth of a revolution. That's equivalent to 45 degrees. All together, we have the following control event specifications:

3. *Create four turn control events:*
   a. *When the left arrow key is pressed, turn left 1/8 revolution.*
   b. *When the right arrow key is pressed, turn right 1/8 revolution.*
   c. *When the up arrow key is pressed, turn backward 1/8 revolution.*
   d. *When the down arrow key is pressed, turn forward 1/8 revolution.*

7. Finally, the fourth specification says that the user needs to be able to find the flying machine if it moves off camera, which we can expect to happen at some point. There are several ways to do this, but one simple way is to choose a key to let the user point the camera at the seaplane whenever that key is pressed. Let's use an easy key—the spacebar. The *find the seaplane* event specification now looks like this:

   4. *Create an event: When the spacebar is pressed, point the camera at the seaplane.*

Let's list all of the more detailed specifications together:

1. *Create a world with a seaplane in it:*
   a. *Select the water template.*
   b. *Add a seaplane to the world.*
   c. *Add and position a few more items—such as an island or two, and a sailboat.*

2. *Create an event: While the world is running do: seaplane move forward one meter, style = abruptly.*

3. *Create four turn control events:*
   a. *When the left arrow key is pressed, turn left 1/8 revolution.*
   b. *When the right arrow key is pressed, turn right 1/8 revolution.*
   c. *When the up arrow key is pressed, turn backward 1/8 revolution.*
   d. *When the down arrow key is pressed, turn forward 1/8 revolution.*

4. *Create an event: When the spacebar is pressed, point the camera at the seaplane.*

Code the World—Specification 1, Create a World with a Seaplane

Now you are ready to create the world. Following the specifications, you need to create a water world with a seaplane in it, similar to Figure 3-22. Note that this specification is a bit subjective. What looks somewhat realistic to one person might not look that way to another.

FIGURE 3-22: A typical world for the Seaplane tutorial

1. First, start the Alice software. If it is already open, close it and restart Alice.
2. When the Welcome to Alice! dialog box appears, select the **water** world from the Templates tab.
3. Once the blank water world opens, click the **ADD OBJECTS** button, and add a **seaplane** to the world from the Vehicles folder in the Local Gallery. Also add a **sailboat** from this gallery and position it somewhere on the water away from the seaplane.
4. Next, add an **island** or two from the Environment Gallery and position the island(s) in the world. The world shown in Figure 3-22 also has a light-house and another boat. You may want to add and position a few additional objects such as these to make the world more interesting, but don't make the world appear too crowded. You may also want to reposition the camera back and up a bit, and then tilt it down toward the seaplane to get a wider view of the world, similar to what is shown in Figure 3-22.

5. When you are finished setting up the world, click the **DONE** button. You can also add a few items from other galleries, such as those shown in Figure 3-22, but don't get carried away.

Code the World—Specification 2, Animate the Seaplane

An event is needed to make the seaplane move continuously. Almost everything is spelled out in the second revised specification—*while the world is running do: seaplane move forward one meter, style = abruptly.*

1. Click the **create new event** button and choose **When the world starts** for the event type.

2. When the new event appears in the Events area, right-click it. From the menu that appears, select **change to**, and then select **While the world is running**.

3. Next, make sure that the **seaplane** is selected in the Object tree and that the **methods** tab is selected. Drag and drop a **seaplane move** tile into the event in place of *None* following the phrase *During*.

4. Choose the values **forward** and **1 meter** for the direction and amount parameters. Also, click the word **more**, and then select **style** from the menu that appears, as was shown in Figure 3-21, and change the style to **abruptly** so that the seaplane will move more smoothly. If the seaplane moves too slowly when the world is tested, remember that you can change the speed by changing the distance parameter for this event.

Code the World—Specification 3, Add Turn Controls

Next, events are needed to add controls to turn the seaplane, one for each of the four arrow keys, as shown in Figure 3-23.

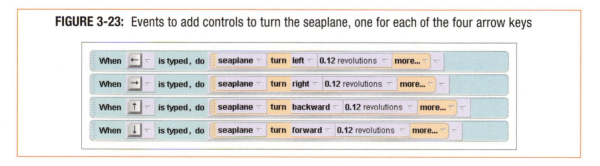

FIGURE 3-23: Events to add controls to turn the seaplane, one for each of the four arrow keys

1. Click the **create new event** button, and select **When a key is typed** as the event type. A new event tile of the form *When a key is typed* will appear in the Events area.

2. Change the *any key* parameter to **left arrow key**.

3. Make sure that the **seaplane** is selected in the Object tree and that the **methods** tab is selected in the Details area. Drag and drop a **seaplane turn** method tile into the new event in place of *Nothing* following the word *Do*, and choose the value **left** for the direction parameter. For the *amount* parameter, select **other** from the amount parameter list. A calculator style keypad will appear. Type **1/8** (as individual characters) and then click **Okay**.

4. Now the world has a control to turn left. In a similar manner, create three more events to provide controls to turn right, up, and down.

Code the World—Specification 4, Add a Find Control

The specifications call for us to create a method to point the camera at the seaplane when the spacebar is pressed.

1. Start by clicking the **create new event** button, and select **When a key is typed** as the event type.

2. When the new event appears, click the **any key** parameter and select **space** from the menu that appears.

3. Next, make sure that the **camera** is selected in the Object tree and that the **methods** tab is selected in the Details area. Drag and drop a **camera point at** method tile into your new event in place of *Nothing*, and select **seaplane, the entire seaplane** when the menu of possible target objects appears.

4. When this step is finished, you should be done coding your seaplane world. Save the world with the name **seaplane** before continuing.

Test the World

Once you are finished coding the world, test it to see if it works properly—that is, according to the specifications. A test plan is often used in professional software development. Such a plan often includes a series of questions based on the specifications. You need to determine if this world meets each of the original specifications, so your test plan might include the following questions:

1. Does the flying machine look like a flying machine in a somewhat realistic environment? (This is a fairly subjective requirement, with a loose standard for what looks realistic.)

2. Is it able to move in three-dimensional space?

3. Are there user controls to turn the object up, down, left, and right while the object is in motion? Do each of these work properly?

4. Can the user find the flying machine if it moves off camera?

To see if the world meets the specifications, play it several times, answering the questions from the test plan as you go along. It might also be good to let someone else, such as a fellow student or your instructor, do so as well. We want to see if it meets the specifications, and if there are any obvious problems or side effects in the finished world.

Debug the World

This might be the hardest part of the entire exercise. If the world does not meet one of the specifications, see if you can isolate the problem and fix it. Usually the problem lies in the code related to the failed specification, but not always—sometimes it is a side effect of other code.

Remember that software development is a cycle. If you find any errors, you need to repeat the steps in the cycle to review the design specifications, code any changes, test, and debug.

Chapter Summary

This chapter consisted of discussions of events and three-dimensional space, followed by hands-on tutorials involving events, camera controls, and construction of a flying machine in Alice.

The discussion of events included the following:

☐ A modern personal computer uses event-driven software for its Graphical User Interface (GUI), which has icons on the computer screen and a mouse to control a pointer that can be used to operate the computer.

☐ An event occurs when an event listener detects an event trigger and responds by running an event handler.

☐ An event listener is a combination of hardware and software that repeatedly checks the computer system for the event trigger.

☐ An event trigger can be any activity or condition that causes an event to occur.

☐ An event handler is a method that is activated when the event trigger occurs. Almost any method can serve as an event handler.

☐ When the event listener detects an event trigger, an event handler is called into action.

The discussion of three-dimensional (3D) space included the following:

☐ A dimension is a way of measuring something. It is an abstract idea invented by people to help us understand something.

☐ Only one dimension is needed to measure the location of a point on a straight line; on a flat plane, two dimensions are needed; and in real physical space, three dimensions are needed.

☐ A three-dimensional space, like the physical world around us, is sometimes referred to as Euclidean 3-space. The 3D worlds of Alice are Euclidean 3-spaces.

☐ The concepts of distance and direction together make up an object's point of view.

☐ A direction or position in relation to a scale of measurement is called absolute, and from the point of view of a specific object, it is called object-relative.

☐ In Alice's Euclidean 3-space, there are six object-relative directions—forward, backward, left, right, up, and down. There are also six object-relative positions—in front of, behind, to the left of, to the right of, above, and below.

In Tutorial 3A, you explored events in Alice and worked with some of Alice's nine different event types that can be used to provide mouse and keyboard controls. You also saw that some events have a BDE format.

In Tutorial 3B, you experimented with events to create camera controls. You saw that a camera can move, pan, tilt, and zoom.

In Tutorial 3C, you created a flying machine in Alice. You applied what you had learned about events and the ideas from Chapter 2 about a program development cycle to design the world before coding and testing it.

Review Questions

1. Define each of the following terms:

   - absolute direction
   - BDE event format
   - Cartesian coordinates
   - command-driven interface
   - dimension
   - Euclidean 3-space
   - event handler
   - event listener

   - event trigger
   - event-driven software
   - frame (verb)
   - Graphical User Interface (GUI)
   - object-relative direction
   - object-relative position
   - ordered pair

   - orientation
   - pan
   - point of view
   - quantification
   - side effects
   - tilt
   - zoom

2. Describe the difference between the terms object-relative position and object-relative direction.

3. Create a drawing of a number line, with three objects at different points on the number line. For each object, list the following:

   a. The point of view of each object
   b. The distance and absolute direction from each object to each other object
   c. The object-relative direction from that object to each of the other two objects

4. Describe the function of each of the blue arrows that appears below the world window in the standard Alice interface.

5. Does the cabin in Alice's *lakeSkaterDemoStart* world have a back door? To answer this question, you need to open the world and manipulate the camera using the camera controls below the world window so that you can see the back of the cabin.

6. Describe an Alice event of the BDE format that will make a ballerina jump up when a key is pressed, spin around for as long as the key is held down, and return to the ground when the user lets go of the key.

7. Individual keyboard events can be created to control the camera. As such, do the following:

   a. Describe a set of two keyboard events to allow the user to pan the camera.
   b. Describe a set of two keyboard events to allow the user to tilt the camera.
   c. Describe a set of two keyboard events to allow the user to zoom the camera in and out.

8. List and describe each of the four style parameters that can be used for **move**, **turn**, and **roll** methods. Why is the abruptly style used in the following event?

   While the world is running, move seaplane forward 1 meter style = abruptly.

9. Why wasn't Alice's built-in event for moving an object with the arrow keys used in the *seaplane* world in Tutorial 3C?

10. Look up the aviation terms *pitch, roll,* and *yaw* in a dictionary, or find a Web site on basic aeronautics, and read about them. How are they related to our seaplane controls?

Exercises

1. Create a simple Alice world to let a user drive a vehicle, such as a car, around on the ground. The Vehicles folder in the Local Gallery has a Zamboni machine, which could be driven around the *lakeSkaterDemoStart* world.

2. Create your own set of camera controls to allow the user to pan, tilt, zoom, and move the camera. The built-in controls do not allow for all of these options. Remember, in Alice we simulate zooming in and out by moving the camera closer or farther away.

3. Alice has a *Take Picture* button to capture the image from the world window while a world is playing. Open the *amusementPark* world and, for each element in the following list, use the camera control arrows to frame the object or group of objects and take the indicated picture:
   a. The octopus ride
   b. The Alice fountain
   c. The roller coaster and carousel together
   d. One of the teacups in the teacup ride
   e. Most of the amusement park, shown from slightly up in the air

4. Modify the *seaplane* world to include a barrel roll control. This would make the plane roll one complete revolution whenever a chosen key is pressed.

5. Modify the *seaplane* world to make the seaplane's propeller spin while the world is running. Does the propeller need to turn or roll to make this work?

6. Modify the *seaplane* world to make the turn events work more smoothly. To do this, we can change the form of each of the turn control events to *While the arrow key is pressed* instead of *When the arrow key is typed*, and change each turn's style to *abruptly*. You might also want to experiment with the `turn at speed` primitive method in place of the `turn` method.

7. Try to create a speed control for the *seaplane* world. This is a little harder than it looks. Here are some ideas:
   a. Create an object variable for the seaplane called *speed*.
   b. Set the initial value of the speed to zero.
   c. Pass the speed variable as the amount parameter to the seaplane's movement method instead of a fixed amount.
   d. Create two controls—one to increase the speed and one to decrease it. You can use a math expression to do this.

8. Create a simple Alice world to fly a pterodactyl instead of a plane. There is a pterodactyl in the Animals folder in the Local Gallery. You could build a method to flap its wings, and then use this as an event handler for an event while the world is in motion. Do the wings need to turn or roll? Should they go up and then down, or down and then up? How far should they move? You should experiment with the pterodactyl and then develop specifications before coding your world.

9. The Environment Gallery contains a bedroom. Create an Alice world with a bedroom that contains things like furniture, a clock, paintings, etc.

   Add events to the world to turn the bedroom into a haunted bedroom. For example, you could make a bed disappear into the floor and have a tombstone pop up whenever someone clicks the bed. You can create events that affect the subparts of an object, to do things like make the clock's hands spin, have dresser drawers open and close on their own, or make a character's head spin around.

10. The people folder in the local Alice Gallery has hebuilder and shebuilder classes to let you create your own Alice characters. These characters will have built-in methods to stand, walk, and show different moods. Experiment with the hebuilder or shebuilder in a simple Alice world to build a character of your own, and then create several events to show what the character can do. For example, create a method to make the character walk when the "W" key is pressed, or show confusion when the "C" key is pressed. You should experiment with the character and then develop specifications before coding your world.

Algorithms

After finishing this chapter, you should be able to:

☐ Provide a brief definition of the following terms: flowchart, linear sequence, branching routine, branch, selection sequence, binary branching, multiple branching, binary bypass, binary choice, structured language, pseudocode, repetition sequence, loop, control variable, pretest loop, posttest loop, count-controlled loop, counter, initial value, final value, increment, sentinel loop, thread, parallel algorithm, and concurrency

☐ List and describe the three major elements of logical structure found in algorithms

☐ List several criteria that should be met by each linear sequence

☐ Describe how binary bypass and binary choice selection sequences (branching routines) work, create simple flowchart segments and pseudocode for each, and implement each in at least one Alice method

☐ Describe how count-controlled and sentinel selections sequences (loops) work, create simple flowchart segments and pseudocode for each, and implement each in at least one Alice method

☐ Describe how pretest and posttest loops differ from one another, and why pretest loops are preferred

☐ Describe what is meant by parallel execution of instructions in an algorithm, and explain how to implement parallel execution in Alice

This chapter includes a discussion of the logical structure of algorithms—including linear sequences, selection sequences, repetition sequences, and parallel execution of instructions in an algorithm. This discussion is followed by three tutorials that will provide you with experience implementing these in Alice.

ELEMENTS OF LOGICAL STRUCTURE

In programming, an object is a collection of properties, along with the methods to manipulate those properties. Methods are algorithms. In order to effectively develop methods, you must understand the nature of algorithms.

Algorithms contain the steps necessary to complete a particular task or solve a particular problem. A recipe for baking a cake will have a list of all the ingredients needed, as well as step-by-step instructions on what to do with those ingredients. In other words, the recipe provides an algorithm for baking a cake.

When young children learn to perform long division, they are learning an algorithm. Professionals, such as engineers, architects, and doctors, apply many different algorithms in the course of their daily work. Some algorithms are simple; some can be quite long and complex. The Holtrop and Mennen Algorithm, which can be used by naval architects to design the optimum propellers for an oceangoing ship, involves several thousand steps and must be run on a computer.

Algorithms are sequential in nature, forming a kind of sequential logic. Modern object-oriented approaches to software development include much more than just algorithm development, yet programmers need to be able to design and implement sequential algorithms. They need to understand sequential logic.

Sequential logic forms patterns, which can be understood as the elements of logical structure. These elements are combined in a myriad of ways to form the complex algorithms found in modern computer software. A programmer who is familiar with the design patterns of logical structure can more easily create and edit software.

Think about how a programmer's work compares to the work of a plumber or an electrician. A person who wants to design a plumbing system for a building, such as a house, has a selection of existing parts from which to choose. We can see these parts in a hardware store or building supply warehouse—elbows, T-joints, different kinds of valves, and so on. Despite differences from one house to another, the plumbing systems will be composed of many of the same parts, which we might think of as the elements of structure for a plumbing system. The architects who design the system need to know how the parts work and how they fit together. The plumbers who build or repair the system need to know how to work with each of the parts.

The same concept is true for an electrical system. The electrical engineers and electricians who design and build such systems need to be familiar with the parts that are available, how they work, and how they fit together. Switches, wires, outlets, junction boxes, circuit breakers, and so on can be thought of as the building blocks of an electrical system.

Now, consider this concept in terms of the elements of the logical structure in an algorithm. They form the building blocks of the algorithm's sequential logic. However, there are only a handful of basic elements of logical structure that programmers need to learn, not hundreds or even thousands of different parts, as in plumbing and electrical systems. In the 1960s, two Italian mathematicians, Corrado Böhm and Giuseppe Jacopini, showed that algorithms are composed of three major structures: linear sequences, branching routines, and loops. These are the building blocks of algorithms that you must understand to be a good computer programmer.

Flowcharts

Böhm and Jacopini used a system they called flow diagrams to describe their work. In Figure 4-1, you can see part of their manuscript showing some of their flow diagrams, which soon became known as flowcharts. A **flowchart** is a diagram that shows the structure of an algorithm. Böhm and Jacopini weren't the first to use such diagrams; however, they formalized the concept of flowcharts and used them in their work on algorithms.

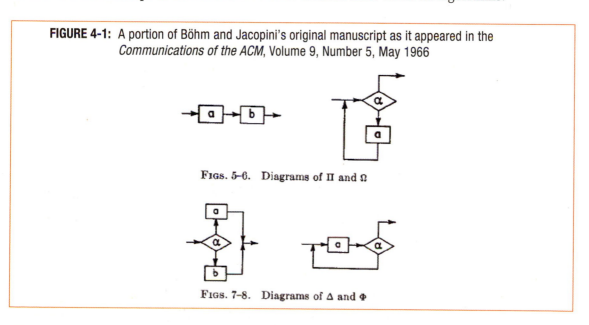

FIGURE 4-1: A portion of Böhm and Jacopini's original manuscript as it appeared in the *Communications of the ACM*, Volume 9, Number 5, May 1966

FIGS. 5–6. Diagrams of Π and Ω

FIGS. 7–8. Diagrams of Δ and Φ

Böhm and Jacopini used a simple system of flowcharting with two symbols: rectangles to show each step in an algorithm, and diamond-shaped boxes to show what they called a logical predicative. More commonly, the diamond symbol for a logical predicative is called a decision diamond, a decision box, or a conditional.

To say that one thing is "predicated" on another means that one thing is determined by another. In other words, there is some condition that will determine what happens next. In an algorithm, these conditions will be either true or false. If the condition is true, one thing happens; if the condition is false, then something else happens. The path through an algorithm each time it is executed is determined by the state of the true or false conditions in that algorithm at that time. Flowcharts are designed to show the possible paths through an algorithm.

Flowcharting Template

Böhm and Jacopini's notion of flow diagrams was relatively simple, but, in practice, flowcharts quickly became complicated as people continued to add more shapes. Figure 4-2 shows a flowcharting template introduced by IBM in 1969. It was accompanied by a 40-page manual showing the proper way to use all of the symbols.

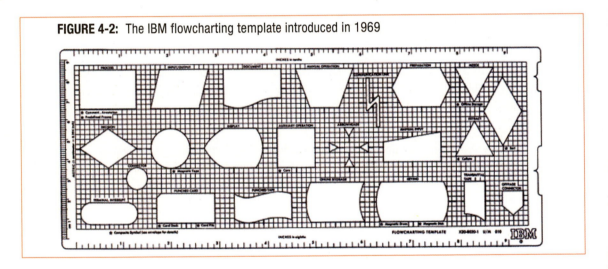

FIGURE 4-2: The IBM flowcharting template introduced in 1969

Flowchart Symbols

In the rest of this chapter, we will use a simple version of flowcharting to help describe the elements of logical structure found in algorithms. We will use only three symbols: rectangles and diamonds—as Böhm and Jacopini did—and an oval-shaped box, which is used to mark the beginning and end of an algorithm, as shown in Figure 4-3.

The oval shape is called a terminator. There should be only one terminator at the beginning of an algorithm and one terminator at the end of an algorithm, because each algorithm should have one beginning, called an entry point, and one end, called an exit point. Usually terminators are labeled with the words "start" or "stop," or sometimes "begin" or "end."

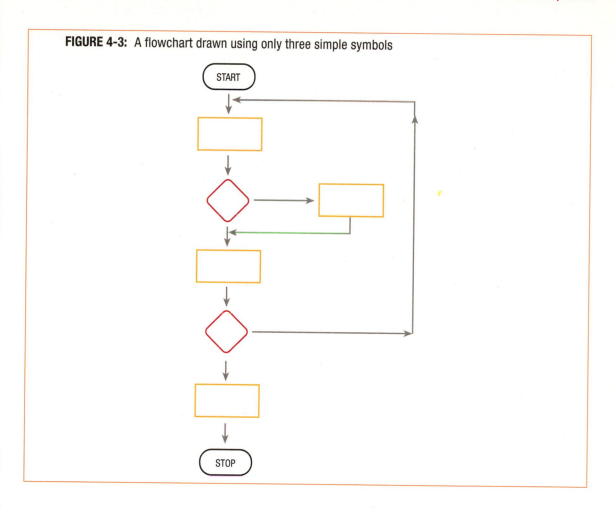

FIGURE 4-3: A flowchart drawn using only three simple symbols

LINEAR SEQUENCES

The simplest element of logical structure in an algorithm is a **linear sequence**, in which one instruction follows another as if in a straight line. The most notable characteristic of a linear sequence is that it has no branching or looping routines. There is only one path of logic through the sequence, which doesn't divide into separate paths, and nothing is repeated.

On a flowchart, this would appear as a single path of logic, which would always be executed one step after another, as shown in Figure 4-4.

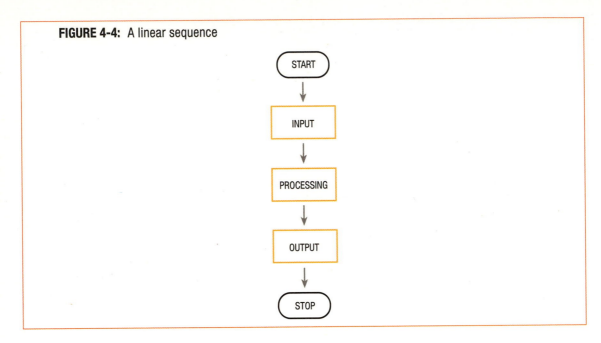

FIGURE 4-4: A linear sequence

Linear sequences are deceptively simple. It doesn't seem very complicated to do one thing, then another, and then another, but it can be. Programmers need to make sure that each linear sequence meets the following criteria:

- The sequence has a clear starting point and ending point.
- Entry and exit conditions is clearly stated. What conditions need to exist before the sequence starts? What can we expect the situation to be when the sequence is finished?
- The sequence of instructions is complete. Programmers need to be sure not to leave out any necessary steps. (This is harder than it sounds. See Exercise 2 at the end of this chapter for an example.)
- The sequence of instructions is in the proper order.
- Each instruction in the sequence is correct. If one step in an algorithm is wrong, then the whole algorithm is wrong.

In short, linear sequences must have clearly stated entry and exit conditions, and they need to be complete, correct, and in the proper order.

SELECTION SEQUENCES—BRANCHING ROUTINES

Sometimes an algorithm reaches a point at which the path through the algorithm can go one way or another. That is, the code can execute a selection sequence. Consider this example of a student who has chemistry lab at 2:00 p.m. on Fridays only:

```
Start
IF (Today is Friday)
THEN (Get to chemistry lab by 2:00 p.m.)
Stop
```

Diagrammed as part of flowchart, it would look like Figure 4-5.

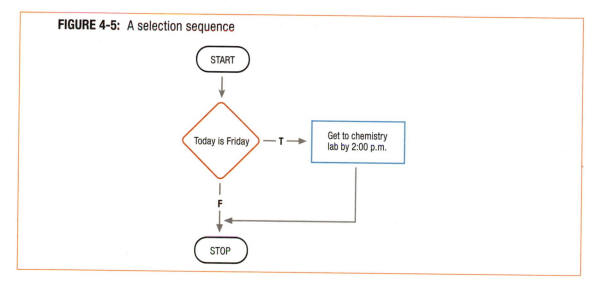

FIGURE 4-5: A selection sequence

This is an example of a branching routine. A **branching routine** occurs whenever the path or flow of sequential logic in an algorithm splits into two or more paths. Each path is called a **branch**. Branching routines are also known as **selection sequences** or selection structures.

Binary and Multiple Branching

If there are two possible paths, then the routine is known as **binary branching**. If there are more than two paths, then it is called **multiple branching**. "Would you like vanilla ice cream?" is a binary question. It has two possible answers, "yes" and "no." "What flavor ice cream would you like?" is a question with many possible answers. Binary branching is similar to the first question; multiple branching is similar to the second.

It is possible to rewrite each multiple branching routine as a collection of binary branching routines. Consider an ice cream parlor with 28 flavors of ice cream. Instead of asking the multiple question, "What flavor ice cream would you like?", a series of binary questions

could be asked, for example: "Would you like vanilla ice cream?" "Would you like chocolate ice cream?" "Would you like strawberry ice cream?" In a similar manner, every multiple branching routine in an algorithm can be rewritten as a series of binary branching
routines.

The Alice exercises in this chapter focus on binary branching rather than multiple branching. In fact, Alice does not have an instruction for multiple branching.

Binary Branching

There are two kinds of binary branching: a **binary bypass** and a **binary choice**. In a binary
bypass, an instruction is either executed or bypassed, as shown in Figure 4-5. In a binary
choice, one of two instructions is chosen, as shown in Figure 4-6. The difference between a
bypass and a choice is subtle but significant. In a binary bypass, it is possible that nothing
happens, whereas in a binary choice, one of the two instructions (but not both) will occur.

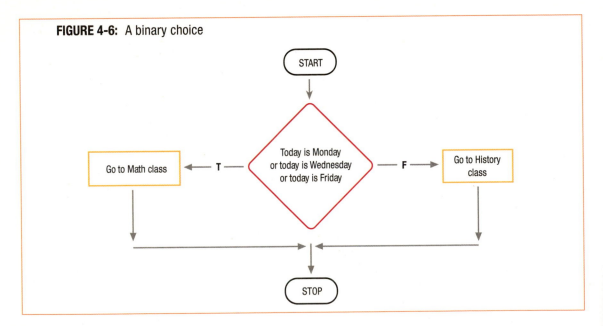

FIGURE 4-6: A binary choice

Pseudocode

Sometimes computer programmers use a more formal language, called **structured language**
or **pseudocode,** to describe algorithms. The term pseudocode comes from the fact that it
looks something like the code in a computer programming language, but not quite. It's like
code, but it's only a tool to help describe and understand algorithms, just as flowcharts are.

In pseudocode, a bypass is equivalent to an IF/THEN instruction of the form IF (*condition*)
THEN (*instruction*). If the condition is true, then the instruction is executed; if the condition

is not true, then the instruction is ignored, and the computer will move on to the next step in the algorithm. The chemistry lab example prior to Figure 4-5 shows a binary bypass.

A binary choice is equivalent to an IF (*condition*) THEN (*instruction A*) ELSE (*instruction B*). If the condition is true, then instruction A is executed; if the condition is not true, then instruction B is executed. Either instruction A or instruction B will be executed, but not both. One of the two always happens, as seen in the example in Figure 4-6, in which a student has Math class on Monday, Wednesday, and Friday, and History class on Tuesday and Thursday. (We will assume the student only needs to consider weekdays and not weekends.) The pseudocode showing an algorithm for the student's day might include the following:

```
IF (today is Monday, or today is Wednesday, or today is Friday)
THEN (go to math class)
ELSE (go to history class)
```

A set of instructions, called a block of instructions or a block of code, could take the place of a single instruction anywhere in an algorithm, including in binary branching routines. In the preceding example, `go to math class` could be a whole series of instructions.

One thing is common to all binary branching routines—there must be a condition to determine what to do. These conditions will be either true or false when the algorithm is executed. They are a form of conditional logic known as Boolean logic, which will be discussed in the next chapter.

REPETITION SEQUENCES—LOOPING

In the branching routines that you saw earlier in the chapter, the algorithms split into different paths that all moved forward; nothing was repeated. A **repetition sequence** occurs when an algorithm branches backward to a previous instruction, and then repeats part of the algorithm. A repetition sequence forms a **loop** in an algorithm, which can be seen on a flowchart, as shown in Figure 4-7. This figure shows both the pseudocode and a flowchart for the algorithm for printing numbers from 1 to 10.

In this algorithm, the word WHILE is used for looping instead of the word IF, which was used for branching. In pseudocode, as in many programming languages, this usage tells the computer to loop back to the conditional expression when the block of code following the WHILE instruction is finished. Each time the condition is true, the computer will execute the block of code, and then come back to the condition again. When the condition is no longer true, the block of code will be ignored, much like a binary bypass, and the computer will move on to whatever comes next in the algorithm.

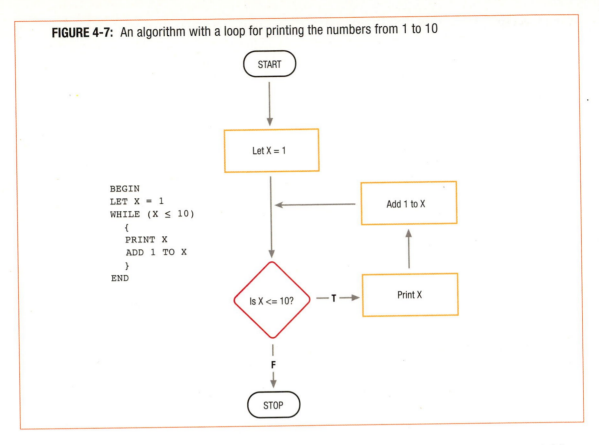

FIGURE 4-7: An algorithm with a loop for printing the numbers from 1 to 10

```
BEGIN
LET X = 1
WHILE (X ≤ 10)
    {
    PRINT X
    ADD 1 TO X
    }
END
```

Like all loops, this loop has a control variable in its condition. In programming, a variable holds a value that can change, much like a variable in algebra, which stands for a number that could change. A **control variable** is a variable whose value controls whether or not a selection sequence will be executed. In this loop, the variable X stands for a number that is used to keep track of how many times a loop should be executed. In this example, we want to print the numbers from 1 to 10. X starts at 1 and increases by 1 each time through the loop. While X is less than 10, the loop is executed and the number is printed. When X reaches 11, we move on to whatever comes next.

Pretest and Posttest Loops

The loop in Figure 4-7 is a **pretest loop,** meaning that the test to determine whether or not to go though the loop comes before the block of code to be executed. Traditionally, there are four parts to every pretest loop:

- Initialization: an instruction that sets the first value of the control variable
- Test: the instruction that looks at the control variable to see if the loop should be executed

- Processing: instructions that define the process to be repeated
- Update: an instruction that changes the value of the control variable

Figure 4-8 shows the example again, this time using COUNT instead of X and highlighting the four parts of the loop.

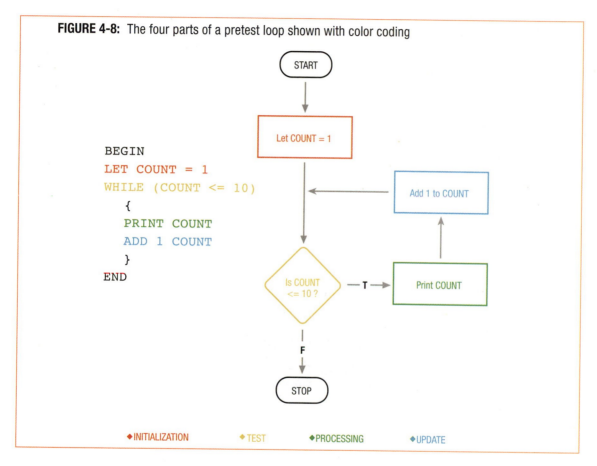

FIGURE 4-8: The four parts of a pretest loop shown with color coding

```
BEGIN
LET COUNT = 1
WHILE (COUNT <= 10)
    {
    PRINT COUNT
    ADD 1 COUNT
    }
END
```

◆INITIALIZATION   ◆TEST   ◆PROCESSING   ◆UPDATE

In a pretest loop, the test to determine whether or not to continue executing the loop comes before any other instructions that are to be repeated. It is also possible to set up a **posttest loop**, with the test to determine whether or not to repeat a loop coming after the instructions that are to be repeated.

Figure 4-1, near the beginning of this chapter, shows diagrams of four different logical structures from Böhm and Jacopini's original manuscript. Look closely at both the upper-right diagram and the lower-right diagram. In both cases, the condition in the diamond-shaped box is labeled with the Greek letter "**α**" (alpha), and the rectangular box representing an instruction to be repeated is labeled with the letter "a." Notice that the upper structure is a pretest loop with the decision diamond before the instruction to be repeated, and the lower structure is a posttest loop, with the decision diamond after the instruction to be repeated.

Some computer programming languages contain a REPEAT (*instruction*) UNTIL (*condition*) structure to create a posttest loop, yet many computer scientists suggest that only pretest loops should be used in programming. To see why they suggest this, consider the following two programs:

1. Program 1—When the computer is turned on, the program erases the first hard drive and then asks "Should I do that again for the next hard drive?" (Of course, this assumes the program will still run after the first hard drive has been erased.)
2. Program 2—When the computer is turned on, the program asks "Do you want me to erase the first hard drive?" If the answer is "yes," it erases the first hard drive, and then it asks if you want to repeat the process for the next hard drive.

The second program is slightly more complicated than the first, but which do you think is a safer program to run?

Unfortunately, people often think very differently than the way a computer works. We tend to do something first, and then ask if it should be repeated, like a posttest loop instead of a pre-test loop—just the opposite of what computer scientists suggest. Alice has a WHILE instruction for pretest loops, but it does not contain any commands to set up a posttest loop.

Count-Controlled and Sentinel Loops

In addition to being a pretest loop, the example in Figure 4-8 is also a count-controlled loop. Every loop in a computer program is either a count-controlled loop, or a sentinel loop. A **count-controlled loop** causes a process to be repeated a specific number of times. A **sentinel loop** causes a process to be repeated until a condition or marker, called a **sentinel**, is encountered.

In a count-controlled loop, the control variable is a called a **counter**. In some programming languages, the counter is also called the **index** of the loop. We need to know the **initial value**, the **final value**, and the **increment** for the counter. The loop starts with the counter at the initial value. The increment is the amount added to the counter each time through the loop. If the increment is positive, then the index increases by the increment each time through the loop. If the increment is negative, then the index decreases by the increment each time through the loop. The final value is the last value processed by the loop. In Figure 4-8, the initial value is 1, the increment is 1, and the final value is 10.

It's important to make sure that the initial value, the final value, and the increment are coordinated. If a computer were programmed to start the counter at 100, and then increase it by 1 each time through the loop until it reached 0, we would probably get some unexpected results.

If the increment is positive, then the final value should be higher than the initial value. If the increment is negative, then the final value should be lower than the initial value.

Alice has a special LOOP instruction for programming count-controlled loops, which automatically handles the counter's increment and final value. Most programming languages have a similar instruction, such as the FOR instruction in Java. However, Alice's LOOP instruction does not let us use a negative increment. That is, you could not use the LOOP instruction to add a negative number to the counter each time through the loop. If you wanted to start at 100 and count backward until you reached zero, then you would need to set up your own count-controlled loop using the WHILE instruction instead of the special LOOP instruction.

NOTE □ □ □ A count-controlled loop is a special case of a sentinel loop, in which the sentinel involves a counter, but the term "sentinel loop" is generally used to refer only to loops that are not count-controlled.

As an example of such a loop, imagine a machine that tests a car door. The machine, which is controlled by a computer program, opens the door, and then closes the door. The machine could be programmed to repeat this a certain number of times with a count-controlled loop. However, it could also be programmed to repeat the process until the door falls off, as shown in the following pseudocode:

```
BEGIN
LET counter = 0
WHILE (door is still on the car)
    {
    open the door
    close the door
    increment counter by 1
    }
PRINT "The door fell off after opening and closing this many times:"
PRINT counter
END
```

The counter in this loop does not control when the loop stops running, so this is not a count-controlled loop, but rather a sentinel loop. It is the sentinel condition, the door still being on the car or falling off the car, that controls when the loop will stop.

In summary, when code in a computer program is repeated, the algorithm contains a repetition structure, which is also called a loop. Algorithms can contain count-controlled loops or sentinel loops that are not count-controlled. Each loop is also a pretest loop or a posttest loop. Alice has a WHILE instruction for pretest loops but does not allow posttest loops. Alice also has a special LOOP instruction for count-controlled loops.

There are two methods of programming that are more appropriate than loops in many situations in which processes are repeated—event-driven programming and recursion. These methods will be discussed in detail in later chapters.

PARALLEL ALGORITHMS

It is possible for one computer, or several computers working together, to work on several parts of an algorithm at the same time. Each path of logic that is being executed is called a **thread** of sequential logic, and algorithms that run multiple threads at the same time are called **parallel algorithms**. The process of running multiple threads is called parallel execution, concurrent execution, or **concurrency**.

Parallel algorithms can be quite powerful, but they can be difficult to design and use. Many problems arise, such as the different threads interfering with each other. It might be easier to run a restaurant kitchen with four chefs instead of one, but if things aren't carefully coordinated, then chaos could ensue.

Concurrency is mentioned here for two reasons: first, it is becoming more common, even in simple programs, and second, concurrency is important in Alice. For instance, you need it when an object should move and turn at the same time, or when two objects should move at the same time.

You have already seen a simple version of concurrency in Alice. In Chapter 3, you used the *Do together* logical structure, which causes parallel execution of separate instructions. Alice also has a *For all together* instruction that can be used with lists, which will be covered in Chapter 9.

TUTORIAL 4A—BRANCHING IN ALICE METHODS

In this exercise, you will modify the *triple jump* world from Chapter 2 to include user input and branching. The world contains three objects, each a character from *Alice's Adventures in Wonderland*. The existing version of the world contains a method to make all three characters jump, one at a time. The algorithm in `world.my first method` is simply a linear sequence. You will modify it to include user input and IF/THEN instructions. The new program will ask the user questions about which character should jump, and then have one of the three characters jump, depending on the answers to those questions.

Alice has a world-level function to ask the user a yes or no question. You are going to add two questions to `world.my first method`. First, the method will ask if the user wants Alice to jump. If the answer is "yes," then Alice will jump. If the answer is "no," then the method will ask if the user wants the White Rabbit to jump. If the second answer is "yes," then the White Rabbit will jump: if the answer is "no," then the Cheshire Cat will jump. The pseudocode and flowchart in Figure 4-9 describe this algorithm.

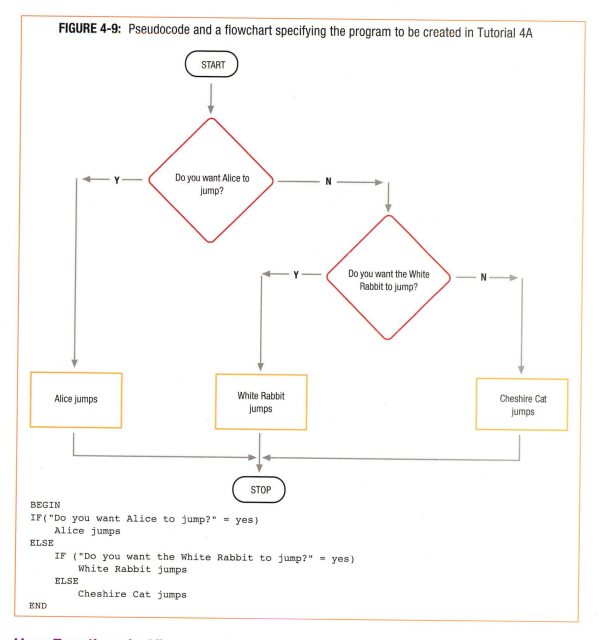

FIGURE 4-9: Pseudocode and a flowchart specifying the program to be created in Tutorial 4A

```
BEGIN
IF("Do you want Alice to jump?" = yes)
    Alice jumps
ELSE
    IF ("Do you want the White Rabbit to jump?" = yes)
        White Rabbit jumps
    ELSE
        Cheshire Cat jumps
END
```

User Functions in Alice

Before you start, you need more information about the user input functions in Alice. There are three world-level functions in Alice to ask the user a question: *ask user for a number, ask user for yes or no*, and *ask user for a string*. Figure 4-10 shows the tiles for these three functions on the functions tab in the Details area for the world.

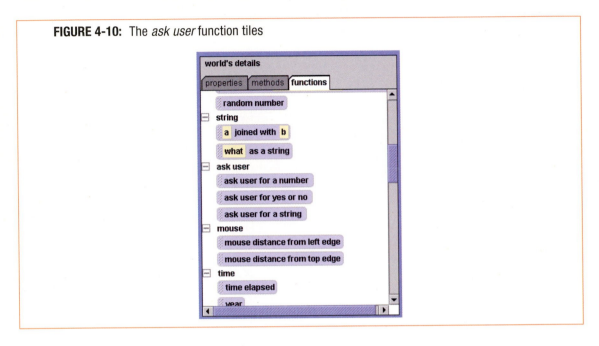

FIGURE 4-10: The *ask user* function tiles

In the following steps, you will use the function to *ask user for yes or no,* which returns a value of true if the user answers "yes" to the question and false if the user answers "no." This function may be used any place in an Alice method where `true` or `false` can be used, such as in a condition in an IF/ELSE instruction.

1. Start the Alice software and open the **triple jump** world created in Chapter 2. If you cannot find the world, then either load the world from the student data files for this book, or complete Tutorial 2B to create and save the world before continuing.

2. Look at the code for `world.my first method`, as shown in Figure 4-11. You can see that there are several instructions that form a linear sequence in the program. You need to add an IF/ELSE instruction to the method. Drag a copy of the **If/Else** tile from the bottom of the Editor area and drop it into the method just below the three jump instructions.

3. A short menu will appear asking you if you want to use a true or false condition in the IF/ELSE instruction. Select **true**, and a light greenish-blue *If/Else* tile will appear in your method, as shown in Figure 4-12.

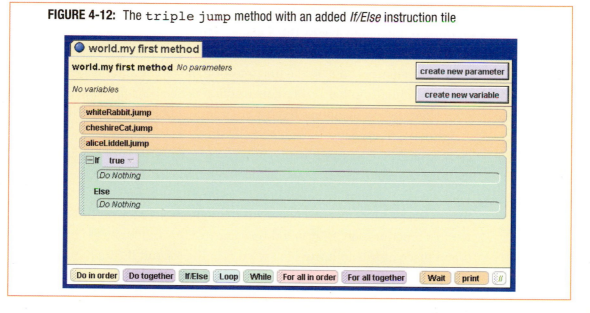

FIGURE 4-11: The *triple jump* world's `world.my first method`

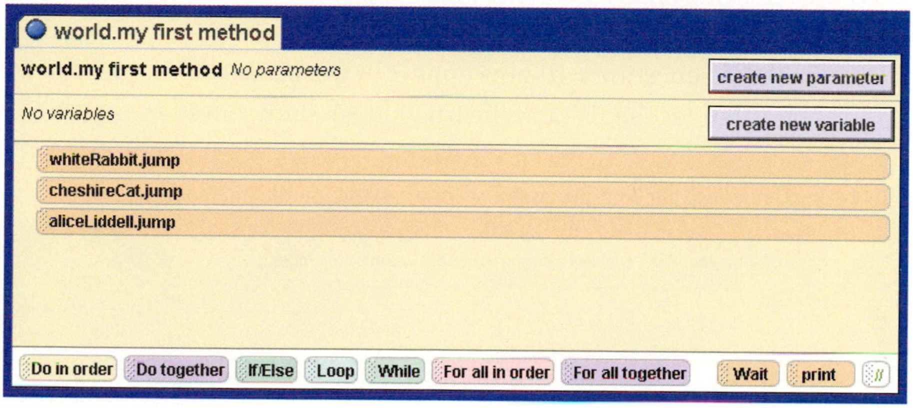

FIGURE 4-12: The `triple jump` method with an added *If/Else* instruction tile

4. Next, you need to replace *true* in the *If/Else* tile with the function to *ask user yes or no*. Select the **world** tile in the Object tree, and then click the **functions** tab in the Details area. Scroll through the list of functions and find the function titled *ask user for yes or no*. Drag and drop a copy of this function into the *If/Else* tile in place of *true* following the word *If*.

5. A short menu will appear with the options *Yes or No?* and *other....* This menu is asking you how you want to word the question that the user will

see. Click **other ...**, and the Enter a string dialog box will appear. The character string entered here will form the text of the question the user will see. Type **Do you want Alice to jump?** as the string, and then click the **OK** button. Your question will now appear in the *If/Else* tile in place of *true* as the condition for the IF/ELSE instruction, as shown in Figure 4-13.

FIGURE 4-13: The *If/Else* tile with the *ask user for yes or no* function in place

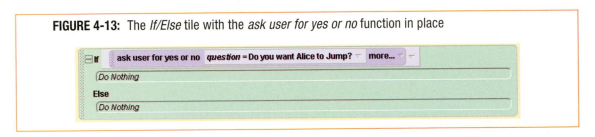

6. Drag the **aliceLiddell.jump** tile from its place in the linear sequence above the *If/Else* tile, and drop it into the IF/ELSE instruction in place of *Do Nothing* immediately below the *If* clause, and above the word *Else*. Now if the user answers "yes" to the question, Alice will jump.

7. If the user answers "no" to the first question, he or she should see a second question. Thus, another IF/ELSE instruction is needed following the word *Else.* Drag and drop another **IF/Else** tile from the bottom of the Editor area and drop it in place of *Do Nothing* following the word *Else*, and then click **True** when the short menu appears. Now you have nested IF/ELSE instructions—one IF/ELSE tile inside another one.

8. You need to put another question in place of true in the second *If/Else* instruction. As before, find the function titled *ask user for yes or no* on the world's functions tab. Drag and drop a copy of this function into the *If/Else* tile in place of *true* following the word *If* in the second IF/ELSE instruction.

9. A short menu will appear. Click **other ...**, and the Enter a string dialog box will appear. Type **Do you want the White Rabbit to jump?** as the string, and click the **OK** button. Your second question will now appear in the *If/Else* tile in place of *true* as the condition for the IF/ELSE instruction.

10. If the user answers "yes," the whiteRabbit should jump. Drag the **whiteRabbit.jump** tile and drop it in the instruction in place of *Do Nothing* below the *If* clause and above the word *Else.*

11. Drag the **cheshireCat.jump** tile, and drop it in the instruction in place of *Do Nothing* below the word *Else.*

12. Your method should look like the code shown in Figure 4-14. You are now ready to test the new program, but first you should save your work. Save the world with the name **jump user choice**.

FIGURE 4-14: The completed `world.my first` method in the *jump user choice* world

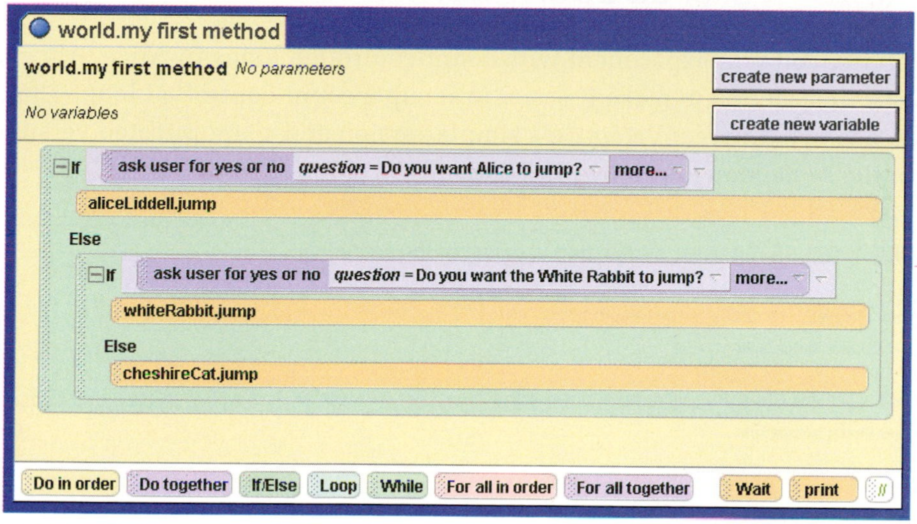

It's a good idea to test the world under all possible circumstances, which in this case means trying the world with all possible combinations of user input. This calls for a testing plan.

The specifications in Figure 4-9 show that there are three possible paths for the logic in the program. The answer to the first question could be "yes" or "no." If it's "yes," then Alice should jump and the program is done. If it's "no," then the second question appears. If the answer to the second question is "yes," then the White Rabbit jumps, and the program ends. If the answer to the second question is "no," then the Cheshire Cat jumps, and the program ends. The testing plan must include three trials, one for each possibility, as follows:

- Trial 1—first answer "yes"
  Expected outcome—Alice jumps

- Trial 2—first answer "no," second answer "yes"
  Expected outcome—White Rabbit jumps

- Trial 3—first answer "no," second answer "no"
  Expected outcome—Cheshire Cat jumps

Test your program according to the testing plan, and see if it works as expected. If it does, you're done; if not, then it's time to debug. Remember to save your world again if you make any significant changes.

TUTORIAL 4B—A SIMPLE COUNT-CONTROLLED LOOP

In this exercise, you will experiment with count-controlled loops in Alice. Alice has a special LOOP instruction to make it easier to set up a count-controlled loop. The LOOP instruction has two different versions: a simple version and a complicated version. Both versions of the same loop are shown in Figure 4-15.

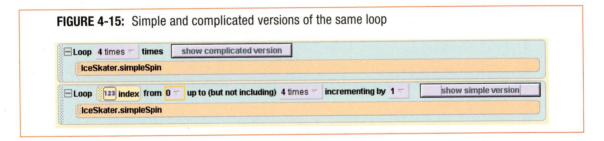

FIGURE 4-15: Simple and complicated versions of the same loop

In the simple version, the programmer simply tells Alice how many times to repeat the loop, and Alice will handle the counter, increment, and final value to stop the loop when it has been executed the specified number of times. In the complicated version, the programmer has access to the initial value, the final value, and the increment.

In the next several steps, you will modify the *triple jump* world created in Chapter 2 using the simple versions of Alice's LOOP instruction to make the characters jump a specified number of times.

1. Open the **triple jump** world created in Chapter 2, or create it again as described in Tutorials 2B and 2C in Chapter 2. A copy of the finished world is in the student data files for this book.

2. In this program, all three characters will jump at the same time. Drag a **Do together** tile from the bottom of the Editor area and place it in your method after the three jump instructions.

3. Drag each of the **jump** instructions into the middle of the *Do together* tile, as shown in Figure 4-16. This is an example of concurrency in an algorithm.

FIGURE 4-16: Parallel execution of the jump instructions

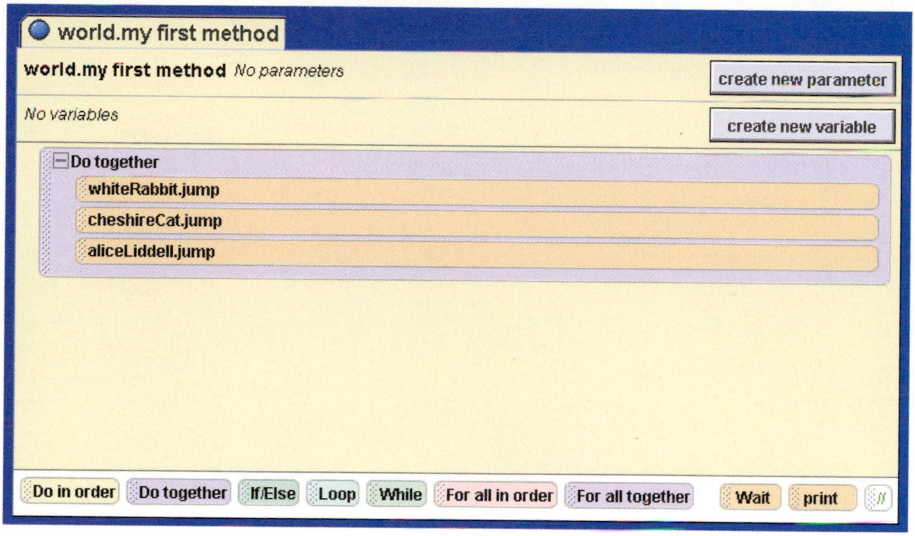

4. Save the world first with the name **triple jump loop,** and then play the world. If all three characters jump at the same time, then move on to the next step. If not, then find and fix the error.

5. Next, you will add a simple count-controlled loop to the program to make the three characters jump a certain number of times. Drag a **Loop** tile from the bottom of the Editor area and drop a copy of it into the method just below the *Do together* tile. When you do this, a short menu will appear asking you how many times you want to repeat the loop. Select **5 times.**

6. Drag the **Do together** tile into the *Loop* tile. Your method is complete and should now look like Figure 4-17.

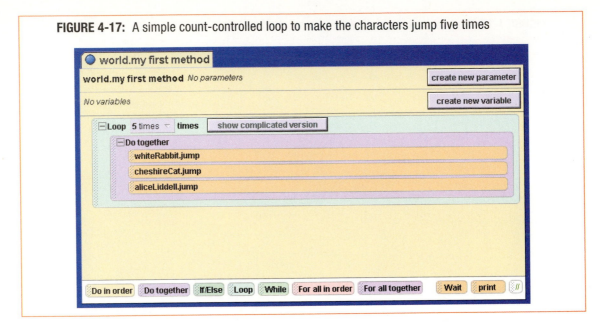

FIGURE 4-17: A simple count-controlled loop to make the characters jump five times

7. You can now test the world again, to make sure that the characters jump together five times. Save the world first, and then play it to see if it works.

This world demonstrates the use of the simple version of a loop instruction. All of the characters should jump together five times. If the program doesn't work properly, review your work to find the error in your program, and then fix it. Once it works, you are finished with this exercise.

 The LOOP instruction in Alice is really intended to be used only in situations where the programmer wants to make something happen a certain number of times, such as jumping five times. Remember that a count-controlled loop is just a special case of a sentinel loop. Whenever a more sophisticated loop is called for, such as one that counts backward, it is best to create your own version of a count-controlled loop with a WHILE instruction.

TUTORIAL 4C—USING THE WHILE INSTRUCTION

In this tutorial, you are going to use the WHILE instruction to duplicate the effect of the LOOP instruction used in Tutorial 4B. Remember that a sentinel loop has a value or condition that tells a loop when to stop executing. A count-controlled loop is just a special case of a sentinel loop.

You will use the *triple jump loop* world from Tutorial 4B as your base world, modifying it to use the WHILE instruction instead of the LOOP instruction, but the new world should function similarly to the old world. Figure 4-18 shows the algorithm for a simple count-controlled loop alongside the new algorithm for the WHILE loop you will create. Notice that the LOOP instruction handles the initialization, test, and update automatically, whereas the programmer must include instructions to deal with these steps in the WHILE loop.

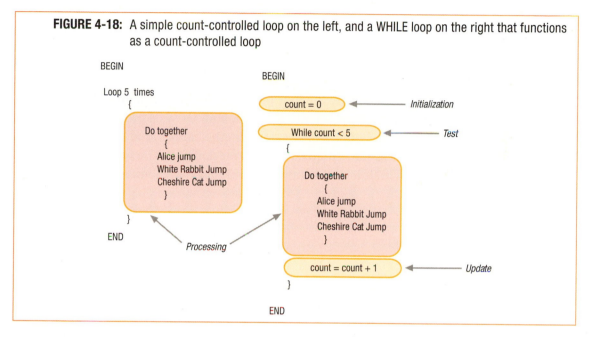

FIGURE 4-18: A simple count-controlled loop on the left, and a WHILE loop on the right that functions as a count-controlled loop

You will need to add a variable to `world.my first method` to function as the control variable, add a WHILE loop to the method, and delete the LOOP instruction.

1. Open the **triple jump loop** world that you saved in Tutorial 4B. If you cannot find the world, then either load the world from the student data files for this book or redo Tutorial 4B to create and save the world before continuing.

2. Select the **world** tile in the Object tree and the **methods** tab in the Details area. Click the **edit** button next to the *my first method* tile on the methods tab; the method `world.my first method` should open in the Editor area.

3. You need to create a new control variable for the WHILE loop that you will add to the program. Click the **create new variable** button, and a dialog box will appear asking you for the name and type of the new variable. Type **count** for the name, select **Number** as the type, and then click the **OK** button.

4. The *variable* tile at the top of the method shows that the count is initialized to 1. Click the **1** and change the value to **0**.

5. Drag a **While** instruction tile from the bottom of the Editor area and drop it in the method below the *Loop* tile. Select **true** from the short menu that appears.

6. Next, drag the **Do together** tile with the three jump instructions from the *Loop* tile and drop it in the *While* tile.

7. Now the *Loop* tile is no longer needed. Right-click the **Loop** tile and click **delete**.

As discussed earlier in this chapter, there are four parts to every pretest loop: initialization, test, processing, and update. Each of these parts of the loop needs to be properly in place for the loop to function as desired. Count is initialized to 0 in the *count* variable tile at the top of the method, so this will suffice as the initialization step for the loop. The three jump instructions are the processing in the middle of the loop. You only need to modify the test and add the update step.

The condition in the WHILE instruction will be the test to see if the loop needs to be repeated. The algorithm in Figure 4-18 shows that the loop should continue while the count is less than 5. It also shows that 1 should be added to count at the end of the loop. You need to modify the code in world.my first method to match this.

1. Drag a copy of the **count** variable tile and drop it into the *While* tile in place of the value *true*. When the menu appears with different choices for the conditional expression, choose **count <** , then **other**, and set the value to **5**. Now the loop will repeat while *count* is less than *5*.

2. Drag the **count** variable tile from the top of the method and drop a copy in the *While* tile after the three jump instructions. When you do this, a short menu will appear asking you how you want to set the value of count. Choose **set value**, choose **expressions**, and then click **count**.

3. Now the tile says *count set value to count.* You need to build a math expression so that the tile will say *count set value to count +1.* Click the second word **count**, and select **math** from the menu that appears. Then select **count +** and then **1**. Now world.my first method should look like Figure 4-19, which matches the specifications in Figure 4-18.

FIGURE 4-19: The completed `world.my first` method with the WHILE loop

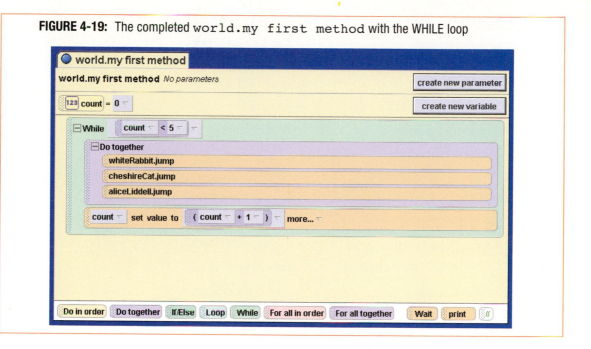

4. You need to save and test the world. Save the world with the name **triple jump while loop**, and then play the world to make sure that the characters jump together five times, just as they did with the simple count-controlled loop in Tutorial 4B. If the program doesn't work properly, review your work to find the error in your program, and then fix it. Once it works, you are finished with this tutorial.

Chapter Summary

This chapter consisted of several readings about the logical structure of algorithms—including linear sequences, selection sequences, repetition sequences, and parallel execution of instructions in an algorithm—followed by three hands-on tutorials.

The readings discussed the following:

☐ Algorithms are sequential in nature; we can think of the instructions in an algorithm as being executed one at a time.

☐ Each element of logical structure is a set of instructions that forms part of an algorithm. Corrado Böhm and Giuseppe Jacopini showed that algorithms are composed of three major structures: linear sequences, selection sequences (branching routines), and repetition sequences (loops).

☐ A flowchart is a diagram showing the structure of an algorithm. Flowcharts are designed to show the possible paths through an algorithm.

☐ The simplest element of logical structure in an algorithm is a linear sequence, in which one instruction follows another as if in a straight line. Linear sequences must have clearly stated entry and exit conditions, and they need to be complete, correct, and in the proper order.

☐ A selection sequence (branching) occurs whenever the path or flow of sequential logic in an algorithm splits into two or more paths.

☐ There are two kinds of binary branching in algorithms: a binary bypass and a binary choice. In a binary bypass, an instruction is either executed or bypassed. In a binary choice, one of two instructions is chosen.

☐ A repetition sequence (loop) occurs when an algorithm branches backward to a previous instruction, and then repeats part of the algorithm.

☐ A control variable is a variable whose value controls whether or not a repetition sequence will be executed.

☐ In a pretest loop, the test to determine whether or not to continue executing the loop comes before any other instructions that are to be repeated. In a posttest loop, it comes afterward. Many computer scientists recommend that only pretest loops be used.

☐ There are four parts to every pretest loop: initialization, test, processing, and update.

☐ Every loop in a computer program is either a count-controlled loop or a sentinel loop. A count-controlled loop causes a process to be repeated a specific number of times. A sentinel loop causes a process to be repeated until a condition or marker, called a sentinel, is encountered. Actually, a count-controlled loop is a special case of a sentinel loop.

☐ It is possible for a computer to execute several instructions from the same algorithm at the same time. This is called concurrency, and algorithms that include concurrency are called parallel algorithms.

In Tutorial 4A, you learned how to use the IF/ELSE instruction to include binary branching in an Alice method, and to use the *ask user a yes or no question* function.

In Tutorial 4B, you learned how to include a simple count-controlled loop in Alice with the LOOP instruction, and used the *Do together* instruction to perform parallel execution of several methods.

In Tutorial 4C, you learned how to create a properly structured WHILE loop.

Review Questions

1. Define the following terms:

    □ binary branching   □ final value   □ pretest loop
    □ binary bypass   □ flowchart   □ pseudocode
    □ binary choice   □ increment   □ repetition sequence
    □ branch   □ initial value   □ selection sequence
    □ branching routine   □ linear sequence   □ sentinel loop
    □ concurrency   □ loop   □ structured language
    □ control variable   □ multiple branching   □ thread
    □ count-controlled loop   □ parallel algorithm
    □ counter   □ posttest loop

2. Create a set of instructions for a simple everyday process that contains a linear seqeuence of steps, such as making a cup of coffee or getting from your school to where you live. Exchange directions with another student, and critique each other's work. In particular, determine if the linear sequences in each algorithm are complete, correct, and in the proper order.

3. Compare the structures created by using an IF/ELSE instruction and a WHILE instruction in pseudocode and on a flowchart. How are they the same? How are they different?

4. To add two fractions, such as 1/2 and 1/3, the fractions must have a common denominator. Using both pseudocode and a flowchart, describe a general algorithm for adding two fractions.

5. What is meant by the term "nested" IF/ELSE instructions? Give at least one example of a nested IF/ELSE instruction using pseudocode and flowcharts to describe your answer.

6. List and describe the four parts of every pretest sentinel loop.

7. The following algorithm was intended to result in the numbers from 10 to 1 being printed. What will it actually do? What is wrong with it, and how can it be corrected?

```
BEGIN
count = 10
While count > 0
    {
    Print count
    Count = count +1
    }
Print "The countdown is finished."
END
```

8. Tutorial 4B shows how to set up a count-controlled loop using the LOOP instruction. Tutorial 4C shows how to do the same thing using a WHILE instruction. What are the advantages to using the LOOP instruction to set up a count-controlled loop? What are the advantages in using the WHILE instruction to set up a count-controlled loop?

9. Describe the difference between a pretest loop and a posttest loop. Which is generally safer to use in a computer program, and why?

10. A data file for a payroll program consists of a set of records. There is one record for each employee, containing the employee's ID number, first name, last name, and hours worked. The last record contains "0000" as the employee number. Using pseudocode and a flowchart, describe an algorithm that will read in and print each record no matter how many records are in the file when the algorithm is executed.

Exercises

1. Alice contains a world-level function that will *ask the user for a number*. Create an Alice world with a character of your choice that will ask the user for a number, cause the character to jump up, use a loop to spin around the number of times specified, and then come back down. Think about how variables will be used as you design the algorithm.

2. Modify the *triple jump loop* world so that Alice jumps if the index is equal to 1, the White Rabbit jumps if the index is equal to 2, the Cheshire Cat jumps if the index is equal to 3, and all three characters jump if the index is equal to 4.

3. Add a tree to the *triple jump while loop* world. Use the tree's height as the sentinel rather than the number 5, so that the loop will execute when the count is less than or equal to the tree's height, but stop when the count passes its height. To do this, you can use the character-level function that returns the tree's height.

4. Modify the *triple jump while loop* world from Tutorial 4C to make the count increase by .5 meters each time through the loop. How does this affect the number of times the characters jump?

5. Make the count in the *triple jump while loop* world start at a higher number and decrease each time until it is less than or equal to a smaller value. For example, the initial value could be 5, the increment could be –1, and the final value could be 1.

6. Modify the *jump user choice* world from Tutorial 4A so that it has three questions and three separate IF instructions, one for each character.

7. Modify the finished *triple jump While loop* world from Tutorial 4C to use the `increment` instruction instead of the instruction that says `count set value to count +1`. To do this, delete the old set value instruction, drag the *count* variable tile, drop it into the code for the method, and select *increment count by 1* instead of *set value*.

8. Alice contains *Hebuilder* and *Shebuilder* class tiles in the People folder of the Local Gallery. You can create your own character objects in Alice using these tiles. The new character will have a method to walk. Create an Alice world with a character of your own creation as an object in the world. Using the `walk`, `move`, and `turn` methods, create an Alice method with a loop to make the character walk around in a complete circle. (You can approximate a circle with a polygon, such as an octagon.)

9. The Animals object gallery contains a pterodactyl. The student data files for this book have a world named *flapping pterodactyl* with a character-level method named `flap` that will cause the pterodactyl to flap its wings. Do each of the following:

   a. Create a method called `pterodactyl fly` that will make the pterodactyl move forward while flapping its wings, and then create a loop in `world.my first method` to make the pterodactyl fly away.
   b. Add controls to your *pterodactyl* world so that the user can steer the pterodactyl.
   c. Add a user control to point the camera at the pterodactyl when the spacebar is pressed.
   d. Modify the world to use an event instead of a loop to make the pterodactyl fly while the world is running. You might need to refer back to Chapter 3, which covers events.

10. In Exercise 9, why is it better to use an event instead of a loop to make the pterodactyl continue flying while the world is running? In general, when should events be used instead of loops in computer programming?

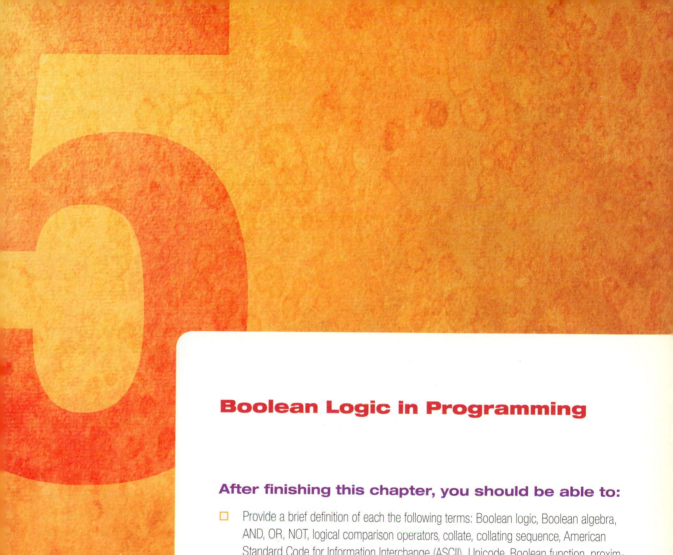

Boolean Logic in Programming

After finishing this chapter, you should be able to:

☐ Provide a brief definition of each the following terms: Boolean logic, Boolean algebra, AND, OR, NOT, logical comparison operators, collate, collating sequence, American Standard Code for Information Interchange (ASCII), Unicode, Boolean function, proximity function, and hardcode

☐ Describe the function of the Boolean operations AND, OR, and NOT, and show how they are used in Alice branching and looping instructions

☐ List and describe the function of the six logical comparison operators, and show how they are used to form Boolean conditions in Alice

☐ Describe what a Boolean function is and how such functions are used in Alice

☐ Create new methods in Alice that use Boolean conditions, Boolean functions, and method parameters

BOOLEAN LOGIC

Branching and looping routines contain conditions that are either true or false. In 1854, George Boole, the first Professor of Mathematics at Queen's College in Cork, Ireland, published a book titled *An Investigation into the Laws of Thought, on Which are Founded the Mathematical Theories of Logic and Probabilities.* In that book, Boole outlined a system of logic and a corresponding algebraic language dealing with true and false values. Today that type of logic is called **Boolean logic,** and his language is called **Boolean algebra**. The conditions that exist in branching and looping routines are a form of Boolean logic, which is the basis for all modern digital electronic technology.

NOTE □ □ □   The *howstuffworks.com* Web site has an article about how computers implement Boolean logic at *http://computer.howstuffworks.com/boolean.htm.* In 1858, Boole's original book was republished as *An Investigation of the Laws of Thought*, which can still be found in many bookstores and online. The complete text of an 1848 paper by Boole titled the "Calculus of Logic" is available at: *http://www.maths.tcd.ie/pub/ HistMath/People/Boole/CalcLogic.* The site is maintained by the University of Dublin's Trinity College School of Mathematics. The school also maintains links to information about George Boole at *http://www.maths.tcd.ie/pub/HistMath/People/Boole.*

Boolean logic is a form of mathematics in which the only values used are true and false. There are three basic operations in Boolean logic—AND, OR, and NOT, as described in Figure 5-1.

FIGURE 5-1: The Boolean AND, OR, and NOT operations

AND	OR	NOT
true *and* true = true	true *or* true = true	*not* true = false
true *and* false = false	true *or* false = true	*not* false = true
false *and* true = false	false *or* true = true	
false *and* false = false	false *or* false = false	

The AND and OR operations are binary operations, meaning that they need two operands. Basically, when two values are combined in the **AND** operation, the result is true only if both values are true. Otherwise, the result is false. In the **OR** operation, if either value is true, then the result is true.

The **NOT** operation is a unary operation, which means that it works on only one operand. It simply reverses the true or false value of its operand. In other words, NOT true yields false; NOT false yields true.

The use of AND, OR, and NOT should be common sense. A statement like "today is Monday AND this is March" can be evaluated for its true or false value; yet people sometimes run into trouble converting the informality of human language into the formality needed for algorithms. Consider the following conversation:

> **BOSS:** Give me a list of all our offices in Pennsylvania and New Jersey.
> **PROGRAMMER:** Let me get this straight—you want a list of our offices located in either Pennsylvania or located in New Jersey, right?
> **BOSS:** Yes, isn't that what I just said?

The programmer, who has experience converting the informality of human language into a formalized computer programming language, knows what would happen if the condition (state = "PA" AND state = "NJ") were used to create the list. If each office is located in only one state, then both conditions cannot possibly be true. What should the programmer do, give the boss a blank sheet of paper? Tell the boss the request is nonsense according to the rules of Boolean logic? The programmer's response in the dialogue clarified the boss's request in an appropriate manner.

Boolean expressions can become long and complex with many nested AND, OR, and NOT clauses layered together. Professional programmers often use Boolean algebra and other formal tools when dealing with the layered complexities of Boolean logic. It won't be necessary to learn Boolean algebra to complete the exercises in this book; however, most students majoring in computer science will need to study it in courses such as "Discrete Mathematics" or "Computer Math and Logic."

COMPARING VALUES

Often the Boolean conditions in branching and looping routines are based on expressions that compare values. Consider the following warning message, which might be found in the documentation for a modern automobile:

The passenger-side air bag may cause injury to children who are under the age of 12 or who weigh less than 48 pounds. They should not sit in the front passenger seat of this car.

The condition in this warning might be expressed in pseudocode like this:

```
IF (age < 12 OR weight < 48)
THEN do not sit in the front passenger seat
```

Two items, each with a true or false value, are joined by the OR operation. The two items are each comparisons of values. The condition "age < 12" is either true or false, as is the condition "weight < 48." When the algorithm is executed, the true or false value of each of these conditions is determined, and then the overall true or false value is determined using the rules for the OR operation.

The symbol "<" in the above example stands for "is less than." There are six such **logical comparison operators** used to compare two values in Boolean logic: equals, is not equal to, is less than, is greater than, is less than or equal to, and is greater than or equal to. Figure 5-2 shows the symbols most commonly used for these operators.

FIGURE 5-2: The six logical comparison operators

Condition	In Mathematics	In Computer Programming
A equals B	$A = B$	$A = B$ or $A == B$
A is not equal to B	$A \neq B$	$A <> B$ or $A != B$
A is less than B	$A < B$	$A < B$
A is greater than B	$A > B$	$A > B$
A is less than or equal to B	$A \leq B$	$A <= B$
A is greater than or equal to B	$A \geq B$	$A >= B$

Notice that several of the computer programming symbols, such as "<>" for "not equals," are composed of two characters. This doubling of characters is required because modern computer keyboards do not include a single symbol for these comparison operators; this is in contrast to standard algebra, in which the symbol "≠" is used for "not equals."

String Comparisons

It's clear that numbers can be compared according to their value, but what about other data types, such as character strings? Most have their own rules for logical comparisons. Character strings, for example, are compared according to the place in a collating sequence for each character of the string. To **collate** means to put a set of items in order. A **collating sequence** is a list that shows the correct order to be used when collating a set of items. The English language alphabet is a collating sequence. It shows us that when putting things in alphabetic order, A comes before B, B comes before C, and so on. Modern computers most often use one of two codes to represent characters in a computer—either the **American Standard Code for Information Interchange (ASCII)** or a newer code called **Unicode**. These codes can also be used as collating sequences for character string values, just as the English language alphabet can. Figure 5-3 shows a portion of the ASCII code.

NOTE□ □ □   The ASCII code is based on the English language, and it includes letters, numeric digits, and some "hidden" characters, such as the Enter key and the Esc key. Each character is given a numeric value, and the binary equivalents of those numeric values are used to store characters in the computer. Unicode is a much larger code, which includes characters for other alphabets, such as the Greek, Hebrew, Arabic, and Cyrillic alphabets. The ASCII code is now actually a subset of the longer Unicode. For more information on the ASCII code, see *www.webopedia.com/TERM/A/ASCII.html*. For more information on Unicode, see *http://www.unicode.org/standard/WhatIsUnicode.html*.

FIGURE 5-3: A portion of the ASCII code

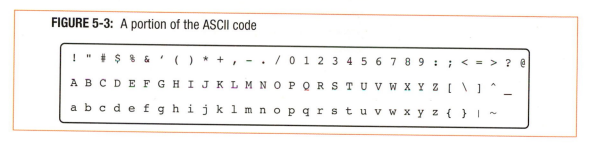

Comparisons using character strings are often used when searching and sorting data stored on a computer. While this is very important in data processing and database management, comparisons using character strings in Alice are rare.

Boolean Functions

The true and false values in computer programming can also come from Boolean functions. A **Boolean function** is a function that returns a true or false value instead of a numeric value. The *ask a user a yes or no question* function used in the last chapter and shown in Figure 5-4 is an example of a Boolean function. When a method using the function is played, a question will appear on the screen. If the user answers "yes," then the function returns the value true. If the user answers "no," then the function returns the value false.

FIGURE 5-4: A Boolean function to ask the user a yes or no question

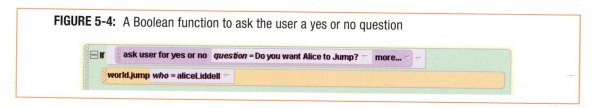

Figure 5-5 shows some spatial relation functions on a seaplane's functions tab in Alice. Each of these functions is a Boolean function that returns a true or false value.

FIGURE 5-5: Spatial relation Boolean functions

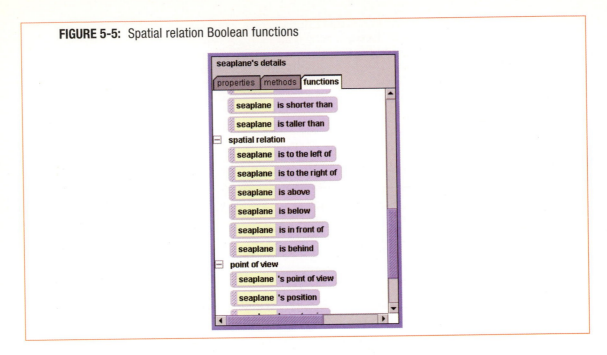

These and other Boolean functions can be used in any place that a true or false value can be used, such as in an IF instruction or a WHILE instruction, as shown in the `seaplane.fly` method in Figure 5-6. The *seaplane is above water* function in the WHILE instruction in this example will return a value of true, and the loop will be executed as long as the seaplane is above the water. Within the loop, there is an IF instruction to cause the seaplane to wave its wings whenever it is close to the island. This instruction uses a Boolean function that will return a value of true if the seaplane is within 10 meters of the island.

FIGURE 5-6: The `seaplane.fly` method, which uses two Boolean functions

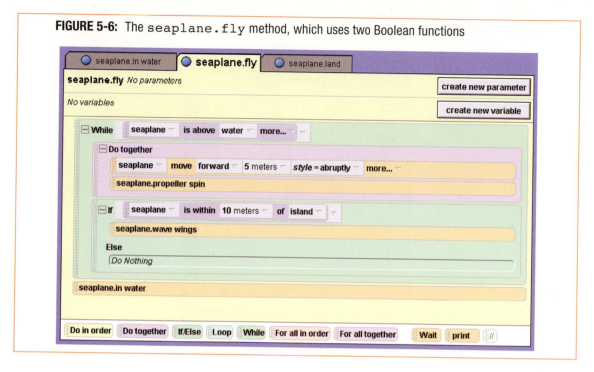

Alice has math comparison functions that can be found on a world's functions tab along with the AND, OR, and NOT functions; these functions can be used to build more complex Boolean expressions. Both function types are shown in Figure 5-7.

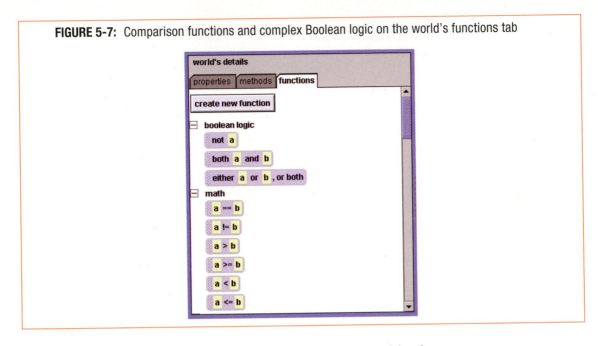

FIGURE 5-7: Comparison functions and complex Boolean logic on the world's functions tab

With the functions in Figure 5-7, you can build expressions like these:

- `If (age < 12 OR weight <48)`

- `While (aliceLiddell distance to whiteRabbit <=10)`

- `While NOT (target = windmill) OR NOT (target = gazebo)`

- `If NOT (seaplane is in front of camera) AND ( (time < 10) OR (time > 30) )`

- `While numberOfGuesses <= log(range)`

The following tutorials will each provide experience with simple uses of Boolean functions in Alice.

TUTORIAL 5A—BRANCHING WITH RANDOM NUMBERS

In this exercise, you will modify the *jump user choice* world from Tutorial 4A to have the computer randomly select who will jump, instead of asking for user input. Alice has a world-level function that will return a random number in a specified range. The numbers that it returns are six-digit numbers, greater than or equal to the lowest number specified and less than the highest number specified. In this exercise, for example, you will ask Alice to return a number between 0 and 3. Alice will return numbers such as 1.83475, 0.41257, 2.89175, and so on. All of the numbers it returns will be greater than or equal to 0, but less than 3.

In this exercise, if the random number is less than 1, Alice will jump. If it is greater than or equal to 1 but less than 2, then the White Rabbit will jump. If it is greater than or equal to 2 but less than 3, then the Cheshire Cat will jump. Figure 5-8 shows the expected results of the program. The logic is very similar to the user input program in Tutorial 4A, with nested IF/ELSE instructions to determine which character will jump.

FIGURE 5-8: The value of the random number will determine who jumps

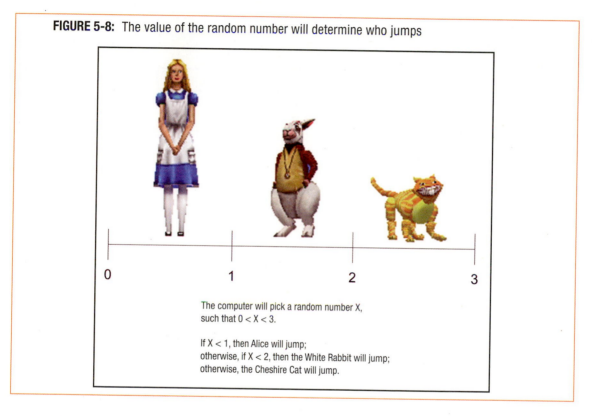

The computer will pick a random number X, such that 0 < X < 3.

If X < 1, then Alice will jump; otherwise, if X < 2, then the White Rabbit will jump; otherwise, the Cheshire Cat will jump.

You will add a variable to the program to hold the random number. Figure 5-9 shows what the code for the method will look like after you do this. You can refer to this image to guide you through the next several steps.

FIGURE 5-9: `World.my first method` with random numbers instead of user questions

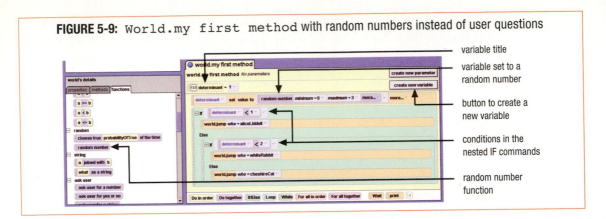

1. Open the **jump user choice** world saved as part of Tutorial 4A, or load the world from the student data files for this book.

2. Click the **create new variable** button on the right side of `world.my first method` to add a variable to hold the random number. Name the variable **determinant** (because it will determine who jumps), select **Number** as the type, and then click **OK**. You will now see a variable tile for *determinant* at the top of the method.

3. Next, you need to tell the computer to set the value of *determinant* to a random number. Drag the **determinant** variable tile down into `world.my first method` as a new first instruction before the IF/ELSE instructions. When you do this, a set value dialog box will appear. Set the value of *determinant* to **1**. The 1 is only a placeholder; you will change it to a random number in the next step.

4. Now you need to tell the computer to set the value of the variable *determinant* to a random number instead of a 1. To do this, select the **world** tile in the Object tree, and then click the **functions** tab in the Details area. Scroll through the list of functions and find the function titled *random number*. Drag and drop a copy of this function into the *set value* tile in place of the number 1.

5. You now need to tell the computer what range of values to use when picking a random number. To do so, click **more** in the blue *random number* tile, and set the *minimum* value to **0**. Click **more** again, and this time set the *maximum* value to **3**. The *set value* tile should now look like the *determinant set value to random number* tile near the top of the method shown in Figure 5-9.

6. The nested IF/ELSE instructions still contain conditions based on the user question. You need to replace these conditions following the word *If* in each of the nested IF/ELSE instructions with conditions based on the random number. To do so, drag the **determinant** variable tile from the top of the method down into the first IF/ELSE instruction in place of the blue *ask user yes or no* condition tile. When you do this, a short menu will appear. Select **determinant <** and **1** as the value. Now the first IF/ELSE instruction tile should look like it does in Figure 5-9.

7. Do the same thing for the second IF/ELSE instruction, but this time, choose **2** as the value. When you are done, the second IF/ELSE instruction should be *if determinant < 2.*

8. The method should now be ready to select a random number and make one of the three characters jump, based on the value of the random number. Save the world as **triple jump random,** and you are ready to test the world.

You need a testing plan for your modified Alice world. If things work correctly, then one of the three characters should jump each time the world is run. Which character jumps depends on the value of the random number that the computer picks for the variable you named *determinant.*

To test the program properly, you would need to run it several hundred or several thousand times, and keep track of how many times each character jumps. Over a long period of time, we would expect each character to jump about one-third of the time the program runs. This will be left as an exercise at the end of the chapter. For now, test the program to make sure that the same character does not jump all the time, and that each of the three characters jumps at least part of the time. Play the world, and then use the restart button several times to replay the world. Because the numbers are random and not part of a pattern, the same character might jump several times in a row, but over the course of several replays, each of the characters can be expected to jump at least once.

TUTORIAL 5B—THE NERVOUS PENGUIN

In this exercise, you will create a world with two penguins. The first penguin will be controlled by the user and may move around freely in the world. The second penguin, the nervous penguin, will flap its wings and jump up and down whenever the first penguin gets close to it. A Boolean **proximity function** returns a value based on the distance from one object to another. In this tutorial, a proximity function will be used to cause the nervous penguin to react.

NOTE □ □ □ | A proximity function returns a value of true or false; however, a numeric proximity function returns the distance between two objects.

1. Start a new Alice world using the **snow** template.

2. Click the green **ADD OBJECTS** button to enter Scene Editor mode, and then add a **penguin** to the world from the Animals folder in the Local Gallery.

3. Move the **penguin** to the left side of the screen and push it back away from the viewer.

4. Add a second **penguin** to the world. Alice will give it the name *penguin2*. Right-click the **penguin2** tile in the Object tree and rename it as **nervousPenguin**.

5. Move **nervousPenguin** to the right side of the world window. The two penguins should now be positioned something like those in Figure 5-10.

FIGURE 5-10: The initial scene for the *nervous penguin* world

6. Now the scene is ready. Click the large green **DONE** button to exit, and save the world with the name **nervous penguin**.

The world will need one method and several events. The method will be the nervous penguin's reaction to the other penguin getting too close. Figure 5-11 shows the method you will need to create.

FIGURE 5-11: The `react` method for the *nervous penguin* world

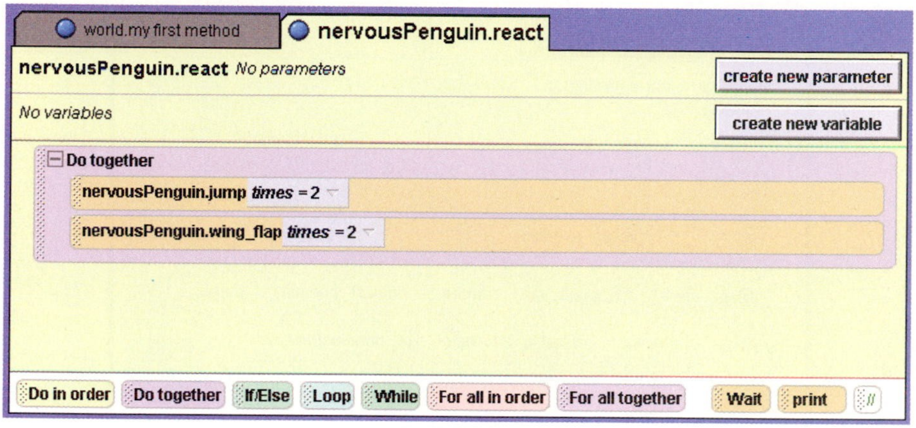

1. `World.my first method` will not be used further, so you can delete it. Then, select the **nervousPenguin** tile in the Object tree and the **methods** tab in the Details area.

2. Click the **create new method** button. When the create new method window appears, type the name **react**, and then click the **OK** button.

3. The nervous penguin will need to jump up and down and flap its wings when the other penguin gets too close. These two actions—jumping and flapping—should happen at the same time. Drag a **Do together** tile from the bottom of the Editor area and drop it in the new method in place of *Do Nothing*.

4. Drag a **nervousPenguin jump times** tile from the methods tab and drop it in the *Do together* instruction in place of *Do Nothing*. When the short menu appears, select **2** as the number of times.

5. Drag a **wing_flap times** tile from the methods tab and drop it in the *Do together* instruction below the *nervousPenguin jump times = 2* instruction. When the short menu appears, select **2** as the number of times. The new method is now complete and should resemble Figure 5-11.

Now it's time to create several simple events that will be needed for this world. You will create methods to provide user controls for the moving penguin, to animate the moving penguin, to let the user point the camera at the moving penguin in case it moves off camera, and to cause the nervous penguin to react when the other penguin is near. Figure 5-12 shows these new events.

FIGURE 5-12: Several events for the *nervous penguin* world

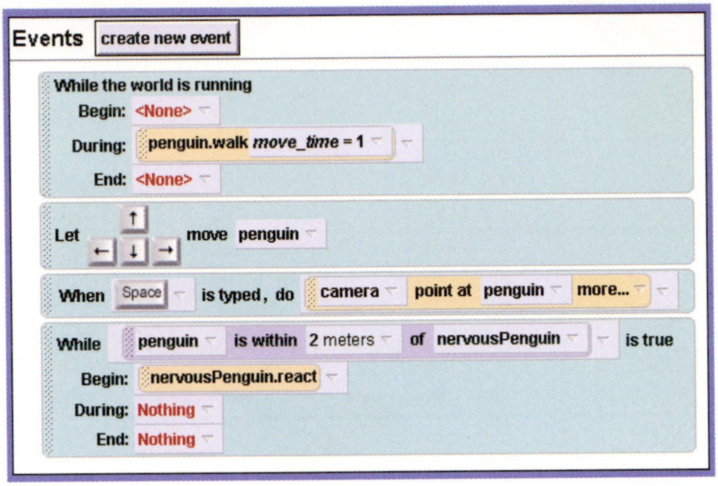

A built-in event can be used to provide control of the moving penguin. A second event can be created to use the *penguin walk move_time* method to animate the penguin. The default event can be modified to serve as this second event.

1. Click the **create new event** button in the Events area. When the menu appears, select **Let the arrow keys move <subject>** as the event type.

2. A new arrow key event will appear in the Events area, as shown in Figure 5-13. Click **camera** in the event tile and select **penguin, the entire penguin**. The event is now set to let the user move the penguin with the arrow keys.

FIGURE 5-13: The arrow key control event

3. Right-click the **When the world starts, do world.myfirst method** default event. When the short menu appears, select **change to, While the world is running**.

4. Select the **penguin** tile in the Object tree and the **methods** tab in the Details area. Drag a copy of the **walk move_time** method and drop it in place of *None* following *During* in the new event. Select **1** from the short *move_time* menu that appears. The event should resemble Figure 5-14. The penguin will now shuffle its feet and waddle even when standing in place.

FIGURE 5-14: The event to animate the penguin

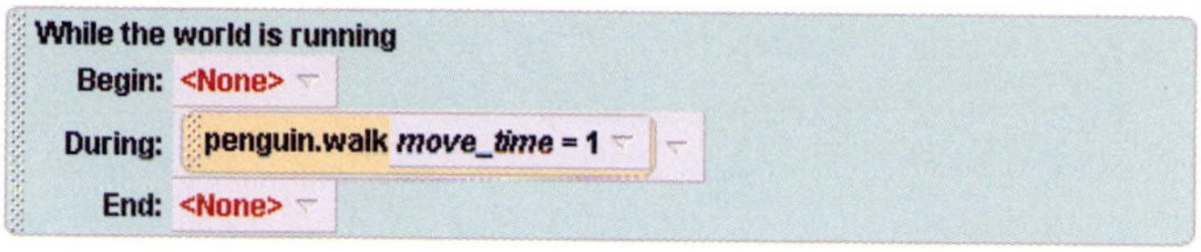

While the world is running
Begin: <None>
During: penguin.walk *move_time* = 1
End: <None>

The first two events are complete. The user can now move the penguin with the arrow keys, and the penguin will waddle and move its feet while the world is running, even when standing in place.

Next, you will add an event to allow the user to point the camera at the penguin in case it moves off camera.

1. Click the **create new event** button in the Events area. When the menu appears, select **When a key is typed** as the event type. A new *When any key is typed do Nothing* event tile will appear in the Events area.

2. Click **any key** and select **Space** from the menu that appears. Your actions will make the spacebar the trigger key for this event.

3. Select the **camera** tile in the Object tree and the **methods** tab in the Details area. Drag a copy of the **camera point at** method tile from the methods tab and drop it in place of *Nothing* in the new event. Select **penguin**, **the entire penguin** from the menu that appears. The event to allow the user to point the camera at the moving penguin is now complete, as shown in Figure 5-15.

FIGURE 5-15: The event to allow the user to point the camera at the moving penguin

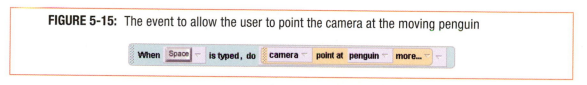

When Space is typed, do camera point at penguin more...

The last event that is needed is the event to cause the nervous penguin to react whenever the moving penguin gets too close. The event trigger will have a Boolean function that will return a value of true if the first penguin is within two meters of the nervous penguin. The event handler will be the `nervousPenguin.react` method. Figure 5-16 shows what the finished event will look like.

> **FIGURE 5-16:** The event to cause the nervous penguin to react
>
> | While | penguin ⌄ | is within | 2 meters ⌄ | of | nervousPenguin ⌄ | ⌄ | is true |
> | :--- | :--- | :--- | :--- | :--- | :--- | :--- | :--- |
> | **Begin:** | nervousPenguin.react ⌄ | | | | | | |
> | **During:** | Nothing ⌄ | | | | | | |
> | **End:** | Nothing ⌄ | | | | | | |

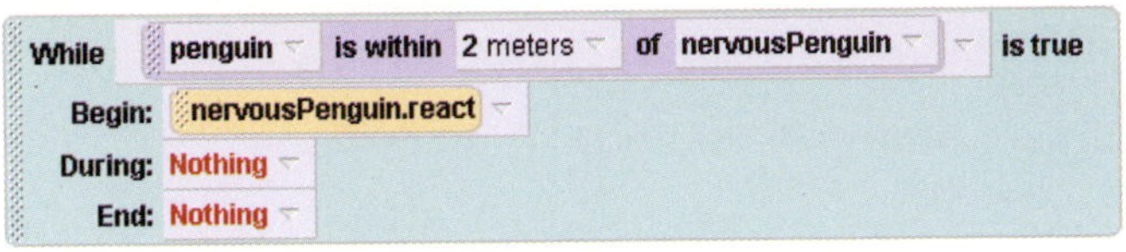

1. Click the **create new event** button in the Events area. When the menu appears, select **When something is true** as the event type. A new *When None is true* event tile will appear in the Events area.

2. Select the **penguin** tile in the Object tree and the **functions** tab in the Details area.

3. Find the *penguin is within threshold of object* tile, shown in Figure 5-16. Click and drag the **penguin is within threshold of object** tile and drop a copy of it in the new event in place of *None* following the word *When*. Select **2 meters**, **nervousPenguin**, and **entire nervousPenguin** from the menus that appear. The trigger for the event is now complete.

4. Select the **nervousPenguin** tile in the Object tree and the **methods** tab in the Details area. Next, drag a copy of the **react** method and drop it in place of *Nothing* following *Begin:* in the new event.

5. The final event is in place. Save the world again before continuing.

The *nervous penguin* world is complete and ready for testing. You should be able to move the penguin around using the arrow keys. Be careful—it moves rather quickly. You should be able to point the camera at the penguin using the spacebar. The nervous penguin should jump up and down and flap its wings whenever the first penguin gets within two meters of it.

TUTORIAL 5C—A SENTINEL SAILING LOOP

In this exercise, you will create a world with a sailboat and several objects. When the world starts, you will be able to click an object, and the sailboat will sail to that object. You will create a `sail to` method that uses a sentinel loop to make the sailboat sail toward the object. The method will use a Boolean condition with a method parameter in the condition. The loop will have the following logic:

```
WHILE (NOT (the sailboat is within 5 meters of the [object]))
    {
    turn to face [object]
    move forward 1 meter
    }
```

The brackets "{" and "}" are used to mark the beginning and end of the block of code within the loop. When this code is executed, the sailboat will turn to face a target object, and then move one meter toward the object. It will continue to do so until it is within five meters of the object. You will write a `sail to` method that will work with any object and that will accept the target object as an input parameter, much like the way the primitive move method accepts direction and amount as parameters.

You will create your world in two steps. First, you will place an island in the world and hardcode the island as the target for the `sail to` method. (To **hardcode** a value in a program means that the programmer puts a specific value in a program instead of a variable or parameter.) Once this method works, you will add an object parameter called *target* and put it in the method in place of *island*.

The Sail to Island World

Let's start by setting the scene for the new Alice world. First, you need to create a water world with a sailboat in it. Then, you need to adjust the camera.

1. Start a new Alice world with a **water** template.
2. Click the green **ADD OBJECTS** button to enter Scene Editor mode, and then add a **sailboat** to the world from the Vehicles folder in the Local Gallery. Your screen should resemble the left side of Figure 5-17.
3. The camera is too close to the sailboat, creating a tight shot in which the boat fills most of the frame. Using the blue camera control arrows at the bottom of the world window, move the camera back from the sailboat and up a little bit so that the world window looks more like the image on the right side of Figure 5-17. You might also want to move the sailboat a little toward the side of the window.

FIGURE 5-17: The world window before and after positioning the camera

before

after

Next, you need to add an island to the world. You can decide where to put the island, but it should not be too close to the sailboat, and it should not be directly in front of the sailboat.

1. Add an **island** to the world from the Environments Gallery.
2. Position the island so that it is away from the sailboat and not directly in front of it. You can use Figure 5-18 as a guide.

FIGURE 5-18: An island has been added and positioned in the water world

3. Now click the large green **DONE** button to exit Scene Editor mode, and save the world with the name **sail to island**.

You are ready to create the new method. In this first version of the world, the sailboat will sail to the island when the world starts. You will need to create a method that is invoked by an event with `When the world starts` as its trigger. The default event does this, but it uses the method `world.my first method` as its event handler. The new method for the default event will be `sailboat.sail to`. Notice that it will be a method for the sailboat object and not a world-level method as is `world.my first method`. You can create the new method, change the event handler in the default event, and then delete `world.my first method`.

1. Select the **sailboat** tile in the Object tree and the **methods** tab in the Details area.

2. Click the **create new method** button. When the create new method dialog box appears, type the name **sail to**, and click **OK**. The new method will appear in the Editor area, and the related method tile will appear in the Details area.

3. Drag the **sail to** tile from the Details area and drop it in the default event in place of `world.my first method`.

4. Now `world.my first` method is no longer needed. Select the **world** tile in the Object tree and the **methods** tab in the Details area. Click and drag the **my first method** tile to the Trash can to delete it.

Now it's time to begin writing the code for the new method. It should contain a WHILE loop that matches the pseudocode shown at the beginning of this tutorial.

NOTE␣␣␣ | Even though we are learning about the sentinel loop in this tutorial, you might have noticed that the process can also be done with events, and without a `sail to` method. Both techniques are acceptable.

1. Select the **sailboat** tile in the Object tree and the **methods** tab in the Details area.

2. Drag a **While** tile from the bottom of the Editor area and drop it into the `sailboat.sail to` method in the Editor area. Select **true** from the short menu that appears.

3. Next, select the **functions** tab in the Details area and find the *sailboat is within threshold of object* tile, as shown in Figure 5-19. This is a Boolean proximity function. Drag a copy of the tile and drop it in the WHILE instruction in place of *true*. Select **5 meters** as the distance and **island, the entire island** as the object.

FIGURE 5-19: The Boolean proximity function *sailboat is within threshold of object*

sailboat is within threshold of object

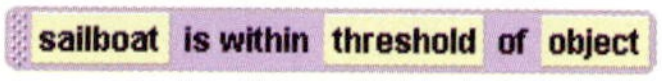

4. The *While* tile now says *While sailboat is within 5 meters of island*. However, you want just the opposite. Select the **world** tile in the Object tree and find the *not* tile on the functions tab. Drag a copy of the tile to the *While* tile, and drop it in place of the condition *sailboat is within 5 meters of island*. Now the condition should be as required, shown in Figure 5-20.

FIGURE 5-20: The modified Boolean proximity function

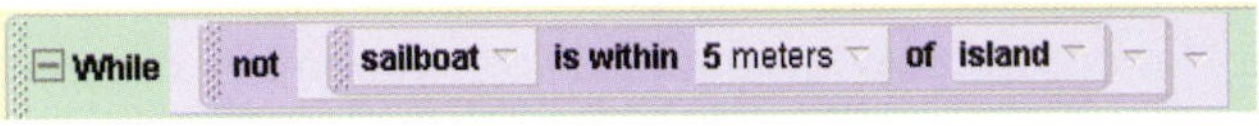

| ☐ While | not | sailboat ▽ | is within | 5 meters ▽ | of | island ▽ | ▽ | ▽ |

The `sailboat.sail` to method now has the correct loop structure and condition in place. Two instructions need to be placed in the loop. One will turn the sailboat and one will move the sailboat. These should be executed together, so they will need to be inside a *Do together* tile.

1. Drag a **Do together** tile from the bottom of the Editor area and drop it into the WHILE instruction in place of *Do Nothing*.

2. Select the **sailboat** tile in the Object tree and the **methods** tile in the Details area.

3. Drag a copy of the **sailboat turn to face** method tile and drop it in the *Do together* tile in place of *Do Nothing*. Select **island, the entire island** as the object, and then click **more** and change the style to **abruptly**.

4. Drag a copy of the **sailboat move** method tile and drop it in the *Do together* tile just below the *sailboat turn to face* tile. Select **forward** as the direction and **2 meters** as the amount, and then click **more** and change the style to **abruptly**.

5. Click **File** on the menu bar, click **Save World As**, and then save a copy of the world with the new name **sail to island**.

6. Play the world to see if it works properly. The boat should sail toward the island and stop before it reaches it. If it does not, then you need to find and fix any errors in your program. If the boat does not move at all, then it may be too close to the island when the world starts.

The Sail to Any Object World

Next, you will use the *sail to island* world as the basis for a new world that will allow the user to sail the boat to any object in the world. You will add additional objects to the world, add an event to allow the user to select a target object, and modify the `sail` to method to include a target variable instead of the island. First, you will save the world with a new name so that the *sail to island* world will be preserved, and then several objects will be added to the world.

1. Click **File** on the menu bar, click **Save World As**, and then save a copy of the world with the new name **sail to object**.

2. Click the green **ADD OBJECTS** button to enter Scene Editor mode, and using the blue camera control arrows, pull the camera back a little farther and up a

bit more so that you can see more open water. As you complete the following steps, note that it might be necessary to adjust the camera further.

3. Add several objects to the world. As you place the objects in the world, you should move them away from each other, positioning them as if they were on the edge of a large circle. Figure 5-21 shows a world with the following objects:

- An island2 from the Environments folder in the Local Gallery
- A pier from the Beach folder in the Local Gallery placed adjacent to the island2
- A lighthouse from the Beach folder in the Local Gallery
- A lifeboat from the Vehicles folder in the Local Gallery
- A shakira (a type of boat) from the Vehicles folder in the Local Gallery

FIGURE 5-21: The *sail to any object* world with several objects added

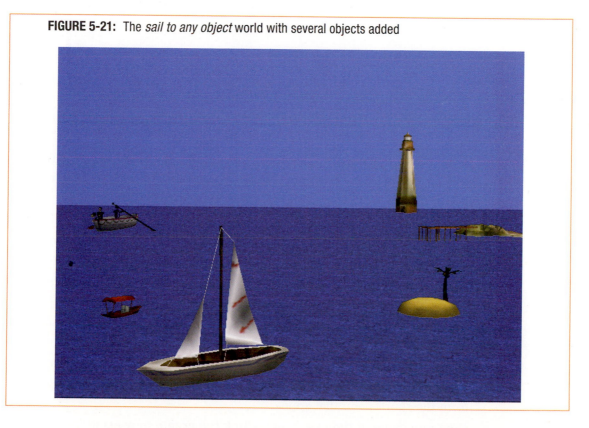

4. When you are happy with the collection of objects in your world, click the large green **DONE** button to return to Scene Editor mode.

Now you are ready to modify the `sailboat.sail to` method and add a new event. You will also need to delete the default event, which will actually prevent the world from playing with the changes that you make. Figure 5-22 shows the `sail to` method with the modifications you will make. The default event should be deleted first.

FIGURE 5-22: The `sail to` method with a *target* parameter added

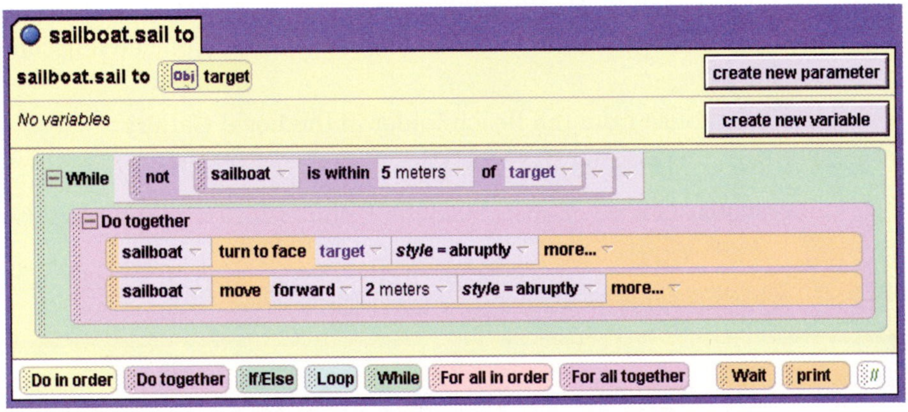

1. Right-click the default event in the Events area and select **delete** from the menu that appears. The event will be deleted.
2. Select the **sailboat** tile in the Object tree and the **methods** tab in the Details area, and then click the **edit** button next to the *sail to* tile. You should be able to see the `sail to` method in the Editor area.
3. Click the **create new parameter** button to add a *target* parameter to the method. When the create new parameter window appears, type the name **target**, make sure that **Object** is selected as the data type, and then click the **OK** button. A tile for the *target* object parameter will appear near the top of the method.
4. Drag the **target** object parameter tile and drop it in the WHILE instruction in place of *island*.
5. Drag the **target** object parameter tile again and drop a copy of it into the *sailboat turn to face island* instruction in place of *island*. Select **target** from the short menu that appears.
6. Now you can add the new event. Click the **create new event** button in the Events area and select **When the mouse is clicked on something** from the menu of event types that appears. A new event similar to Figure 5-23 will appear.

FIGURE 5-23: A *new mouse click* event tile

When 🖱 is clicked on anything ⌄ , do Nothing ⌄

7. Click and drag the **sail to target** tile from the methods tab and drop a copy of it in the new event in place of the word *Nothing*. When the target menu appears, select **expressions** and then **object under mouse cursor**. Your new event should now look like Figure 5-24; the modifications to the world are now complete.

FIGURE 5-24: The new event to cause the sailboat to sail to the selected object

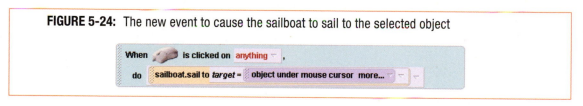

When 🖱 is clicked on anything ⌄ ,

do   sailboat.sail to *target* = object under mouse cursor more... ⌄ ⌄ ⌄

8. Save the world before continuing.

You can now test your new world. The sailboat should sail to whatever object you select with the mouse. If you click the water, it will sail toward the center point of the world. If you click the sky background, then the world will stop playing, and Alice will show you an error message telling you that the target value must not be null. This means that there is no value for the target parameter because you clicked nothing.

NOTE □ □ □ | The sailboat moves rather slowly from object to object in the sail to any object world. You can use the speed **slider control** in the playing world window to speed things up a bit as you test your new world.

You might also notice that the sailboat will sail through objects to get to its target. To correct this, you would need to create methods for collision detection and avoidance in your world, which is rather time consuming; as such, it is not part of this tutorial.

Chapter Summary

This chapter consisted of a discussion of Boolean logic, including the comparison of values and Boolean functions, followed by three tutorials. The discussion of Boolean logic included the following:

☐ Branching and looping routines both contain conditions that are either true or false. These conditions are a form of Boolean logic.

☐ Boolean logic is a form of mathematics in which the only values used are true and false.

☐ There are three basic operations in Boolean logic: AND, OR, and NOT.

☐ When two values are combined in the AND operation, the result is true only if both values are true. Otherwise, the result is false. In the OR operation, if either value is true, then the result is true.

☐ The NOT operation is a unary operation, which means that it works on only one operand. It simply reverses the true or false value of its operand: NOT true yields false, and NOT false yields true.

☐ People sometimes run into trouble converting the informality of human language into the formality needed for algorithms.

☐ Often the Boolean conditions in branching and looping routines are based on expressions that compare values.

☐ There are six logical comparison operators used in Boolean logic: equals, is not equal to, is less than, is greater than, is less than or equal to, and is greater than or equal to.

☐ Numbers can be compared according to their value, but other data types, such as character strings, have their own rules for logical comparisons.

☐ Character strings are compared according to the place in a collating sequence for each character of the string. To collate means to put a set of items in order. A collating sequence is a list that shows the correct order to be used when collating a set of items.

☐ Modern computers most often use one of two codes to represent characters in the computer—either the American Standard Code for Information Interchange (ASCII), or a newer code called Unicode. These codes can also be used as collating sequences for character string values, as can the English language alphabet.

☐ A Boolean function is a function that returns a true or false value instead of a numeric value.

☐ Boolean functions can be used in any place that a true or false value can be used, such as in an IF instruction or a WHILE instruction.

☐ The AND, OR, and NOT functions in Alice can be found on the world's function tab, along with functions to compare values.

In Tutorial 5A, you modified the *jump user choice* world from Tutorial 4A to have the computer randomly select who will jump, instead of asking for user input. You created Boolean conditions that involve random numbers.

In Tutorial 5B, you created a *nervous penguin* world with a Boolean function used in an event trigger.

In Tutorial 5C, you created two worlds: one to make a sailboat sail to an Island and one to make a sailboat sail to any object. Each world contained a `sail to` method that used a sentinel loop with a Boolean condition in the loop's WHILE instruction.

Review Questions

1. Define the following terms:

   - American Standard Code for Information Interchange (ASCII)
   - AND
   - Boolean algebra
   - Boolean function
   - Boolean logic
   - collate
   - collating sequence
   - hardcode
   - logical comparison operators
   - NOT
   - OR
   - Proximity function
   - Unicode

2. Truth tables are often used to describe the result of Boolean expressions. Fill in the correct values in each of the following truth tables. For each cell in the table, apply the operation for the table to the values at the top of the row and at the beginning of the column for that cell, just as you would fill in values in a multiplication table.

AND	*true*	*false*
true		
false		

OR	*true*	*false*
true		
false		

NOT	*true*	*false*

3. The following three Boolean operations are composite operations, which means they are combinations of AND, OR, and NOT. All three of these are important in designing the logic circuits inside computer chips. Create truth tables similar to those in Question 2 for each of these operations:

   a. XOR – A OR B, but not both.
   b. NOR – NOT (A or B)
   c. NAND – NOT (A and B)

4. Parentheses can be used in Boolean logic to clarify the order of operations, just as in ordinary arithmetic. Assuming that the height of a palm tree is 5 meters, the height of a lighthouse is 25 meters, and the height of a beach house is 10 meters, rewrite the following expression exactly as it is three times, but with parentheses in different places each time. Determine whether each of the new expressions is true or false.

   Height of the beach house is less than the height of the lighthouse and not height of the lighthouse is less than the height of the tree or height of the beach house equals the height of the tree.

5. Boolean conditions are important when using library search engines. Usually a library search engine has fields such as title, subject, author, year, and publisher. A typical search condition would be something like this: (author = "Lewis Carrol" AND year < 1865). Write Boolean conditions for searches to find books about each of the following:

    a. Martin Luther King Jr., written between 1968 and 1978

    b. About Martin Luther King Jr., written before 1968, but not by Martin Luther King Jr.

    c. Microsoft Excel, published by Course Technology, or accounting, published by Delmar, after 1998

    d. Careers in nursing or health care or medicine

    e. London, Ontario, not London, England, not London, Great Britain, not London, UK, written using the word NOT only once

6. Boolean conditions are also important in Internet searches. Write Boolean conditions for searches to find Web pages about each of the following:

    a. John D. Rockefeller and Ida Tarbell

    b. Abraham Lincoln and Jefferson Davis, but not schools or parks

    c. Cooking a turkey, but not in a microwave or deep-fat fryer

    d. George Boole and either Charles Babbage or Herman Hollerith

7. Which of the following does not contain a valid Boolean expression, and why?

    a. If (distance to alice < distance to caterpillar OR queen)

    b. If (count > 10 AND count < 20)

    c. While (count < 5 AND >1)

    d. While height < count OR height < 12.5

    e. If (message = "Hello, World." OR "Hello, World!")

8. Write Boolean conditions to make WHILE loops continue to function until the following occurs:

    a. A car door has been opened and closed 1,000 times, or the door falls off the car.

    b. A penguin in an Alice world is within 5 meters of an igloo or an Eskimo, or is more than 100 meters away from the camera.

    c. A sailboat is moving at a speed between 5 and 10 meters per second.

9. Write the following rule as a Boolean expression:

I before E except after C, or when sounding as A as in "neighbor" or "weigh"

10. In most states in the United States, a vehicle must stop at an intersection with a traffic light when the traffic light is red, except when making a right turn, in which case the driver can pause and then make a right turn on red if the way is clear, unless otherwise posted. At a particular intersection there is a sign that says, "No right turn on red, 6 am to 6 pm, except Saturdays and Sundays." Write the set of rules and conditions for this intersection as an IF/ELSE instruction with a single Boolean expression.

Exercises

1. Assume that we have an Alice world similar to the *nervous penguin* world, but with a strangePenguin and a motherPenguin as well as the nervousPenguin. Write code for Boolean conditions that could be used to trigger events to make the nervousPenguin react in each of the following situations:

    a. The strangePenguin is within 2 meters of the nervousPenguin and the motherPenguin is more than 2 meters away.

    b. The strangePenguin is within 2 meters of the nervousPenguin or the motherPenguin is more than 2 meters away.

    c. The strangePenguin is closer than the motherPenguin.

2. Chicago's Wrigley Field is a baseball field with a vine-covered wall in the outfield, that has a railing above the wall. A ball that hits the wall and does not leave the playing field is sometimes still in play and sometimes a double according to the following rules: A ball striking the railing and rebounding onto the playing field is still in play. A ball that lodges in the screen that is attached to the bleacher wall is a double. A ball that lodges in vines on the bleacher wall is a double. A ball entering the vines on the bleacher wall and rebounding onto the playing field is still in play. Rewrite this as a single Boolean condition of the form:

    A ball that hits the wall is ruled a double IF (condition), else the ball is still in play.

3. Years that are evenly divisible by four are leap years, unless they are evenly divisible by 100, in which case they are not leap years, unless they are also evenly divisible by 400, in which case they are leap years. Write a single Boolean expression that can be used to determine if a year is a leap year.

4. The last paragraph in Tutorial 5A suggests that you would need to run the *triple jump random* world many times and keep track of how many times each character jumps to properly test the world. Modify the world to include a loop that will do this, with number variables to keep track of how many times each character jumps, and print statements after the loop to show the values. Test your world to see if one character jumps more than the others, or if the jumps are uniformly distributed. How do the results compare to each other if you run the test several times?

 For Exercises 5, 6, and 7, create a new Alice world with a grass template and five objects from the people gallery: aliceLiddell, blueBallerina, handsomePrince, maleBalletDancer, and pinkBallerina. Exercises 5, 6, and 7 will refer to this world as the *dancer* world.

5. Using the *dancer* world, create a method to print the height of each character with the print instruction and the height function for that character. Using the information shown when the world is played, determine which of the following is true:

    a. aliceLiddell is taller than handsomePrince or shorter than blueBallerina.

    b. blueBallerina is taller than pinkBallerina or shorter than pinkBallerina.

    c. maleBalletDancer is shorter than handsomePrince and taller than blueBallerina.

    d. aliceLiddell is (shorter than pinkBallerina and shorter than maleBalletDancer) or (taller than blueBallerina).

    e. aliceLiddell is (shorter than pinkBallerina) and (shorter than maleBalletDancer or taller than blueBallerina).

6. Using the *dancer* world, create a method that will allow the user to select any two of the objects, and that will then cause the taller of the two objects to spin. If they are the same height, then both should spin. (*Hint:* An object variable can be used to store the object a user has selected.)

7. Using the *dancer* world, create a method that will allow the user to select any three of the objects, and that will then cause the tallest of the three objects to spin. If more than one is the tallest, then the first of the tallest objects selected should spin.

8. Sometimes complicated Boolean expressions can be simplified, or rewritten in a different form. One rule that explains how to do this is DeMorgan's Law. See if you can find information online about DeMorgan's Law and then use that information to rewrite each of the following using only one NOT operation:

    NOT(today is Monday) OR NOT (today is Wednesday)

    NOT(subject = History) AND NOT (subject = Biology)

9. The logic in the following code can be implemented with a single event with a compound Boolean condition, or with two events with simple Boolean conditions. What are the advantages and disadvantages of each approach? When can separate events be combined into one event, and when must separate events be kept as separate events?

    ```
    IF (mouse is clicked on island OR mouse is clicked on pier)
    THEN sail to pier
    ```

10. Create an Alice guessing game world according to the instructions below. The world should have two characters of your choice. (*Hint:* Create a flowchart or pseudocode to help design your world.)

    a. Pick a random number X, such that 1 <= X < 100. In the instruction to pick the random number, click "more" and select "integer only = true" so that the random number tile looks like something this:
        [X set value to random number (minimum = 1 maximum= 100) integerOnly = true]
    b. Ask the user to guess the number. Alice has a world level function to ask the user for a number.
    c. Have one of the characters tell the user if the guess is too low. Have the other character tell the user if the guess is too high.
    d. Set up a sentinel loop to repeat the process while the user's guess is not equal to the number the computer picked.
    e. Have both characters tell the user when the guess is correct and react, such as with a dance.

Text and Sound

After finishing this chapter, you should be able to:

- ☐ Provide a brief definition of the following terms: text, dialog balloon, thought bubble, personification, typeface, font, breakpoint, billboard, HSB, RGB, and tessellation
- ☐ List and describe the different ways to add text to an Alice world
- ☐ Use the `say` and `think` methods to add text messages to an Alice world
- ☐ Place messages in a special zone below Alice's playing world window with the *print* instruction
- ☐ Add 3D text objects to an Alice world
- ☐ Create a billboard from a picture file and manipulate it in an Alice world
- ☐ Add sound to an Alice world

ADDING ELEMENTS OF LANGUAGE TO AN ALICE WORLD

Even in a visually rich, three-dimensional, animated, virtual world, it is still important to be able to communicate using words—both visually and verbally. In Tutorial 1B in Chapter 1, the first Alice world you created was a version of the traditional Hello, World! program. As you may recall, this program contained a text message. The word **text** is used to describe the visual use of words (that is, the written language) in a computer program.

You can show text in an Alice world by:

- Using the `say` and `think` methods to show an object's speech and thoughts.
- Using the *print* instruction to show messages in a special zone below the playing world window.
- Adding 3D text as an Alice object.
- Placing a picture file with an image of text in an Alice world as a billboard.

The remainder of this chapter includes a brief discussion of each of these items. In addition, you will learn about sound files, which contain verbal messages that can be added to an Alice world and then played using an object's `play sound` method.

The discussions in the chapter are then followed by tutorials showing you how to use the respective techniques.

THE `say` AND `think` METHODS

Let's start with a discussion of the `say` and `think` methods. Figure 6-1 shows a scene from an Alice world, with text produced by the `say` and `think` methods. The text created by these methods appears in what animators call balloons or bubbles, much like text appears in cartoons in a newspaper or magazine. A **dialog balloon** shows words that are supposed to have been spoken by an object, and a **thought bubble** shows words that reflect an object's thoughts. In Figure 6-1, Alice is shown saying "Simon says 'Jump'!" in a dialog balloon produced by a `say` method, while the Cheshire Cat's thoughts are shown in a thought bubble produced by a `think` method.

FIGURE 6-1: The effects of the say and think methods

The say and think methods can be used with every object in Alice, including inanimate objects like rocks, trees, buildings, and vehicles. Figure 6-2 shows a thought balloon associated with a beach chair. The process of giving human qualities, such as feelings, thoughts, or human-like movements, to inanimate objects is a form of **personification**.

FIGURE 6-2: A `think` method has been used to give the beach chair human-like qualities

Personification has a long tradition in literature, often being used by poets and playwrights. Shakespeare's *Romeo and Juliet* contains the line "An hour before the worshipped sun peered forth from the golden window of the East." The sun is portrayed as looking through a window, like a person would do. Shakespeare, like other writers, often used personification when describing things like a smiling moon. In television cartoons, such as Warner Brothers' *Looney Tunes*, objects like trees, hammers, and anvils often walk, run, or speak. The use of the `say` and `think` methods with nonhuman objects in computer animation, such as Alice worlds, is an extension of this tradition.

The Alice `say` and `think` methods work almost identically, with a parameter to allow you to change the message itself. You can also change the font used for the text, the size of the text, the color of the text, the color of the bubble in which the text is displayed, and the amount of time that the message stays on the screen. Tutorial 6A will show you more about using the `say` and `think` methods.

NOTE □ □ □ In typography, a **typeface** is a full range of type of the same design, such as *Times New Roman* or *Hevetica*. A **font** is a set of characters of the same typeface, size, and style. *Times New Roman* is a typeface; *Times New Roman Bold 12 pt.* is a font. However, many people (and a certain large computer software company) use the terms interchangeably.

THE *PRINT* INSTRUCTION

The *print* instruction can be used to display messages or the value of variables and parameters in a special text zone at the bottom of a running Alice world. Figure 6-3 shows an Alice world with a text (or print) zone at the bottom of the window for the playing world.

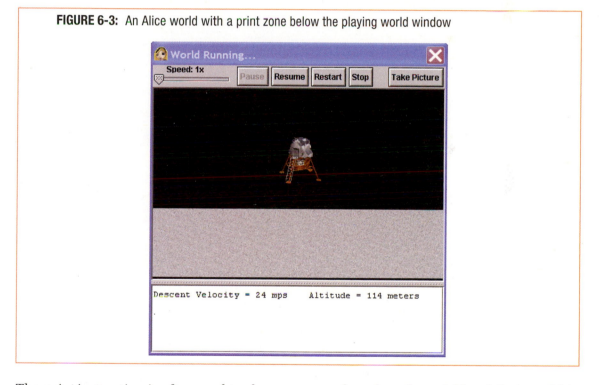

FIGURE 6-3: An Alice world with a print zone below the playing world window

The *print* instruction is often used to show someone the value of a variable while a world is playing. For example, in a world with a moving vehicle, such as a car, the object's location in three-dimensional space and its speed could be displayed.

A programmer can choose to display the value of a variable using the *print* instruction while debugging a world. The *print* instruction can then be removed once the program is debugged. For instance, this could be done in the *nervous penguin* world from Tutorial 5B. The world contains two penguins, a nervous penguin and a moving penguin. The nervous penguin is supposed to react whenever the moving penguin comes within 2 meters of the nervous penguin. The distance from the moving penguin to the nervous penguin could be displayed using a *print* instruction. That way, the programmer could note the distance between the two penguins when the nervous penguin begins to react to the presence of the other penguin, as shown in Figure 6-4. Tutorial 6B will show you more about the *print* instruction.

FIGURE 6-4: The result of using a *print* instruction in the *nervous penguin* world from Tutorial 5B

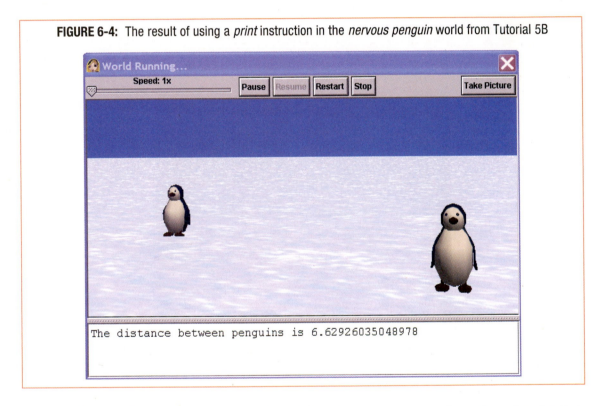

You can also use the *print* instruction when debugging a program to show that a breakpoint has been reached. A **breakpoint** is a spot in a computer program just before or just after some action occurs. For example, if a printed message shows that a point has been reached where a bunny should jump, but the bunny does not jump, then that information helps to isolate the spot in the code where the problem occurred. This is especially useful in the case where one method calls another method. The person debugging the software can tell if a problem is in the method doing the calling, or in the method being called. As with many things about learning Alice, this use of the *print* instruction is more useful in long, complex programs than in short, simple programs.

3D TEXT IN ALICE

Unlike the text used with the `say` and `think` methods or the text in a *print* instruction, 3D text is implemented in Alice as its own object. It can be used to communicate with the user or as an integral element of an Alice world. For example, the 3D text could be an object that is used as part of a story. However, most often, 3D text is used for titles, such as the opening title at the beginning of an Alice world, or for the phrase "The End" at the end of a narrative Alice world. Figure 6-5 shows an example of 3D text in an Alice world.

FIGURE 6-5: 3D text in an Alice world

The Alice Local Gallery contains a folder to create 3D text objects. Because 3D text is implemented as an Alice object, methods such as `move`, `turn`, and `roll` can be used to animate the text. User-created methods can also be developed to provide special effects for 3D text, just as they can with any other object. Although 3D text can be resized like any other object, it does have several special properties which other objects do not have, such as font and extrusion, which affect the way the text is displayed on the screen. The font property works like the font property of any other text, while the extrusion property controls the depth of the text, from front to back.

In Alice, unlike in many other programming languages, you cannot create an instance of an object in a world while the world is running. This means that 3D text in an Alice world must be kept off-camera or made invisible until it is needed on-screen. Each object in Alice has a Boolean *isShowing* property that can be set to false to make an object invisible. An object's *opacity* property, which determines if the object is solid or transparent, also can be changed to make an object invisible. Tutorial 6C will provide you with more details about 3D text.

PICTURE FILES AS ALICE BILLBOARDS

A picture file can be added to an Alice world as a billboard. A **billboard** is a flat two-dimensional object with length and width, but no depth. Once placed in an Alice world, the image from the picture file will be seen on both the front and back of the billboard. Like the 3D text described in the preceding section, billboards are objects that can be manipulated with primitive methods, like `move`, `turn`, and `roll`, as well as with user-created methods. Figure 6-6 shows a photograph of the Mona Lisa that has been added to an Alice world as a billboard.

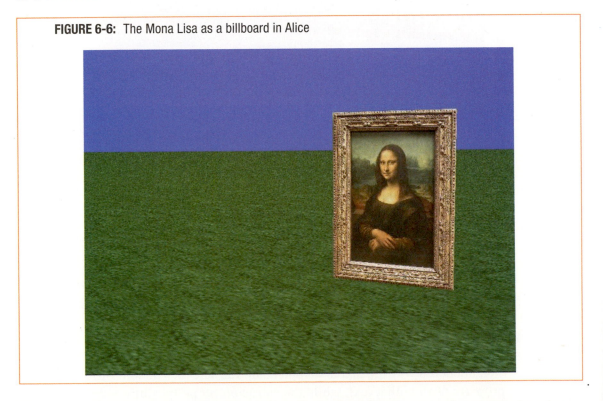

FIGURE 6-6: The Mona Lisa as a billboard in Alice

The current version of Alice (Version 2.2) easily imports files in several common imaging formats, including the Graphics Interchange Format (GIF), the Joint Photographic Experts Group format (JPG), the bitmapped file format (BMP), the Tagged Image File Format (TIF), and the Portable Network Graphics (PNG) format. Anyone who adds pictures to an Alice world as billboards should keep in mind that some image files are very large and may add significantly to the size of the Alice world.

Many graphics-manipulation programs, even simple programs like Microsoft Paint, allow a user to create and save text as an image file. Titles, credits, and instructions for users can be presented in an Alice world as a billboard that was created and saved as a picture file. Figure 6-7 shows instructions for playing a guessing game that have been placed in an Alice world as a billboard. These instructions were first typed in Microsoft Word and then cut and pasted into an image in Microsoft Paint; the saved picture file was then imported into Alice as a billboard. The Snipping Tool in *Microsoft Windows 7* also can be used to capture an image of text from a Word document.

FIGURE 6-7: An Alice billboard with instructions for playing a guessing game

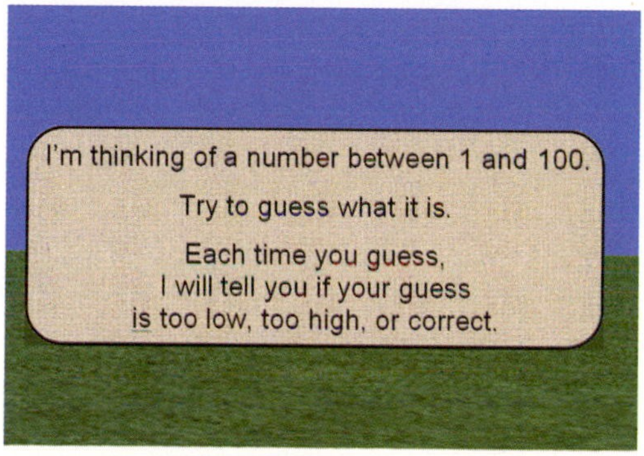

SOUNDS IN ALICE

Each object in an Alice world has a primitive `play sound` method that can be used to play a sound file. Sound files are most often used in Alice worlds to add special effects, such as the sound of a doorbell, or to play background music as a scene unfolds. A pop-up menu showing Alice's prerecorded sounds appears when the `play sound` method is used, as shown in Figure 6-8.

FIGURE 6-8: A menu showing the prerecorded sounds for the Alice `play sound` method

Notice that the menu also includes options to import a sound file and to record a new sound. Prerecorded sound files in the WAV or MP3 formats can be imported into Alice, and new sound files can be recorded directly using the Alice interface. Sound files are stored as properties of an Alice object, but a sound file stored as part of one object can be played by any other object in Alice as well.

You can record someone speaking and then use the recording to represent the voice of an object or to provide audio instructions for the user of an Alice world. For example, an event could be created to play a recording of someone speaking to provide directions on how to use the controls for a flight simulator. The directions could be recorded and saved as a property of the airplane, with an event in place to play the recording whenever someone presses the H key for help. The use of the `play sound` method in Alice is covered in Tutorial 6E.

TUTORIAL 6A—USING THE say AND think METHODS

In this short tutorial, you will revisit the Hello, World! program from Chapter 1 to learn more about the `say` and `think` methods. `World.my first method` in the program from Tutorial 1C already contains two *bunny say* tiles, as shown in Figure 6-9. In this tutorial, you will learn how to manipulate the text in these two `say` methods.

NOTE □ □ □ | The `think` method functions almost identically to the `say` method, except that its text is displayed in a thought bubble instead of in a dialog balloon.

FIGURE 6-9: `World.my first method` in the Alice world from Chapter 1

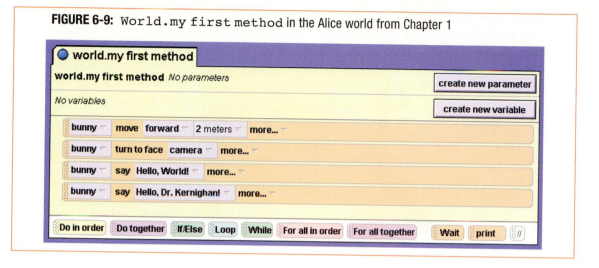

1. Open the **hello world** Alice world created in Tutorial 1C, or open a copy of the world from the student data files for this book.

2. If you cannot see the instructions in `world.my first method`, select the **world** tile in the Object tree and the **methods** tab in the Details area, and then click the **edit** button next to the name of the method on the methods tab. You should see the method displayed in the Editor area.

3. Click the word **more** following the phrase *Hello, Dr. Kernighan!* in the second *say* instruction. You should see a short menu, as shown in Figure 6-10, with several additional parameters for the `say` method. The `think` method has the same parameters.

FIGURE 6-10: A menu showing the parameters used with both the `say` and `think` methods

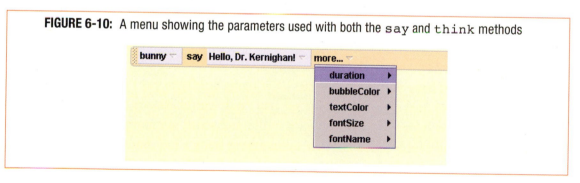

4. Select **fontSize,** and then **30**. Note that the choice of 20 is the default size for all `say` and `think` text in Alice.

5. Save the world again, and then play it to see the effect of your change.

The *duration* parameter determines how long, in seconds, the message will remain on the screen. It is used just like the duration parameter in many primitive Alice methods, such as `move` and `turn`. The *bubbleColor* parameter affects the background color, and the *textColor* parameter affects the font color for the messages displayed by the `say` and `think` methods. The default value for all durations in Alice is 1 second; the default for `say` and `think` method bubbles is black text on a white background, and the default font for all text-based items in Alice is Arial. The number for the *fontSize* parameter refers to the point size of the text, but the actual size depends on the size of the window in which the world runs, as well as the computer's screen resolution. The *fontName* parameter is the name of the chosen font.

Let's take a look at how to change these values.

1. Click the word **more** after *Hello, World!* in the *say Hello, World!* instruction, and then select **bubbleColor** from the menu that appears.

2. A color menu will appear with 16 different options, including *no color* at the top, a list of 14 colors, and *other* at the bottom, as shown in Figure 6-11. Select **yellow** as the new bubbleColor. Notice that the color of the *bubbleColor* parameter box in the *say* tile is now yellow.

FIGURE 6-11: A menu showing the colors available for dialog bubbles and thought balloons

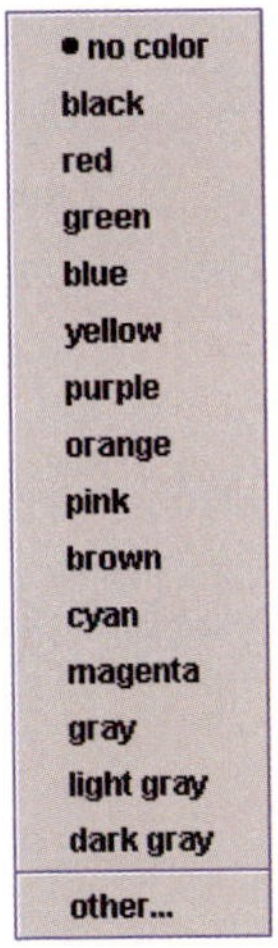

- no color
black
red
green
blue
yellow
purple
orange
pink
brown
cyan
magenta
gray
light gray
dark gray
other...

3. Now, click the word **more** after the *bubbleColor* parameter and change the *textColor* to **brown**.

4. Play the world to see the effect of the changes you made.

5. Leave the world open for use in the next set of steps.

The *other* option on the *bubbleColor* and *textColor* menus will take you to a custom color dialog box, which will let you set the color in one of three different ways: by picking a swatch from a predefined palette of colors, by using HSB color values, or by using RGB color values. **HSB** stands for Hue, Saturation, and Brightness. (Brightness is also called Brilliance.) **RGB** stands for Red, Green, and Blue. These are two different color models for describing the color of a pixel on a computer screen, which is determined by blending red, green, and blue light. The color of a pixel can also be described by setting the hue for the pixel's color, the color saturation, and its brilliance, as shown in the following steps:

1. Click the **bubbleColor** parameter in the *say Hello, World!* instruction tile and select **other** from the menu that appears. You should see the Swatches tab in the Custom Color window, as shown in Figure 6-12.

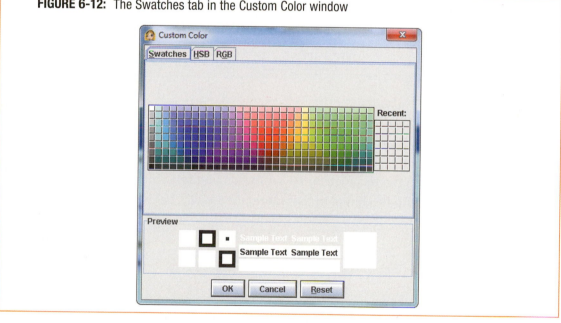

FIGURE 6-12: The Swatches tab in the Custom Color window

2. Pick a light green color from those available on the palette, click **OK,** and then play the world again to see the effect.

3. Next, click the **bubbleColor** parameter and select **other** again. This time, click the **RGB** tab. Figure 6-13 shows the RGB tab. You can set the color on this tab by entering values in the input boxes for red, green, and blue, or by using the slider controls. The effect of your changes can be seen in the previews at the bottom of the window. Experiment a bit with the colors before continuing.

FIGURE 6-13: The RGB tab in the Custom Color window

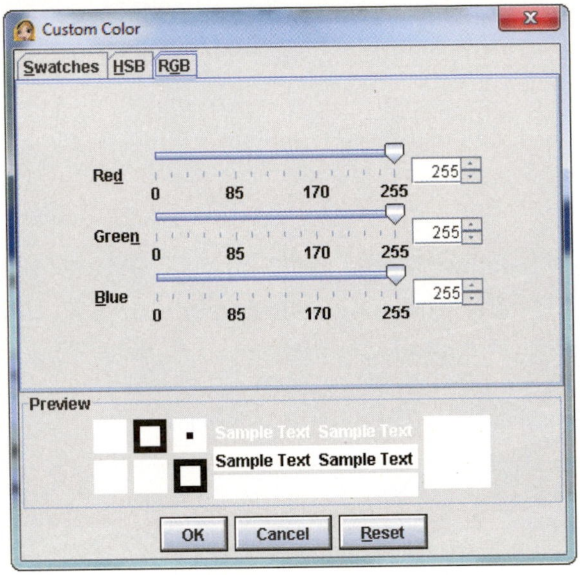

4. Select the **HSB** tab, and you will see the HSB color controls, as shown in Figure 6-14. You can enter numbers in the input boxes for hue, saturation, and brightness or slide the hue control arrow up and down, and then click a spot on the rectangle to set saturation and brightness. The equivalent RGB values will be shown in the information boxes below the HSB input boxes.

FIGURE 6-14: The HSB tab in the Custom Color window

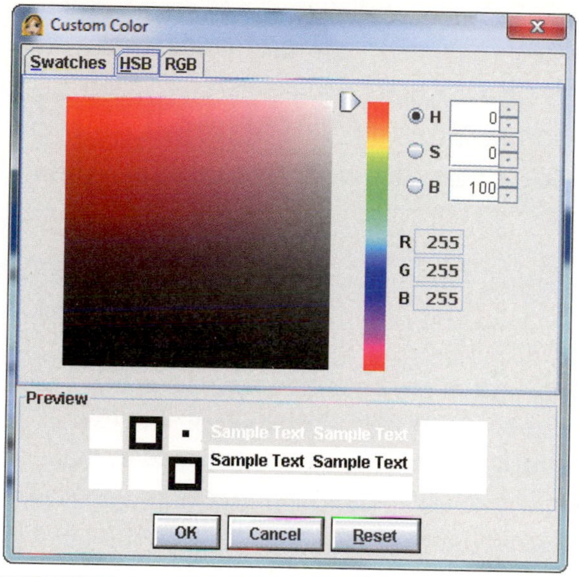

5. Click the **S** (for **saturation)** radio button, and you will see that the slider control now affects saturation. Note that clicking the rectangle will affect hue and brightness.

6. Click the **B** (for **brightness)** radio button, and you will see that the slider control now affects brightness. Note that clicking the rectangle will affect hue and saturation.

7. The *textColor* parameter is changed the same way as the *bubbleColor* parameter. Experiment with setting the colors and playing the world before continuing. Be careful—if the *textColor* and *bubbleColor* parameters are the same, the text will be invisible. Select colors that you like or change them back to black and white before continuing.

You can use the *fontName* parameter to set the typeface for the say and think methods. The default typeface is Arial. The available typefaces are determined by the Alice software and how it interacts with your computer's operating system. Not every typeface that is available on your computer system in programs such as Microsoft Word or Internet Explorer will work with the Alice say and think methods. Figure 6-15 shows a few of the typefaces that work with the current version of Alice in a variety of environments.

FIGURE 6-15: Some of the typefaces that work with the *fontName* parameter

Arial	Haettenschweiler
Book Antigua	*Monotype Corsiva*
Comic Sans MS	Palatino Linotype
Courier New	Times New Roman

The only way to be sure which typefaces will work on your system is by trial and error; however, Arial and Times New Roman will almost always work. The following steps will show you how to change the typeface by changing the *fontName* parameter.

1. Click the word **more** after the text in the *bunny say Hello, Dr. Kernighan!* tile.

2. Select **fontName** from the menu that appears, and then select **other**.

3. You should now see a small window that will allow you to enter a string. This is one of the weakest parts of Alice. You must type the name of the typeface you want to use, rather than selecting it from a list as with other parameters. Type **Times New Roman** as the new fontName, and then click **OK**. Capitalization is not important, but spelling and spacing are.

4. Play the world, and you should see the first message in the Arial typeface and the second in the Times New Roman typeface.

5. Try experimenting with some of the typefaces shown in Figure 6-15 to see if they work on your system before continuing.

The `say` and `think` methods can be used to display information about the world, although they are more commonly used as elements of an Alice world's story or simulation. Many fonts almost have a personality of their own, and particular fonts can be used for particular characters in a story or for particular situations.

Some special typefaces for characters from languages other than English don't work, but Arabic, Hebrew, and Cyrillic characters can often be cut from Microsoft Word or from a Web browser and pasted as the text for the `say` and `think` methods. Figure 6-16 shows an example of this. The Greek phrase *Γειάσου κόσμος* (translation: *Hello World!*) has been cut from Microsoft Word and pasted into a `say` method. The appearance of specific characters, particularly from languages other than English, may depend on which font you are using.

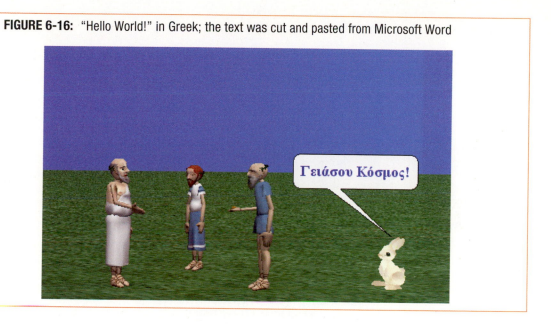

FIGURE 6-16: "Hello World!" in Greek; the text was cut and pasted from Microsoft Word

TUTORIAL 6B—THE *PRINT* INSTRUCTION

The *print* instruction can be used to display information in a special print zone below the playing world window, as shown in Figure 6-17. The text displayed here is very simple plain text and cannot be formatted. You can print any text string as a message in the print zone, or you can print the names of objects and the values of variables and parameters from a running world.

FIGURE 6-17: A playing world window with the print zone showing

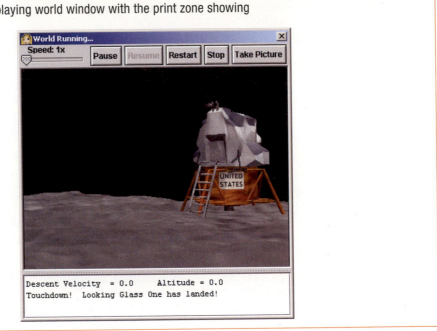

In this tutorial, you will print the distance between two penguins in the *nervous penguin* world. You will also print a message showing when the point in the program has been reached where the nervous penguin should jump.

1. Open the **nervous penguin** world that was created as part of Tutorial 5B, or open a copy of the world from the student data files for this book.

2. Select the **nervousPenguin** tile in the Object tree and the **methods** tab in the Details area.

3. Click the **edit** button next to the *react* method tile on the methods tab, and the method should be displayed in the Editor area. It contains instructions to make the nervous penguin jump up and to flap its wings.

4. Drag a **print** instruction tile from the bottom of the Editor area and drop it in the method in front of the instructions that are already there.

5. A short menu will appear with two options, *text string* and *object*. Select **text string** and an Enter Text String window will appear. Type **begin reaction** and click the **OK** button.

6. Now play the world and use the arrow keys to control the moving penguin. When it gets close to the nervous penguin and the `react` method is called, the *begin reaction* message should be displayed in the world window. In this case, because the code should work, the nervous penguin will start to react at the same time, but you can see how this might be useful if the nervous penguin were not reacting.

7. It is not necessary to save the world before continuing, but if you do so, use the **Save World As** menu option and give the world a new name to preserve the original *nervous penguin* world.

Another useful debugging technique is to display the value of a variable or parameter while a world is running. Let's add an instruction to the *triple jump random* world from Tutorial 5A to display the value of the index variable, which determines which character will jump.

1. Open the **triple jump random** world from Tutorial 5A or open a copy of the world from the student data files for this book.

2. If you cannot see `world.my first method` in the Editor area, select the **world** tile in the Object tree and the **methods** tab in the Details area, and then click the **edit** button next to the name of the method on the methods tab.

3. `World.myfirst method` contains an instruction to randomly set the value of the variable *determinant*, which will determine which character jumps. Drag the **print** instruction from the bottom of the Editor area and drop it in `world.my first method` just below the tile that sets the value of the determinant.

4. When the print menu appears, select **object**, then **expressions**, and then **determinant**. The *print* instruction tile should now say *print* determinant, as shown in Figure 6-18.

FIGURE 6-18: `World.my first method` with an instruction to print the value of the variable *determinant*

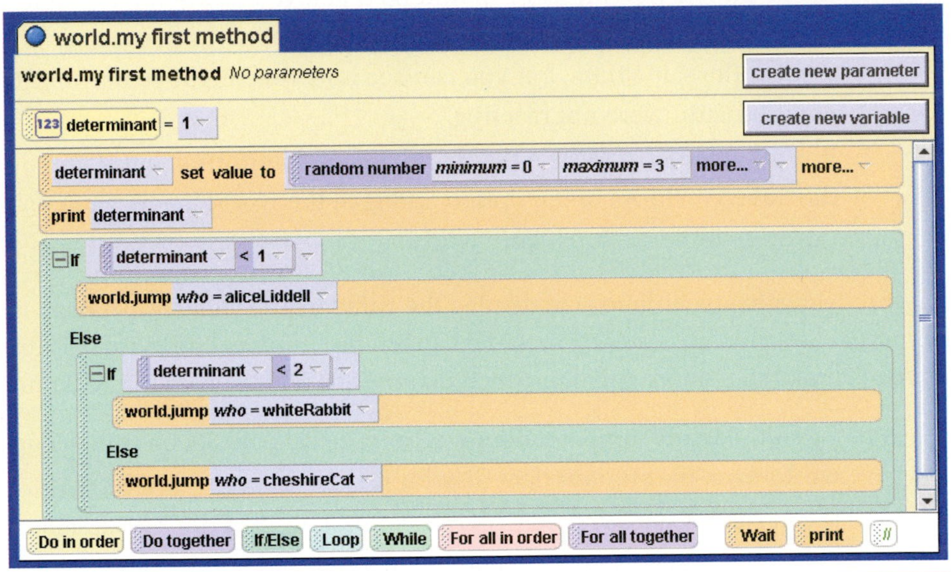

5. Try playing the world several times. You should see messages that display the value of the *determinant* variable appearing in the print zone. It is not necessary to save the world, but if you want to do so, save it with a different name to preserve the copy of the world without the *print* instruction.

TUTORIAL 6C—THREE-DIMENSIONAL TEXT

In this tutorial, you will add opening titles to the *triple jump* world created in Chapter 2. Messages and titles can be added to an Alice world as three-dimensional text. Once in the world, they can be animated and manipulated just like any other Alice object by using primitive methods or creating new methods of your own.

You can add 3D text to a world through the object gallery or by using the *Add 3D Text* option on the File menu. Both ways of starting the process take you to the same place and produce the same results. In the first part of this exercise, you will add an opening title using the object gallery.

1. Open the **triple jump** world created in Tutorial 2B, or open a copy of the world from the student data files for this book.

2. Click the **ADD OBJECTS** button to enter Scene Editor mode and see the object galleries. Scroll through the Local Gallery until you find the *Create 3D Text* tile. It's on the far-right side of the Local Gallery.

3. Click the **Create 3D Text** tile, and you should see the Add 3D Text window, as shown in Figure 6-19. It has a place to enter your text, a button with a pull-down menu to select a font for the text, and buttons for boldface and italicized text effects. Your window may look different, depending on the system fonts installed on your computer. If the typeface shown is not *Arial*, then click the arrow next to the typeface name and change it to Arial.

FIGURE 6-19: The Add 3D Text window

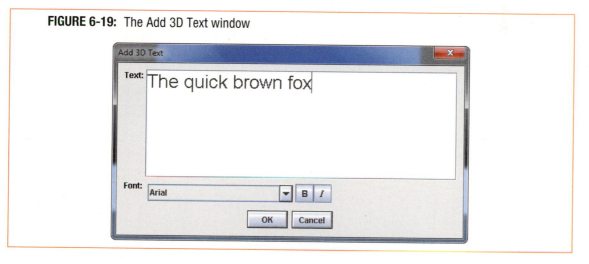

4. Click the **OK** button, and you will see the text appear in the Alice world. In addition, a tile for the text object will appear in the Object tree. The tile will have the name *3D Text*.

5. Right-click the **3D Text** tile in the Object tree and rename the tile **openingTitle**.

6. Now that the object has been created, you can change the text to be what the opening title should say. Click the **openingTitle** tile in the Object tree and then click the **properties** tab in the Details area.

7. Click the words **The quick brown fox** next to the *text* property on the properties tab and change the text to **Triple Jump**. Press the **Enter** key after you have finished changing the text. Notice that the text has changed in the Alice world window, but the object retains the name *openingTitle* in the Object tree.

You can get back to a window similar to the Add 3D Text window through the *font* property on the properties tab at any time to change the typeface of the 3D text. However, there is no property for size. Because 3D text is an object in Alice, it is resized like other objects, by using the primitive `resize` method. Let's take a look at the *font* property.

1. Click the button next to the *font* tile on the properties tab in the Details area. The button is labeled with the name of the font. This will open the Choose a Font window, as shown in Figure 6-20. Notice that it looks very much like the Add 3D Text window shown in Figure 6-19. You can see the text in the Choose a Font window, but, unlike the Add 3D Text window, you cannot change the text. You can only make changes to the text's appearance by using the buttons near the bottom of the window.

FIGURE 6-20: The Choose a Font window

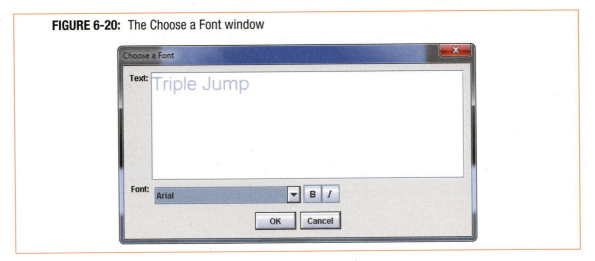

2. Click the **typeface** button, and a scrolling menu with the names of all the typefaces currently available will appear. This is much more convenient than the way in which the *fontName* parameter is changed for the text for the `say` and `think` methods, as you saw in Tutorial 6A.

3. Take a moment to try a few of the typefaces from the list. You will notice that several of the more uncommon typefaces won't work because Alice has not been programmed to render 3D text using them. More common fonts, such as Arial, Times New Roman, and Courier New, should work.

4. Before continuing, select a typeface and color for your title by changing the *font* property and the *color* property on the properties tab.

Next you will position the *openingTitle* title in the Alice world. This can be done in Scene Editor mode or by running primitive methods directly. In the next several steps, you will use the primitive methods approach.

1. Right-click the **openingTitle** tile in the Object tree, select methods, select the **openingTitle move** method, select **up**, and then select **2 meters**. If 2 meters is not an available option, select **other** and type **2** in the Custom Number dialog box, and then press **Enter**.

2. Again right-click **openingTitle** in the Object tree, select **methods,** and run the **openingTitle turn to face** method to make the text face the **camera**.

3. If the entire title does not fit in the world window, right-click **openingTitle** in the Object tree, select **methods,** and run the **openingTitle move** method to move the title backward a few meters. If you go too far back, or not far enough, you can use the `move` method again to move it a little more forward or backward. Don't forget that you can also use the *Undo* button. It may take a few minutes to line it up in a way that looks just right. Position the text so that you think it looks good in relation to the three characters. Figure 6-21 shows one possibility. Keep in mind that when you play the world, the text will disappear before the three characters begin to jump, so it's okay if the text overlaps the characters.

FIGURE 6-21: A 3D text title in the *triple jump* world

A 3D text title looks nice, but normally we don't want the text to remain on the screen for the entire time a world is running. The text can be made to turn, roll, move, etc., including moving off-camera, by creating methods and events as desired. The text can also be left in place, but made invisible. In the next few steps, you will add instructions to make the title disappear a few seconds after the world starts playing. There are two ways to make the title invisible: by changing the *isShowing* property or by changing the *opacity* property. You will try both.

1. Select the **world** tile in the object tree and the **methods** tab in the Details area. Click the **edit** button next to *my first method*, and `world.my first method` should appear in the Editor area.

2. Drag a copy of the **Wait** instruction tile from the bottom of the Editor area and drop it into `world.my first method` as the first instruction in the method. When the menu appears, set the duration to **2 seconds**.

3. Next, click the **openingTitle** tile in the object tree, and then click the **properties** tab and drag a copy of the **isShowing** property tile into the method below the *Wait* instruction. Select **false** from the menu that appears. Dragging a property tile into a method will create an instruction to change that property's value. The method should now look something like Figure 6-22.

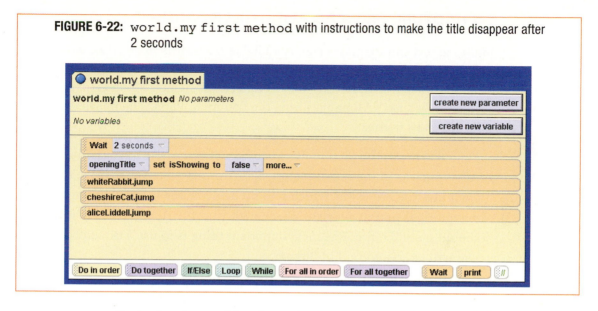

FIGURE 6-22: `world.my first method` with instructions to make the title disappear after 2 seconds

4. Now play the world and watch what happens. If you have followed the steps correctly, then the title should disappear after two seconds.

If you played the world again, you would notice that the title disappears very abruptly. In film and video production, this abrupt change is called a cut. A director may cut from one scene to another or cut a title from a scene. The term fade applies to a more subtle transition in which an object or a scene slowly disappears. In Alice, you can cause a fade to occur by using the *opacity* property.

1. First, right-click the **openingTitle set isShowing to false** instruction tile in the Editor area and select **delete** from the menu that appears. The tile should disappear from `world.my first method`.

2. Select the **openingTitle** tile in the object tree and the **properties** tab in the Details area.

3. Drag a copy of the **opacity** property tile into the method below the *Wait* instruction. Select **0%: invisible** from the menu that appears.

4. Now play the world again, and you should see the title fade away instead of disappearing abruptly.

This world will not be used further in this book, but you may want to experiment with it a little on your own. You can experiment with the font and with the bold and italic effects. You can resize the text in the Scene Editor mode, just as you would any other object. In fact, you may want to add a second title that says "created by *<your name>*", and then have the text fade or move on-screen and then off from the side, from above, or even from below.

TUTORIAL 6D—PICTURE FILES AS ALICE BILLBOARDS

Picture files containing text and diagrams can be added as billboards in an Alice world. In this tutorial, you will add a picture file to a new Alice world to see how this is done. To aid you in this tutorial, the student files for this book contain a file named Mona Lisa.jpg. This is an image of Leonardo DaVinci's Mona Lisa from the Louvre in Paris. The image is a photograph of the painting in its frame.

1. You need to put the picture file someplace it can easily be found inside Alice, such as in the root directory on the primary hard disk drive of the computer you are using, which will probably be the C: drive. If you are doing this as part of a course, check with your instructor to see where you should place the file. The most important thing is to use a directory that you will be able to find in Step 4.

2. Start a new Alice world with a **grass** template.

3. Click **File** on the menu bar, and then click **Make Billboard**. Your screen should resemble Figure 6-23.

FIGURE 6-23: The dialog box to import a picture file for use as an Alice billboard object

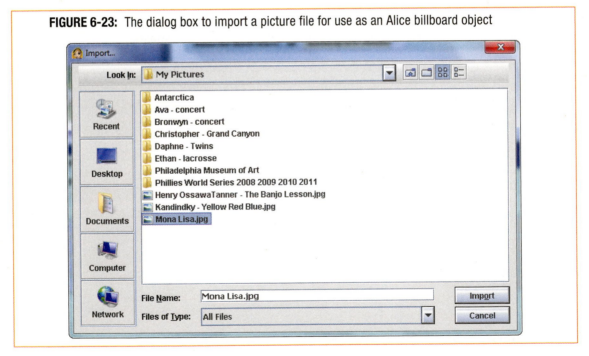

4. Find the directory where you stored the file Mona Lisa.jpg. Click the name of the file, and then click the **Import** button. The picture should appear in the world, as shown in Figure 6-6 earlier in this chapter.

The picture file may now be manipulated like any other object, using the tools in the Scene Editor mode, primitive methods, or any user-created methods that you write for the object. You may want to experiment with the Scene Editor tools and perhaps use a few methods to make the picture move around a bit. You can also use the *opacity* property to make the picture opaque or invisible, as was shown with 3D text in the previous tutorial. If you rotate the object, you will notice that it has no depth, that it is flat like a sheet of paper, and that the original image appears on both sides.

A curious side effect of adding a picture file to an Alice world as a billboard is that the image is now available as a texture map that can be used for other objects. To see how this works, you can try the following:

1. Click the **ground** tile in the Object tree, and then the **properties** tab in the Details area.

2. Click **ground.GrassTexture** next to the *skin texture* tile.

3. A small menu will appear, and you will notice that *Mona Lisa.Mona Lisa_texture* appears as an item on the menu. This is the image from the original *Mona Lisa.jpg* picture file. Select this as the skin texture for the ground, and the Mona Lisa with its frame will now be used as the image file for the surface of the ground.

4. Save the world as **tessellation sample** before continuing.

A repeated pattern of an image on a surface is called a **tessellation** of the surface. The Mona Lisa is now being used to form a tessellation on the ground. You may want to enter Scene Editor mode and move farther above the surface to look down to get a better view of the tessellated ground.

You can use any image as the surface for the ground. Figure 6-24 shows an Alice world tessellated with an image of the White Rabbit. In a similar manner, you could use an image file as the surface for any object, such as the shapes found in the Local Gallery's shapes folder. The image will be distorted to fit the surface of the shape, but in some cases, it may be recognizable.

FIGURE 6-24: Alice in a world tessellated with the image of the White Rabbit

NOTE Using image and sound files in Alice raises the issue of copyrights. You must be careful when using copyrighted material, such as text, sound, and images, in an Alice world or in other computer programs that you create. Section 107 of the U.S. copyright law (Title 17, U.S. code) describes the doctrine of fair use of copyrighted material, which covers the educational use of such material. The concept of fair use is explained on the Web at: *http://www.copyright.gov/fls/fl102.html*. The courts have generally agreed that students and teachers may use copyrighted material for instructional use provided that the material is used only for "educational purposes in systematic learning activities at nonprofit educational institutions," and that the material satisfies certain "portion limitations." An educational presentation may include the following:

- Up to 10% or 1,000 words, whichever is less, of a copyrighted text work. For example, an entire poem of less than 250 words may be used, but no more than three poems by one poet, or five poems by different poets from any anthology.
- Up to 10%, but in no event more than 30 seconds, of the music and lyrics from an individual musical work.
- Up to 10% or three minutes, whichever is less, of a copyrighted motion media work (for example, an animation, video, or film image).
- A photograph or illustration may be used in its entirety, but no more than five images by an artist or photographer may be reproduced. When using photographs and illustrations from a published collective work, no more than 10% or 15 images, whichever is less.

■ Up to 10% or 2,500 fields or cell entries, whichever is less, from a copyrighted database or data table may be reproduced. A field entry is defined as a specific item of information, such as a name or Social Security number, in a record of a database file. A cell entry is defined as the intersection where a row and a column meet on a spreadsheet.

One excellent comprehensive source of information about copyright and fair use is the Stanford University Libraries' Copyright and Fair Use Web site at: *http://fairuse.stanford.edu/*.

TUTORIAL 6E—SOUND IN ALICE WORLDS

In this short tutorial, you will add sound to a very simple Alice world using a sound clip that comes with Alice. In addition to using the prerecorded sounds that are supplied as part of the Alice software, you may also import sound clips from an external file or record your own sound clips.

There are three tiles for three sound clips shown in Figure 6-25: one named *Pacino*, one named *sylvester*, and one named *instructions*. Next to each is a green triangular button that you can use to preview a sound directly before using it in your world.

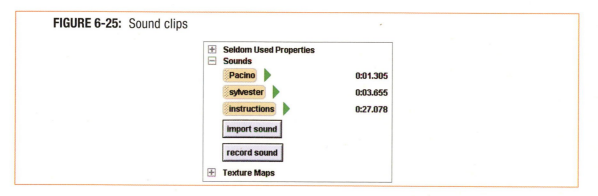

FIGURE 6-25: Sound clips

NOTE □ □ □ You can also rename a sound clip by right-clicking the sound clip tile and then changing the name, and you can delete a sound by dragging it to the Trash can.

Of course, to play sounds in Alice you need to have a computer with speakers and an active sound card, and to record sounds, you need to have a properly working microphone connected to your computer. Check with your instructor or the person who maintains the computer you are using to find out about its sound card and microphone. If your computer does not have sound, you should still read through the tutorial to get a feeling for how sound works in Alice. In these steps, you will add a chicken to a new Alice world and set up an event so that the chicken will make a chicken sound whenever the spacebar is pressed.

1. Start a new Alice world with a **grass** template.

2. Click the **ADD OBJECTS** button to enter Scene Editor mode and add a **Chicken** to the world from the Animals folder in the Local Gallery.

3. Click the **DONE** button after you have added the Chicken to the world. Notice that the *Chicken* is one of the few objects whose instance name starts with a capital letter. There is no special reason for this other than that the programmer who created the *Chicken* class of objects did so.

4. Click the **create new event** button in the Events area and select **When a key is typed** from the menu that appears.

5. Click the **any key** box in the tile for the new method and select **Space** from the menu that appears.

6. Next, make sure that **Chicken** is selected in the Object tree, and then click the **methods** tab.

7. Drag a copy of the **Chicken play sound** tile from the methods tab and drop it in the new event in place of the word *Nothing*.

8. A menu of available sounds will appear. Select **chicken** from the list that appears.

9. Play the world, and whenever you press the spacebar, the chicken sound will be played.

10. The *play sound* tile has parameters that will let you adjust the duration and volume of the sound, which can be accessed by clicking **more** on the play sound tile. You may want to experiment with the volume level, or add some instructions to your world to animate the Chicken.

Chapter Summary

This chapter consisted of a discussion of the various uses of text in an Alice world, followed by a short discussion of sound in an Alice world and five tutorials.

The discussions included the following:

- [ ] There are different ways in which you can show text in an Alice world: by using the `say` and `think` primitive methods, by using the *print* instruction, by adding 3D text as an Alice object, and by placing a picture file with an image of text in an Alice world as a billboard.

- [ ] In addition to using visual text, sound files containing verbal messages can be added to an Alice world and then played using an object's `play sound` method.

- [ ] The text created by the `say` and `think` methods appears in what animators call balloons or bubbles, much like text appears in cartoons in a newspaper or magazine. A dialog balloon shows words that are supposed to have been spoken by an object, and a thought bubble shows words that reflect an object's thoughts.

- [ ] The `say` and `think` methods can be used with every object in Alice, including inanimate objects like rocks, trees, buildings, and vehicles. The Alice `say` and `think` methods work almost identically, with parameters to allow you to change the message itself, as well as the font used for the text, the size of the text, the color of the text, the color of the bubble in which the text is displayed, and the amount of time that the message stays on the screen.

- [ ] The *print* instruction can be used to display messages or the value of variables and parameters in a special text zone at the bottom of a running Alice world. It is most often used to show someone the value of a variable while a world is playing. Sometimes the value of a variable is displayed using the *print* instruction while debugging a world. You can also use the *print* instruction when debugging a program to show that a breakpoint has been reached.

- [ ] 3D text is implemented in Alice as its own object. It can be used to communicate with the user or as an element in an Alice world. The Alice Local Gallery contains a folder to create 3D text objects.

- [ ] Picture files can be added to an Alice world as a billboard. The current version of Alice can easily import GIF, JPG, BMP, PNG, and TIF files.

- [ ] Each object in an Alice world has a primitive `play sound` method that can be used to play a sound file. Sound files are most often used in Alice worlds to add special effects, such as the sound of a doorbell, or to play background music as a scene unfolds.

- [ ] Several sound recordings are included with Alice. Other prerecorded sound files in the WAV or MP3 formats can be imported into Alice, and new sound files can be recorded directly using the Alice interface.

In Tutorial 6A, you explored the use of the `say` and `think` methods in Alice and how to manipulate the appearance of the methods' dialog balloons and thought bubbles.

In Tutorial 6B, you saw how the *print* instruction can be used to display the value of a variable and to show when a playing Alice world has reached a certain spot. These techniques are often used to debug a program.

In Tutorial 6C, you experimented with the creation and manipulation of 3D text as an object in an Alice world.

In Tutorial 6D, you imported a picture file into an Alice world as a billboard object that can be manipulated with methods just as other objects are.

In Tutorial 6E, you added a sound clip to an Alice world.

Review Questions

1. Define the following terms:

   - ☐ billboard
   - ☐ breakpoint
   - ☐ dialog balloon
   - ☐ font
   - ☐ HSB
   - ☐ personification
   - ☐ RGB
   - ☐ tessellation
   - ☐ text
   - ☐ thought bubble
   - ☐ typeface

2. List and briefly describe the different ways that text can be shown in an Alice world.

3. Describe how to change the typeface for each of the following: text in an Alice dialog balloon or thought bubble, Alice 3D text, and text displayed by the Alice *print* instruction.

4. Describe how to change the size of each of the following: text in an Alice dialog balloon or thought bubble, Alice 3D text, and text displayed by the Alice *print* instruction.

5. Describe how the *print* instruction can be useful in debugging methods in an Alice world.

6. Which common picture file formats work best for importing images into Alice as billboards?

7. How can a picture file that has been imported into Alice for use as a billboard be used to tessellate the ground in an Alice world?

8. Describe the notion of "fair use" of copyrighted material for educational purposes. How much of each of the following can probably be used in an Alice world or other student work based on how courts have ruled in the past on this doctrine?

    a. Poems by Langston Hughes
    b. A recording of "Use Somebody" by Kings of Leon
    c. An early recording of Gershwin's *Rhapsody in Blue*
    d. Beethoven's *Symphony No. 5* from the 1996 recording by the Vienna Philharmonic
    e. Images of artwork from the Guggenheim Museum's Web site
    f. Scanned images of pictures from a recent book about art in the Louvre

9. List the recorded sounds that are supplied as part of Alice for use by the `play sound` method. How can other sounds be used in Alice?

10. Colors in Alice can be described using the RGB (Red, Green, Blue) color model or the HSB (Hue, Saturation, Brightness) color model. The term HSL (Hue, Saturation, Luminance) is also used for the HSB color model. Using the Internet as a research tool, find the meaning of the terms hue, saturation, and brightness (or luminance), and how these color models are related to the CMYK and Pantone color schemes.

Exercises

1. Add text in dialog balloons or thought bubbles to an existing Alice world. Change the *bubbleColor*, *textColor*, *fontSize*, and *fontName* properties to give the text a look and feel that enhances the world. In addition, the text should match the personality of the character with whom it is associated or the tone of the message itself.

2. The *ask user for a string* function and the *ask user for a number* function are often used with string and number variables in a manner similar to the *ask user for yes or no* function, discussed in Chapter 4. Using these functions and the `say` method discussed in this chapter, create a simple Alice world with a dialog in which a character asks the user for his or her name, says "hello" to the person by name, asks how old the person is, and then tells the person approximately how many days old he or she will be on his or her next birthday.

3. Create a title sequence for an existing Alice world of your choice. The titles should be added as 3D text objects, with animation sequences for the text. The world should have an entry sequence for when the text appears and an exit sequence for when the text disappears. To get some ideas for entry and exit sequences, you might want to look at Microsoft PowerPoint. The list of effects on the animations schemes or custom animations on the Slide Show menu in PowerPoint might give you some ideas for your title sequences in Alice.

4. Foreign language text can sometimes be cut and pasted from Microsoft Word, from other programs, or from a Web site into Alice *say* and *think* method tiles or as Alice 3D text. For example, the Greek language phrase "Ἀριστοτέλης ἥταν σπονδαστής Πλάτωνα" (Aristotle was a student of Plato) can be cut and pasted from Word into Alice as the text for a 3D text object. The Altavista Babel Fish Translation Web site (*www.babelfish.altavista.com*) is one of many sites you can use to translate text from English into another language. Some of the translated text will work in Alice, and some will not, depending on the language and the typeface used to display the language. Create a simple Alice world with text in one or more languages other than English. Start by picking a few simple phrases, enter them into the Babel Fish Web site, and translate them to see how well they work. You can reenter them into Babel Fish and cut and paste the translation from Babel Fish into Alice as needed while you develop your world.

5.   Images from most digital cameras can be saved as .JPG files, which can be imported into Alice as a billboard. Create an Alice world in which an image of you or someone you know plays a role.

6.   Create an Alice world that is a short tutorial teaching the user about the sound clips built into Alice. Your world should contain keyboard events to allow the user to trigger each sound, along with either a menu of the built-in sounds, or a character who tells the user to press a particular key to hear a sound. The world should have a variety of objects to demonstrate the use of the sounds with matching animations. As always, remember to use good design techniques as you create the world.

7.   You can record a dialog or narration for an Alice world using the record sound feature found on the properties tab of an Alice object. You can also import sound into Alice from an existing sound file. Select a segment of a song or other piece of music of your choice, import it into Alice as a sound file, and then create a short music video sequence in Alice with the sound you added as background. Remember to use proper design techniques as you create the world.

8.   Create a 15- to 30-second animated commercial advertisement for a product or service of your choice as an Alice world. The world should use some of the features discussed in this chapter. You should begin by selecting the subject of your advertisement, and then create an outline or storyboard for the advertisement. Once you have the outline or storyboard, you can write pseudocode as refinement of the specifications for the world, and then code the world based on the pseudocode. Remember to use good modular design as you develop your world.

9.   The Television program *Sesame Street* often uses the theme of commercial endorsements to teach young children about the alphabet, such as segments on the program that are supposedly "… brought to you by the letter W …" Create an Alice world that picks up on this theme to teach children about a letter of the alphabet in a world with animation and sound.

10. Fairytales, myths, stories from history, and urban legends are all good subjects for Alice worlds with a voiceover narration. Create an outline or storyboard for such a world, then write pseudocode for the world, and then write the code itself. Be sure to keep the story short, so that the narration is not too long. You may want to start by looking through both the Alice Local Gallery and the Alice Web Gallery to find characters for your story. There are three different approaches you can use to match the timing of the narration to the world:

a. You could record the narration first, and then make the action in the world match the narration.
b. You could animate the story first, and then record a voiceover to match the action.
c. You could record the narration in short sound bytes that are played as required while the action is occurring.

Recursive Algorithms

After finishing this chapter, you should be able to:

- ☐ Provide brief definitions of the following terms: recursion, recursive method, iterative process, iteration, overhead, linear recursion, exponential recursion, infinite recursion, conditional recursion, base condition, and base case

- ☐ Describe what is meant by recursion in an algorithm, and how to implement recursion in Alice

- ☐ Describe how recursion differs from iteration, including the cost of recursion, and how to tell when one might be more appropriate to use than the other

- ☐ Describe the difference between infinite recursion and conditional recursion

- ☐ Create a recursive method in Alice

- ☐ Convert an iterative Alice method into a linear recursive method

WHAT IS RECURSION?

Recursion is an important concept in computer programming. Generally, something is said to be recursive if each of the parts that make up the thing have a structure—in other words, a design or pattern—that repeats the structure of the whole thing itself. Consider the fern in Figure 7-1. Each leaf of the fern has a pattern that is virtually identical to the overall fern itself. In fact, if you look closely at the leaf, you can see that the parts that make up the leaf have patterns that match the leaf itself. If you were to go deeper and deeper into the structure of the fern, you would see that the same pattern is repeated again and again, each time on a smaller scale, each time in more detail. The fern has a recursive structure—parts of the fern have structures that mirror the overall structure of the fern itself. There are many such examples of recursion in the natural world.

FIGURE 7-1: A fern with a recursive structure

Recursion is not a simple concept, so often it takes a while for someone who has never seen it before to really understand it. This chapter is not intended to make you an expert on recursion, but only to expose you to the topic. By the time you are done, you should have a basic understanding of what a recursive algorithm is. Before going on, let's take a look at another example. Can you see how the following very short story is recursive?

Once upon a time a young princess was sitting with her father, the king. She said to her father, "My Royal Father, can you read me a story?"

"Yes, my Royal Daughter," said the king, as he opened the *Royal Storybook*. He began to read, "Once upon a time a young princess was sitting with her father, the king. She said to her father, 'My Royal Father, can you read me a story?'"

"Yes, my Royal Daughter," said the king, as he opened the *Royal Storybook*. He began to read, "Once upon a time a young princess was sitting with her father, the king. She said to her father, 'My Royal Father, can you read me a story?' . . ."

RECURSIVE ALGORITHMS

Throughout this book you have seen how one method can call another method. Consider Figure 7-2a. The primitive method `bunny.move` is one of several methods called from within `world.my first method`. In computer programming, an algorithm that calls itself is said to be recursive. A **recursive method** is a method that calls itself. Figure 7-2b shows a simple example of a recursive method, `bunny.hop to carrot`, which calls itself. A part of the algorithm is identical to the overall algorithm because the method being called *is* the overall algorithm. In a sense, the method is nested within itself, just as the recursive structure of the fern is nested within itself in the example above.

FIGURE 7-2: A method that calls another method, and a method that calls itself

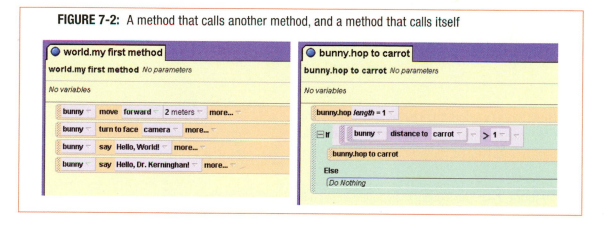

Let's take a look at another example of a recursive algorithm. Almost everyone knows about the famous ceiling of the Sistine Chapel in Rome, painted by Michelangelo, but do you know about its floor? The marble floor of the Sistine Chapel has patterns in the tiles that look like Figure 7-3. This pattern is an example of a mathematical design called a Sierpinski gasket.

FIGURE 7-3: A Sierpinski gasket

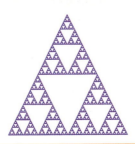

Here is the algorithm for drawing a Sierpinski gasket:

```
Begin with an equilateral triangle
Sierpinski (triangle)
    Start
    Find the midpoint of each side of the triangle
    Draw lines connecting the midpoints, which will form four
        smaller triangles that can be called triangles A, B, C,
        and D, with D in the center and the others around it.
    Color in (or cut out) the center triangle  // triangle D
    Do Sierpinski (triangle A)
    Do Sierpinski (triangle B)
    Do Sierpinski (triangle C)
    Stop
```

The Sierpinski gasket algorithm splits the triangle into four smaller triangles, and then calls itself for three of the four smaller triangles. Figure 7-4 shows the result of the algorithm through five levels of recursion.

FIGURE 7-4: The Sierpinski algorithm through five levels of recursion

In the figure, you can see that the process of dividing the triangle into smaller triangles and then coloring in (or cutting out) one of them is repeated over and over again, each time at a smaller level, each time in more detail. The result is a complex structure created by a small, efficient algorithm.

The Sierpinski gasket algorithm demonstrates the power of recursion in drawing complex structures, but the power of recursion in computer programming is the way in which computer scientists use recursive algorithms to analyze and solve complex problems. An algorithm is really just a set of instructions describing how to complete a process. Recursion can describe a very sophisticated process with a simple and efficient set of instructions. Many of the most important algorithms in computing, such as those used to search large databases quickly, to perform matrix algebra, and to play games such as chess, depend on the use of recursion. As a student in an introductory computer programming course, you don't yet have the skills to write such programs; however, you can spend some time learning about some basic ideas associated with recursion so that you will be able to use recursion appropriately when the time comes to do so.

It's also worth learning about recursion because of its importance in the world around us. Blood vessels in the human body have a structure that can be best described by recursion; blood vessels continue to divide into smaller and smaller vessels until they are tiny capillaries only a few blood cells wide. The pattern of seeds on the head of a sunflower, the geometry of a snail's shell, and even DNA gene sequencing all appear to be recursive structures. The newly emerging fields of Fractal Geometry and Chaos Theory are largely based on recursion. Seemingly random events, such as the electronic interference in a telephone circuit, can be described using recursive functions. There is also some evidence that the human brain is recursive. A basic understanding of recursion will not only help you to become a better computer programmer, but it may also help you to better understand the world around you.

RECURSION COMPARED TO ITERATION

An **iterative process** is one that uses a loop to repeat a set of instructions, so **iteration** is just another name for looping. In many cases, either iteration or recursion can be used to do the same thing. The `bunny.hop to carrot` method shown earlier in this chapter is a good example of such a case. Figure 7-5 shows the recursive `bunny.hop to carrot` method on the left, with an iterative version of the same method using a WHILE loop on the right. Both methods do the same thing, but one uses recursion, and the other uses iteration.

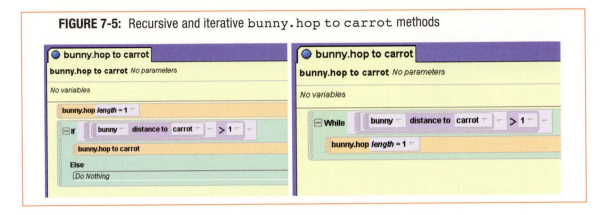

FIGURE 7-5: Recursive and iterative `bunny.hop to carrot` methods

This brings us to an important question—if both iteration and recursion can be used to do the same thing, then when should iteration be used, and when should recursion be used? To answer that question, you need to know a little more about some of the characteristics of recursive methods, including the cost of recursion and the difference between linear and exponential recursion.

The Cost of Recursion

Overhead is the processor time and storage space in a computer's memory needed to manage a method as it runs. The computer must set up a section in its memory every time a new method is called—even if the new method is a copy of an existing method. We don't see this happening, yet it does consume time and space in the computer's memory. In the `bunny.hop to carrot` example, the computer must set up a new section in its memory each time the recursive `bunny.hop to carrot` method is called. If the bunny hops five times, then five new sections will be needed in the computer's memory to manage the five copies of the method. It if hops a thousand times, then a thousand new sections in memory will be required. The iterative `bunny.hop to carrot` method does not have such overhead, so it is more efficient.

People, such as mathematicians, who deal with theoretical algorithms, almost always think recursion is a good idea. In the world of computer programming, the overhead associated with recursion must be considered. Often it is better to use iteration than recursion for methods that can be written using a simple loop. But before giving up on recursion completely, let's go back to the Sierpinski gasket algorithm to see the difference between linear recursion and exponential recursion.

Linear Recursion and Exponential Recursion

Linear recursion occurs when a method calls itself only once each time through the method. **Exponential recursion** occurs when a method calls itself more than once in each pass through the method. The graphs in Figure 7-6 compare the two types of recursion. The graph on the left shows the number of copies of the method running for each level of recursion in an algorithm that calls itself once. The graph on the right shows the same thing for an algorithm that calls itself twice. You can see that the linear recursion graph looks like a straight line. Only one additional copy of the algorithm is created at each level of recursion. Look how much more quickly the number of copies of the exponential algorithm grows. At each level of recursion, the number of copies of the program doubles. If it called itself three times, then the number of copies would triple at each level, and so on. A method that uses exponential recursion can very quickly generate many copies of itself to work simultaneously on smaller examples of the overall problem.

FIGURE 7-6: The growth of linear and exponential recursion

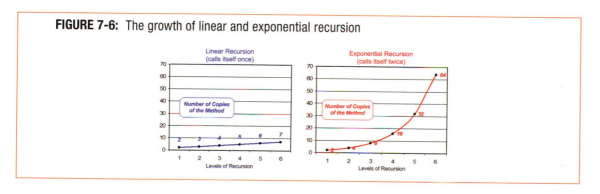

The recursive Sierpinski gasket algorithm is an example of exponential recursion because it calls itself three times. The number of triangles triples with each level of recursion. It is very unlikely that an algorithm using iteration could do the same thing more efficiently. In this case, recursion probably is the best solution. Generally, a method that uses exponential recursion—that is, a method which calls itself more than once—is often very difficult to replace with a more efficient iterative solution. Exponentially recursive algorithms are often far more efficient than iterative solutions because they can repeatedly break a problem into several smaller parts and then attack those smaller parts in a way that an iterative algorithm cannot. Even taking into account the overhead, recursive algorithms are usually far more efficient than iterative solutions.

We now have a rough answer to our question about when to use recursion. For simple tasks that can be described with linear recursion, iteration seems to be better because of the overhead of recursion, but for complex problems that can be broken down into smaller parts, exponential recursion usually works much better.

INFINITE RECURSION AND CONDITIONAL RECURSION

There's one more important concept about recursion that computer programming students should understand—the difference between infinite recursion and conditional recursion. **Infinite recursion** means that an algorithm calls itself repeatedly without stopping. Infinite recursion occurs when an algorithm does not contain any instructions about when to stop the recursion. On a computer, infinite recursion continues until all available memory is used, or until it triggers some time-out mechanism in the operating system. The version of the Sierpinski gasket algorithm presented earlier is an example of infinite recursion. If you examine the algorithm carefully, you will see that the *Stop* instruction is never executed.

Recursion that is not infinite is called **conditional recursion** because the algorithm must contain some condition that will stop the recursion. The condition that stops the recursion is called the **base condition** or the **base case**. The algorithm usually contains an IF/ELSE instruction that causes the algorithm to keep calling itself until the base condition is met. In the recursive `bunny.hop to carrot` method, the algorithm continues to call itself until the bunny is within 1 meter of the carrot. The base condition is that the distance between the bunny and the carrot is 1 meter or less. The IF/ELSE command is set up to continue the recursion while the bunny is more than 1 meter away from the carrot.

A properly structured recursive algorithm should always contain a Boolean expression in a selection sequence to test for the base condition in the same way that the IF/ELSE instruction in the `bunny.hop to carrot` method does. In the case of `bunny.hop to carrot`, the algorithm simply stops when the base condition occurs. In other algorithms, something can be added to the ELSE part of the instruction to tell the computer what to do when the base condition has occurred.

In conditional exponentially recursive algorithms, the recursive step breaks the problem into smaller parts, and then calls the algorithm itself for each of those parts, continuing to do so until the base case is reached. Sometimes that is enough to solve the original problem; sometimes another step is needed to combine all of the small solutions into one big solution. It is such conditional exponentially recursive algorithms that lead to sophisticated and highly efficient solutions to large programming problems. Unfortunately, they are often used with complex data structures, such as trees, graphs, and matrices, which are not easily demonstrated in introductory Alice programming, although the underlying software (in particular, the operating system) that runs Alice worlds does use them.

In the tutorials in this chapter, you will work with simple linear recursive methods to get a feeling for recursion and to compare recursive methods to methods that do the same thing with simple loops.

TUTORIAL 7A—CREATING A RECURSIVE METHOD

In this tutorial, you will create a recursive method to make an airplane taxi from the end of a runway to a spot near an airplane hangar. Let's start with the specifications for the world. You must set up a scene with an aircraft that has just landed at an airport. The aircraft must taxi from the end of the runway to a spot near an airplane hangar. The task is to create a method that will enable an object to move from wherever it is when the method is called to a specific spot. In this case, the aircraft should taxi to within 1 meter of the part of the airport named garage02.

For a good programmer, a few things will come immediately to mind when presented with this situation:

1. This seems to be the kind of programming project that is part of a larger project. You will be building a short method for a very specific task. A good programmer in this situation will think of reusable code. The method could be constructed with a target parameter instead of hard coding garage02 into the method.

2. The specifications do not call for you to build an airport, so either one already exists, or someone else will create one as a separate part of the project.

3. What's an aircraft? The vehicles folder in the local Alice object gallery has several airplanes, including a biplane, a jet, a navy jet, and a seaplane. The gallery also has a helicopter and a blimp, which might be considered aircraft. In a situation like this, the programmer would need to go back to whomever provided the specifications to get more information.

4. Finally, there are no internal specifications for the method, only functional specifications. This means that the specifications tell the programmer what the new method should do, but not how the method should do it. They don't say anything about what techniques can be used inside the method. The specifications don't say, for example, "use a loop to ...". This gives the programmer more flexibility in designing the internal workings of the method, but a good programmer will ask about this to be sure that there really is some flexibility here. Sometimes specifications don't tell you everything.

After reading the specifications, a good programmer will put together a set of questions for the person who provided them. Communication like this among the members of a team working on a software development project is important. In this case, the programmer would ask which airport should be used, which aircraft should be used, and whether any particular techniques should be used or avoided inside the method. The answers to these questions are that the airport in the buildings folder in the local Alice object gallery should be used; the biplane should be used as the aircraft; and the only restriction on the techniques to be used in the method is that recursion should be used.

Now that things are a little clearer, you can begin. In a real situation, a programmer would probably create an iterative method or simply use the existing primitive `move to` method for this project, but your purpose in this tutorial is to experiment with recursion.

Setting the Scene

First you need to build the scene for the new world.

1. Start Alice, and open a new world with a **grass** background.
2. Click the **ADD OBJECTS** button to enter Scene Editor mode, and find the Airport object class in the Buildings folder within the Local Gallery.
3. Click the **Airport** tile, but pause for moment before adding it to the world. Notice that the Airport class information window, shown in Figure 7-7, says that the size of the object is 753 kilobytes, and that it has 44 parts. This is a large and complex object. Also notice that there are no methods listed in the window, so the object only includes the standard primitive methods. Click the **Add instance to world** button to add an airport to the world.

FIGURE 7-7: The Airport object class information window

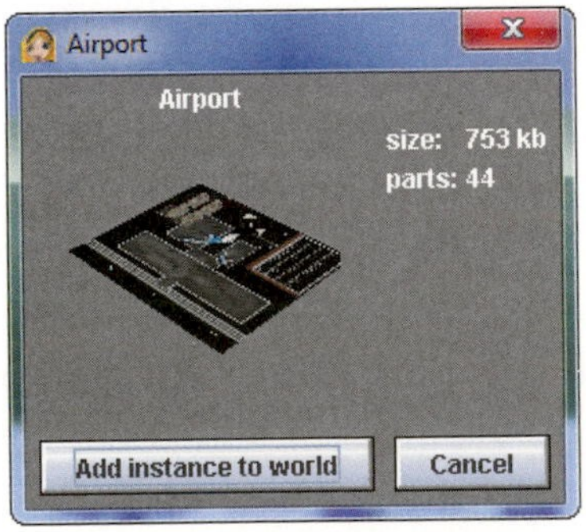

4. Note that a tile for the airport appears in the Object tree, and the view of the airport in the World window will probably look something like Figure 7-8. The view is as if you were standing on the ground at the airport.

FIGURE 7-8: The World window after adding an airport

5. You need to position the camera to get a better view of the airport. Using the blue camera control arrows, move, tilt, and pan the **camera** so that the view of the airport looks more like Figure 7-9, but without the red plane. The trick is to move the camera and not the airport. This will probably take a few minutes to do unless you are very familiar with the Scene Editor. Remember the magic of the *Undo* button, which can be used if you are unhappy with one of your moves. Both the right end of the runway and the hangars on the left should be visible in the window when you are done.

FIGURE 7-9: The World window after positioning the camera, with a red airplane on the runway

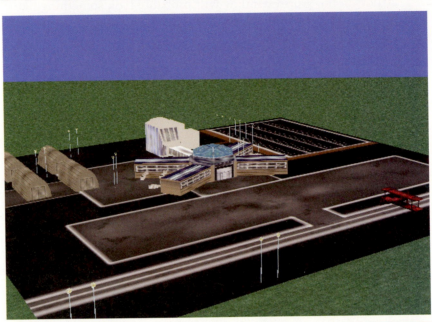

6. Next, add a biplane to the world, and position it near the right end of the runway, similar to the way the red plane is shown in Figure 7-9. Your biplane won't be red; the one in the picture is red so that you can see it better in the printed image. The biplane should look as if it just landed and is about three-fourths of the way down the runway. You will need to move and turn the biplane.

7. Now that the scene is ready, click the **DONE** button to exit Scene Editor mode, and save the world with the name **airport setup.** This will protect you from needing to re-create the scene in case something goes wrong.

Coding the Recursion

Now that the scene is ready, you can create a recursive `taxi` method to make the biplane move as desired. Here is the pseudocode modified for the `taxi` method:

```
biplane.taxi (target)
Start
If  ( [biplane.distance to target]  > 1 meter)
    {
    biplane.point at target
    biplane.move forward 1 meter
```

```
biplane.taxi (target)
        }
    Stop
```

It seems fairly straightforward, so let's create the method. You can start by creating the method and putting the IF/ELSE command in place.

1. Select the **biplane** tile in the Object tree and the **methods** tab in the Details area.

2. Click the **create new method** button, type **taxi** as the method name, and then click the **OK** button. The method `biplane.taxi` should appear in the Editor area.

3. The method will need a parameter named *target* with the data type *object.* Click the **create new parameter** button, type the name **target,** make sure that **object** is selected as the data type, and then click the **OK** button.

4. Drag an **IF/ELSE** tile from the bottom of the Editor area and drop it in the new **taxi** method in place of *Do Nothing.* Select **true** as the condition. Your method should now look like Figure 7-10.

FIGURE 7-10: The taxi method with a *target* parameter and a blank If/Else instruction

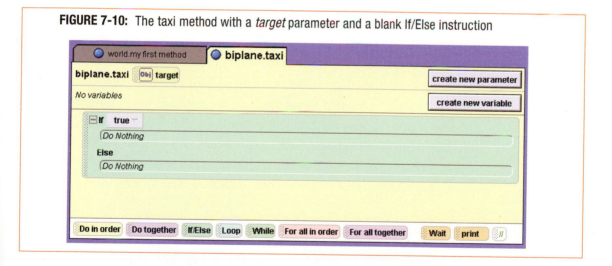

5. The Boolean condition needs to be a comparison of two values using the *greater than* operator. Select **world** in the Object tree and the **functions** tab in the Details area. One of the functions listed under math is *a > b.* Drag a copy of this tile and drop in into the IF/ELSE instruction tile in place of *true.* Select **1** as the value for *a* and **1** as the value for *b* from the short menus that appear.

6. You need to replace the first *1* with the biplane's *distance to* function. Select **biplane** in the Object tree and drag and drop a copy of the **distance to** function in place of the first number *1* in the condition in the IF/ELSE tile.

7. When the menu appears asking for an object, select **expressions**, and then **target**. The instruction should now match the pseudocode on the previous page.

Now you need to add the instructions that belong inside the IF/ELSE structure. The pseudocode shows that there are three of them: biplane.point at (target), biplane.move forward 1 meter, and biplane.taxi (target). You can add them in the order in which they will occur.

1. Select the **methods** tab in the Details area and drag and drop a copy of the **biplane turn to face** instruction tile into the IF/ELSE tile in the Editor area in place of the words *Do Nothing* between IF and ELSE. When the menu appears asking you for the target, select **expressions**, and then **target**. Also, click **more** and change the style to **abruptly**.

2. Next, drag a copy of the **biplane move** tile from the methods tab in the Details area and drop it into the new method just below the *biplane turn to face* instruction. Select **forward** as the direction and **1 meter** as the amount, and then click **more** and change the style to **abruptly**. Note that when you play the finished world, this value of 1 meter will affect the speed of the plane as it taxis. You can come back to this instruction and change the amount to make the plane move more quickly or more slowly.

3. Now drag a copy of the **taxi target** tile from the methods tab in the Details area and drop it into the new method just below the *biplane move forward* instruction. When the menu appears, select **expressions** and then **target**. When you do this, a Recursion Warning window similar to the one in Figure 7-11 will appear, warning you that you are about to create a recursive method.

FIGURE 7-11: The Recursion Warning window

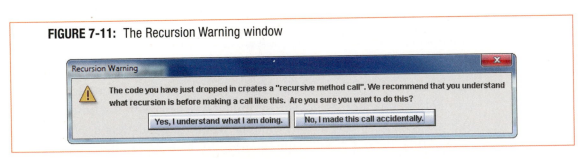

4. Click the **Yes, I understand what I am doing.** button, and the instruction tile will pop into place in the method.

5. Finally, the method will work more smoothly if the *biplane turn to face* and *biplane move* instructions happen at the same time. Drag a **Do together** tile from the bottom of the Editor area and drop it into the method between the *biplane move forward* instruction and the *biplane.taxi* instruction, and then drag the **biplane turn to face** and **biplane move** instruction tiles into the *Do together* tile. The method is complete and should now be similar to Figure 7-12.

FIGURE 7-12: The completed recursive `biplane.taxi` method

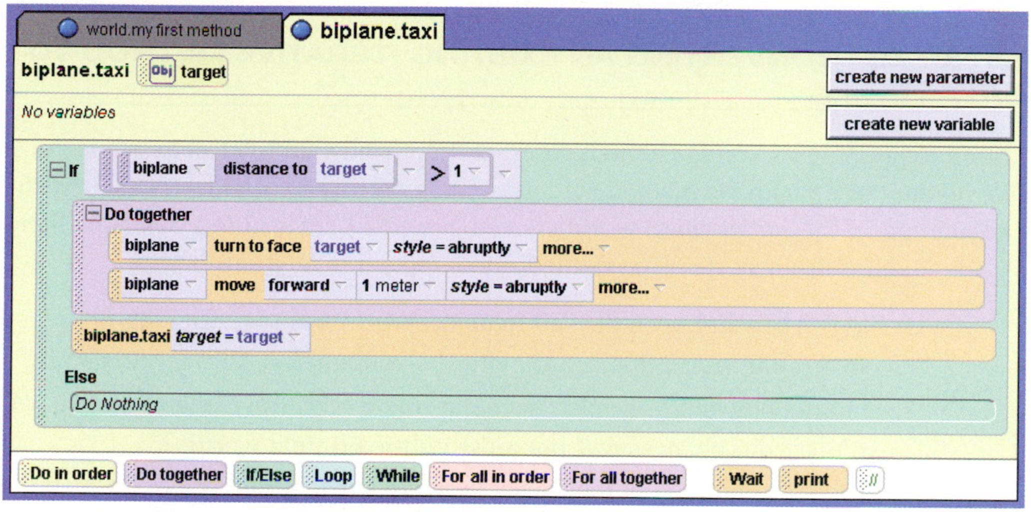

To test the method, you need to call it from `world.my first method`, so `world.my first method` needs to be modified to call `biplane.taxi`. Also, let's add an instruction to make the biplane turn to face the camera after it moves. There are two reasons for this: first, it will help you see if everything is normal after the `taxi` method is finished, and second, it looks a little more interesting. This can only be done outside the `taxi` method; otherwise it would interfere with `taxi` meeting its specifications. In a sense, `world.my first method` is being used as a testing shell for `biplane.taxi`.

1. First, select **world.my first method** in the Editor area.

2. Drag a copy of the **taxi target** tile from the methods tab in the Details area and drop it into `world.my first method` in place of *Do Nothing*. When the menu appears, select **airport,** then **runwayandParking,** and then **garage02.** Garage02 is the name for the part of the airport object to which the biplane should move. Actually, it is a sub-part of the *runwayandParking* object, which is part of the *airport* object.

3. Drag and drop a copy of the **biplane.turn to face** tile in the methods area on the Details tab into world.my first method below the *biplane.taxi* instruction. When the menu appears, select **camera** as the target.

4. Now save the world with the name **recursive taxi**.

You can now test the world, and see if it works as expected. When you do so you may notice that the biplane passes through part of the airport terminal. Exercise 3 at the end of this chapter deals with this. Try the world a few times to see if it works. If it does not work properly, then track down the error and fix it.

TUTORIAL 7B—CONVERTING AN EXISTING ITERATIVE METHOD TO RECURSION

In addition to creating recursive methods from scratch, it's useful to be able to rewrite an iterative method as a recursive method, and vice-versa. In this tutorial, you will modify the sail to method in the *sail to object* world created as part of Tutorial 5C; you will change the sail to method from an iterative method into a recursive method.

1. Start Alice and open the **sail to object** world from Tutorial 5C, or open a copy of the world that comes with the student data files for this book.

2. Before doing anything else, save the world with the name **recursive sail to** so that your changes will not mess up the original world.

3. Select the **sailboat** in the Object tree and the **methods** tab in the Details area, if necessary.

4. Click the **edit** button next to the sail to method tile; the sailboat.sail to method should appear in the Editor area, as shown in Figure 7-13.

FIGURE 7-13: The iterative sail to method in the Editor area

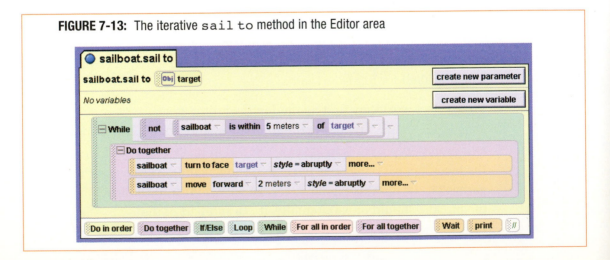

The pseudocode for the existing iterative method and the pseudocode for a new recursive method that does the same thing are shown below:

```
Sailboat.sail to (target)
While( not [sailboat is within 5 meters of target] )
    {
    Do together
        {
        sailboat.turn to face target
        sailboat.move forward 2 meters
        }
    }
Stop


Sailboat.sail to (target)
Start
If   ( not [sailboat is within 5 meters of target] )
    {
    Do together
        {
        sailboat.turn to face target
        sailboat.move forward 2 meters
        }
        sailboat.sail to (target)
    }
Stop
```

Comparing the two versions of the `sail to` method, you can see that an IF/ELSE instruction is needed instead of a WHILE loop, and a recursive call needs to be added inside the method. Let's continue our task with the next set of steps.

1. Drag an **IF/ELSE** instruction tile from the bottom of the Editor area and drop it in the method below the WHILE instruction tile. Select **true** as the condition from the menu that appears.

2. Drag the **Boolean** condition tile that starts with the word ***not*** from the WHILE tile and drop it into the IF/ELSE tile in place of *true*. If you have done this correctly, then your method should look like Figure 7-14. If it is not correct, then use the **Undo** button to back up and try again.

FIGURE 7-14: The `sail to` method after moving the Boolean condition from While to If

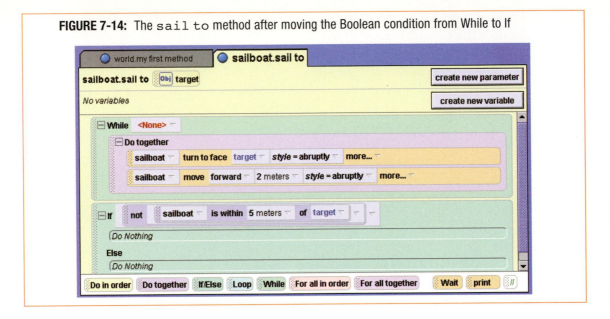

3. Drag the **Do together** tile with the *sailboat turn to face target* and *sailboat move forward 2 meters* instructions from the WHILE tile, and drop it into the IF/ELSE tile in place of *Do Nothing* between IF and ELSE.

4. Now you are ready to add the recursive call to the method. Drag a copy of the **sail to target** method tile from the methods tab in the Details area, and drop it in the IF/ELSE instruction below the *Do together* tile but above ELSE. Select **expressions**, and then **target** from the menu that appears. When you do this, a Recursion Warning window similar to the one in Figure 7-11 in Tutorial 7A will appear. The window is warning you that you are about to create a recursive method and asks you if this is what you intended.

5. Click the **Yes, I understand what I am doing** button, and the instruction tile will appear in the method.

6. The last thing you need to do is to get rid of the WHILE tile, which should now be empty and is no longer needed. Either right-click the **While** tile and select **delete**, or drag the tile to the trash can.

7. The changes to the method are now complete, and it is ready for testing. The method should look like Figure 7-15. Save the world before continuing.

FIGURE 7-15: The completed recursive `sail to` method

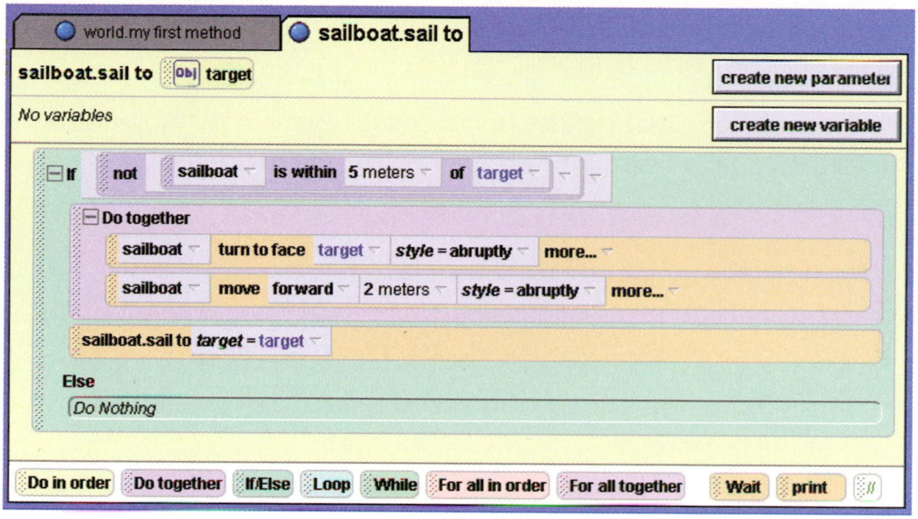

Play the world and see how your new method works. If all is well, it should appear to function no differently than the old *sail to object* world did. The changes are all internal and will not really be seen by the user unless a problem occurs.

Chapter Summary

This chapter consisted of a discussion of recursive algorithms, including a comparison of recursion and iteration, a look at linear and exponential recursion, and a look at infinite and conditional recursion, followed by two tutorials. The discussion of recursive algorithms included the following:

☐ Generally, something is said to be recursive if each of the parts that make up the thing have a structure—in other words, a design or pattern—that repeats the structure of the whole thing itself.

☐ In computer programming, an algorithm that calls itself is said to be recursive.

☐ An iterative process is one that uses a loop to repeat a set of instructions, so iteration is just another name for looping. In many cases, either iteration or recursion can be used to do the same thing.

☐ Overhead is the processor time and storage space in a computer's memory needed to manage a method as it runs. The computer must set up a section in its memory every time a new method is called—even if the new method is a copy of an existing method.

☐ Often it is better to use iteration than recursion for methods that can be written using a simple loop because of the overhead associated with recursion.

☐ Linear recursion occurs when a method calls itself only once each time through the method.

☐ Exponential recursion occurs when a method calls itself more than once in each pass through the method. Exponentially recursive algorithms are often far more efficient than iterative solutions because they can repeatedly break a problem into several smaller parts, and then attack those smaller parts in a way that an iterative algorithm cannot.

☐ For simple tasks that can be described with linear recursion, iteration seems to be better because of the overhead of recursion, but for complex problems that can be broken down into smaller parts, exponential recursion usually works much better.

☐ Infinite recursion means that an algorithm calls itself repeatedly without stopping. Recursion that is not infinite is called conditional recursion because the algorithm must contain some condition that will stop the recursion.

☐ The condition that stops the recursion is called the base condition or the base case. A properly structured recursive algorithm should contain a Boolean expression in a selection sequence to test for the base condition.

In Tutorial 7A, you created a new world with a recursive method.

In Tutorial 7B, you converted an existing iterative method into a recursive method.

Review Questions

1. Define the following terms:

    □ base case   □ infinite recursion   □ overhead
    □ base condition   □ iteration   □ recursion
    □ conditional recursion   □ iterative process   □ recursive method
    □ exponential recursion   □ linear recursion

2. What is the difference between recursion and iteration?

3. Why will a program with infinite recursion eventually crash on a computer system?

4. In a case in which both iterative and recursive solutions to a programming problem exist, how can a programmer tell whether to use iteration or recursion?

5. The recursive `biplane.taxi` method in Tutorial 7A works only with the biplane. How can this be modified so that it will work with any object?

6. The following joke was all the rage in fourth grade classrooms last year. Explain how this is related to recursion. "There were three men in a boat, Joe, Pete, and Repeat. Joe and Pete fell out. Who was left?"

7. Write the pseudocode for both an iterative and a recursive method that will multiply any two positive integers using only addition.

8. It was recently discovered that the famous graphic artist M.C. Escher used the "Droste effect" in at least one of his drawings. Using the Internet, find out what the Droste effect is, how it is related to recursion, and why it's called the Droste effect.

9. Assume that a computer student wants to impress his father, who is a computer security expert for the CIA, by writing a program like the one below. The parameter for the program is the network address of a computer system.

```
Search for dad's account at (computer system)
    Start
    If dad has an account on this computer
        Print "Hello dad, I found your computer."
    Else
        Find two other computers connected to this one
        Search for dad's account at (first computer)
        Search for dad's account at (second computer)
    Stop
```

The preceding code is enough to cause some issues between father and son; however, assume that the student plays with it some more and then makes a mistake, leaving out the IF/ELSE instruction so that the algorithm looks like this:

```
Search for Dad's account at (computer system )
    Start
    Print "Hello Dad, I found your computer."
    Find two other computers connected to this one
    Search for Dad's account at (first computer)
    Search for Dad's account at (second computer)
    Stop
```

a. What kind of recursion is within this program?
b. Assuming that the student knows enough systems programming to make the instructions work, what will the program actually do?
c. If it takes 10 seconds for the algorithm to run, including the time it needs to connect to other computers, how many copies of the program will be running 1 minute after the program first starts? After 2 minutes? After 1 hour? After 6 hours?
d. What would something like this do to the Internet?
e. What sentence did U.S. District Court Judge Howard G. Munson give Cornell University graduate student Robert Tappan Morris when he was convicted of doing something similar to this in November, 1988?

10. An important technique in mathematics is proof by induction. We start a proof by induction by proving that if something is true for one number, then it must be true for the next number also. In other words, if what we are trying to prove is true for n, then it must be true for n+1. This is called the inductive step in the proof. Next, we show that it is true for the number 1. This is called the base step in the proof. Putting the base step and the inductive step together, we can then see that the item in question must be true for all positive integers because if it is true for 1, then it must be true for 1+1, then for 2+1, then 3+1, and so on. How is a proof by induction similar to conditional linear recursion?

Exercises

1. The Alice people gallery has hebuilder and shebuilder classes of objects that include a `walk` method. Create a simple Alice world with a few objects of your choice, including a character that you create with hebuilder or shebuilder, and create both iterative and recursive methods to make the character walk to a target object.

2. In the story *Alice's Adventures in Wonderland*, there is a part in which Alice grows smaller, and then bigger. Create an Alice world with aliceLiddell standing between a tall flower and a short flower and with an infinitely recursive method to keep repeating the following process:

    a. She touches the tall flower and then shrinks.
    b. She touches the short flower and then grows.
       (*Hint:* Use the resize primitive method.)

3.   Mutual recursion occurs when method A calls method B, and method B calls method A. Together, they function like a single recursive method. Rewrite the solution to Exercise 2 using mutual recursion.

4.   The biplane in the *recursive taxi* world created in Tutorial 7A moves right though part of the airport to get to its spot near the hangar. See if you can correct this by adding a cone to the world from the shapes gallery, and positioning the cone on the tarmac. Then, have the plane move twice, first to the cone, and then from the cone to its final spot. Once it works, you can then make the cone invisible by changing its opacity property.

5.   In Tutorial 7B, you converted an existing iterative method into a recursive method. Starting with the *recursive sail to* world from the end of that tutorial (or the copy of that world that comes with the student data files for this book) convert the recursive `sail to` method in the world back to an iterative method.

6.   A recursive algorithm can be written to draw a spiral, starting in the middle and expanding outward with each revolution. A similar algorithm can be written to draw a "spirally increasing pseudo-square" like that shown in Figure 7-16. Such an algorithm could be used for a search pattern to search for a lost object, or for a robotic lawn mower that could be left in the middle of a large field and then programmed to start mowing the field from the center outward. Create a "recursive Zamboni" Alice world with a snow background and a Zamboni with a recursive method to make the Zamboni follow the spirally increasing pseudo-square pattern just described. A Zamboni is the machine that is used to clean an ice-skating rink, such as at a hockey game between periods. The Alice vehicle gallery has a Zamboni.

FIGURE 7-16: A spirally increasing pseudo-square

7.   The Fibonacci sequence is one of the most commonly found patterns in all of nature. The sequence starts with 0 and 1, and then each term in the sequence is generated by adding the previous two terms. The first few terms in the sequence are 0, 1, 1, 2, 3, 5, 8, 13, 21, and 34. Numbers that appear in the sequence are called Fibonacci numbers.

   a. Write a recursive algorithm in pseudocode to generate the Fibonacci sequence.
   b. Write an iterative algorithm in pseudocode to generate the Fibonacci sequence.
   c. Which algorithm would probably work better on a computer, and why?
   d. Write an algorithm in pseudocode to test a number to see if it is a Fibonacci number.
   e. Create an Alice world with a Count penguin and a Fibonacci penguin. Count penguin will simply start counting slowly when the world starts. The Fibonacci penguin will jump up and down and flap its wings while saying "Fibonacci, Fibonacci, (n) is Fibonacci!" when Count penguin says a number that is part of the Fibonacci sequence. The Fibonacci penguin should say the actual number in place of (n).

8.   Images generated by certain recursive algorithms are sometimes called fractal images.

a. Draw the figure generated by the following algorithm:

```
Start with a square
Fractal (square)
      Start
      Divide the square into four smaller squares
      Fill in the upper-left square and the lower-right square
      If the squares are still big enough to draw in, then
            Fractal (upper-right square)
            Fractal (lower-left square)
      Stop
```

b. Using pseudocode, write your own recursive algorithm to generate a fractal image.

c. Search the Internet for fractal geometry to see some very interesting fractal images.

9.   Here is an example of a very short recursive story (which was already discussed in the main part of the chapter):

> *Once upon a time a young princess was sitting with her father, the king. She said to her father, "My Royal Father, can you read me a story?"*
>
> *"Yes, my Royal Daughter" said the king, as he opened the* Royal Storybook. *He began to read, "Once upon a time a young princess was sitting with her father, the king. She said to her father, 'My Royal Father, can you read me a story?' . . ."*

Create an Alice world that contains a very short recursive story. Start with either an outline or storyboard, and consider how camera moves can add to the very short story. The Alice Local Gallery's Objects folder contains Book, Monitor, Picture Frame, and TV classes. One of these may prove helpful in your story.

10.   One well-known puzzle that has a recursive solution is the "Towers of Hanoi" puzzle, which can be seen on the Internet at *www.mazeworks.com/hanoi/*. See if you can write a simple recursive algorithm in pseudocode as a solution to the problem. Your solution should work no matter how many discs there are. You should be warned however, that even though the algorithm is only a few instructions long, it could take a while to figure it out.

Lists and Arrays in Alice

After finishing this chapter, you should be able to:

☐ Provide brief definitions of the following terms: data structure, queue, binary tree, node, root node, list, iterate a list, array, index value, matrix, vector, and Array Visualization Object

☐ Describe what a data structure is, and give several examples of data structures

☐ Generally describe why there are so many different data structures, and how programmers decide what data structures to use for different programs

☐ Describe the simple data structure known as a list, and how it is implemented in Alice

☐ Describe the data structure known as an array, how it differs from a list, and how it is implemented in Alice

☐ Create a list of objects in an Alice world and methods that perform operations on the list items one at a time and all at once

☐ Create methods in Alice that can manipulate the parts of objects contained in a list

☐ Describe the purpose of the Array Visualization Object in Alice

DATA STRUCTURES IN ALICE

A **data structure** is a scheme for organizing data in the memory of a computer. A set of names, addresses, and phone numbers stored as a table is an example of a data structure. Some of the more commonly used data structures include lists, arrays, stacks, queues, heaps, trees, and graphs. Data structures can be simple, or they can become quite complex.

The Need for Different Data Structures

Computer programmers decide which data structures to use based on the nature of the data. Programmers also decide the operations that need to be performed on that data because the way in which the data is organized affects how a program performs different tasks. As an example of this, let's take a look at two data structures, a queue and a binary tree, and see how the differences between the two affect how computer programmers use them.

A **queue** is a set of data items with a beginning and end, called the front and back of the queue. Data enters the queue at one end and leaves it at the other. Because of this, data exits the queue in the same order in which it entered the queue, like people in a checkout line at a supermarket. A queue has many uses in the world of computers. It would, for example, be a good data structure to use in a program for keeping track of documents waiting to be printed on a network printer, as shown in Figure 8-1.

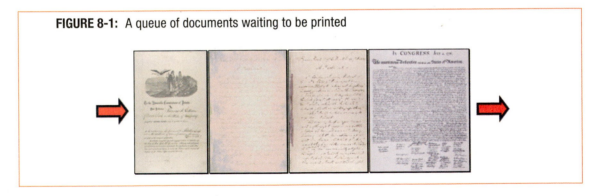

FIGURE 8-1: A queue of documents waiting to be printed

A **binary tree** is a data structure that looks like an upside-down tree. Each spot on the tree, called a **node**, holds an item of data, along with a left pointer and a right pointer, as shown in Figure 8-2. The pointers are lined up so that the structure forms the upside-down tree, with a single node at the top, called the **root node**, and branches increasing on the left and right as you go down the tree. The nodes at the bottom of each branch, with two empty pointers, are called the leaf nodes.

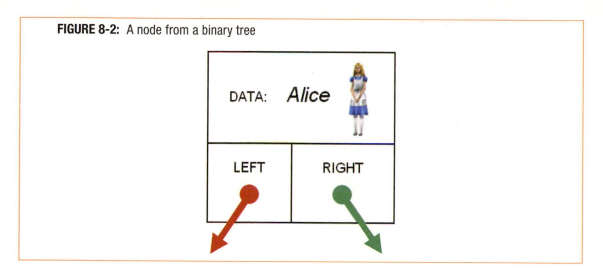

FIGURE 8-2: A node from a binary tree

A binary tree is used when it is necessary to keep a set of data items sorted in a particular order and to be able to quickly find items in the set. The middle item from the set of data is put in the root node, with anything before the middle item stored in the left branch of the tree, and anything after it stored in the right branch of the tree, as shown in Figure 8-3. A binary tree is good for storing information that needs to be searched quickly, such as a dictionary or phone directory.

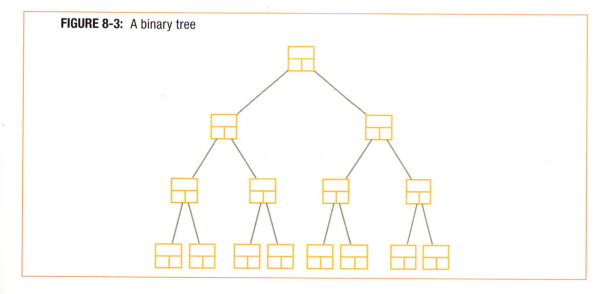

FIGURE 8-3: A binary tree

By comparing the queue with the binary tree, you can see how the structure of the data—in other words, the way in which the data is organized—affects what can be done efficiently with the data. The queue works well for keeping track of documents waiting to be printed on a networked printer because it will keep them in the order in which they were sent to the printer. The first document sent to the print queue will be the first document to leave the queue and be printed, the second document will be printed second, and so on.

On the other hand, the queue is not a good data structure to use for a set of objects that needs to be searched quickly. To find an item in the queue, you need to start at one end of the queue and go through each item in the queue one at a time until you find the item for which you are searching. If the object of your search is the first item in a queue of 1,000 items, then you will only need to look at one item to find it; whereas, if it happens to be the last item, then you will need to look at all 1,000 items before finding it. On average, you will need to look at 500 items to find a single object in a queue with 1,000 items.

Now let's look at searching a binary tree. You always start searching the binary tree by looking at the root node. If it does not contain the data item you want, then you follow one of the pointers to either the node to the left of the root node, or the node to the right of the root node, depending on how the item for which you are searching compares to the item in the root node. For example, if you were searching by name for Alice, and the root node had an object named Cheshire Cat, then you would know to go to the left branch of the tree to find Alice because it comes before the Cheshire Cat. At the next node you would do the same thing—if the node does not contain Alice, then you go to that node's left branch or right branch, and so on until you find Alice. The efficiency of the binary tree comes from the fact that each time you look at a node, you either find the item you want, or move down one level in the tree. This cuts the remaining data to be searched in half, because you now only need to look to the left or to the right of the item you want. With a set of 1,000 objects, you could always find an object in the tree in 10 tries or fewer.

If it takes 1/100th of a second to look at an item, then finding an item in a queue of 1,000 items could take anywhere from 1/100th of a second if it is the first item, to 10 seconds if it is the last item. In a binary tree with a thousand items, the longest it would take to find any item is 1/10th of a second. So, you can see that a binary tree is a much better data structure to use in a situation where objects need to be retrieved quickly.

Thus, if a programmer needs to organize data so that the first item placed in a data structure will be the first item to leave the data structure, then a queue is a quick and simple way to do this, but if a programmer wants to organize data so that any item can be retrieved quickly, then a more complex binary tree would be better. A programmer chooses a data structure based on how the data will be used. Someone who wants to become an effective professional programmer must become familiar with many different data structures and their characteristics.

It's impossible to learn all about data structures in an introductory course in programming, although you can start to learn about the simple and commonly used data structures known as lists and arrays, which are the focus of the remainder of this chapter.

Lists in Alice

One of the simplest of all data structures is a **list**, which is an ordered set of data. It is often used to store objects that are to be processed sequentially, meaning one at a time in order. In fact, lists are often used to set up queues such as the print queue described earlier.

Alice has a number of instructions that can be used to manipulate lists, some of which are shown on the menu in Figure 8-4. You can see that there are commands to insert or remove items from the beginning of the list, the end of the list, or at any position in the list, which in this example is named *world.bunnies*.

FIGURE 8-4: Alice commands for manipulating lists

Alice also has two instructions to manipulate lists—*For all in order* and *For all together*, as shown in Figure 8-5. *For all in order* will perform an operation on each item in a list one at a time, beginning with the first item in the list and going through the list in order. To **iterate a list** means to go through the list in this manner.

FIGURE 8-5: List commands at the bottom of the Editor area

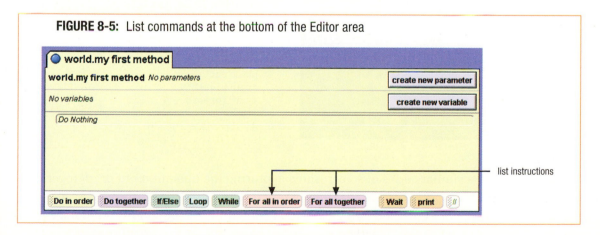

For all together will perform an operation on all of the items in a list at the same time. Notice how *For all in order* and *For all together* are different from the *Do in order* and *Do together* instructions that you saw in earlier chapters. *Do in order* and *Do together* operate on a set of instructions. *For all in order* and *For all together* operate on a set of objects. Of course, the *Do* and *For all* instructions can be combined to perform sets of instructions on sets of objects.

Figure 8-6 shows a series of screen shots from an Alice world window capturing the operation of *For all in order* on a list of cars. You can see that the cars each turn and begin to move away one at a time in order. The same instructions are being executed one at a time on each object in the list; the first car turns and moves, then the second car turns and moves, and so on.

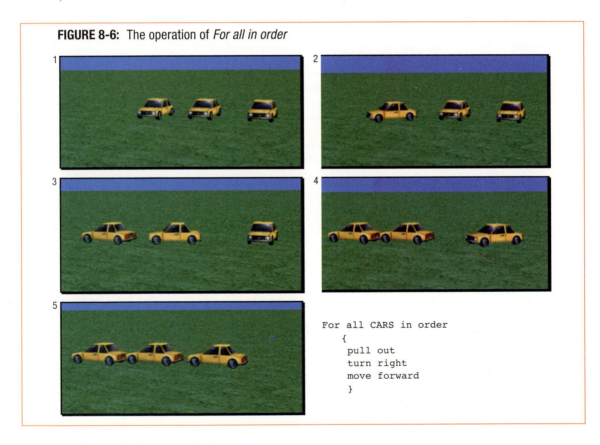

FIGURE 8-6: The operation of *For all in order*

```
For all CARS in order
    {
    pull out
    turn right
    move forward
    }
```

Figure 8-7 shows a similar series of screen shots capturing the operation of *For all together* on the same list of cars. You can see that the cars each turn and begin to drive away all at the same time. In Tutorial 8B, you will create a list containing a group of toy soldiers, and use *For all in order* and *For all together* to make the soldiers perform a drill routine.

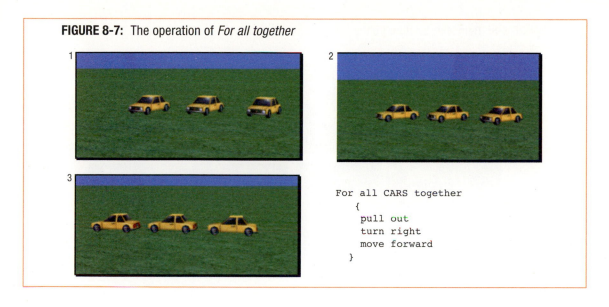

FIGURE 8-7: The operation of *For all together*

```
For all CARS together
  {
    pull out
    turn right
    move forward
  }
```

Arrays in Alice

An **array** is a set of indexed variables, each containing objects of the same data type. For example, if we wanted to store a list of five phone numbers for use by a computer program, we might call them $phone_{[0]}$, $phone_{[1]}$, $phone_{[2]}$, $phone_{[3]}$, and $phone_{[4]}$. The value in brackets after each occurrence of phone is the **index value** for that item. There is not one phone variable, but several phone variables, each identified by its unique index value. Notice that the index values start with 0 rather than 1. This is true in almost all programming languages.

> **NOTE** □ □ □
>
> In mathematics, especially matrix algebra, index values for elements in an array are usually subscripted—which means they are placed half a line below the other characters in the name of the variable, much like the *2* in H_2O, the chemical formula for water. In many programming languages, however, they are simply placed in brackets. An array of the names of four cities might be referred to as $city_0$, $city_1$, $city_2$, and $city_3$, or as $city[0]$, $city[1]$, $city[2]$, and $city[3]$. Sometimes both brackets and subscripting are used. In any case, such variables are often referred to as subscripted variables, even when brackets are used without true subscripting.

At first glance, it might seem that there is little difference between an array and a list; however, a list is a set of objects, while an array is a set of variables that hold objects. It is as if a list were a collection of things, and an array were a collection of boxes that hold things. If we remove an item from the middle of a list, then the list simply gets smaller by one object; whereas, if we remove an item from a "box" in an array, then that "box" is simply empty. Figure 8-8 shows this. If we remove the second item in a list, then the old third item becomes the new second item, and so on for all of the rest of the items in the list. If we remove the second object from an array, then the second "box" in the array is simply empty. The third item will remain in the third "box," and so on throughout the array.

FIGURE 8-8: Removing an item from a list and from an array

There is one other crucial difference between an array and a list: a list is linear, while an array may be multidimensional. To say that a list is linear means that we can think of it as a straight line. It has one item, then a second, then a third, and so on, as if in one continuous straight line. To say that an array has more than one dimension means that each object in an array could have more than one subscript, referring to its location in the array in different dimensions. Recall from Chapter 2 that a dimension is simply a way of measuring something, such as the length, width, and height of three-dimensional objects. A two-dimensional array, for example, could be thought of as having rows and columns, with one subscript for the row and one for the column. Such a two dimensional array is sometimes called a table or a two-dimensional **matrix**. A simple one-dimensional array is sometimes called a **vector**.

You won't be working with any two-dimensional arrays in Alice, but in Tutorial 8D, you will look at a world that sorts the objects in a simple linear array. The world uses a special object in Alice called an **Array Visualization Object**, which is used to show us an array in an Alice world, rather than just creating it in the memory of the computer.

TUTORIAL 8A—EIGHT BALLERINAS

In this tutorial, you will create a list with eight ballerinas in the list, and then write a method to make the ballerinas perform movements individually and all at once. The purpose of the exercise is to learn how to create lists in Alice as well as how to use the *For all in order* and *For all together* instructions tiles.

Exploring the Ballerina Movement Methods

You will begin by opening a world that already has eight ballerinas in it, with methods to enable the ballerinas to perform some individual movements. You will explore the methods this world contains before creating and working with a list of the ballerinas.

1. Start the Alice software and open the **eight ballerinas** world from the student data files for this book.

2. Notice that the world contains eight ballerinas, whose names can be seen in the object tree: *Bronwyn, Ava, Addie, Mardi, Evelyn, Daphne, Kristen,* and *Meagan.* The opening scene from the world is shown in Figure 8-9. Click the **world** tile in the Object tree and the **methods** tab in the Details area, and you will see that in addition to `my first method`, there are generic instructions to make any ballerina jump, put its arms up or down, spin, jump and move at the same time, and bow. Before creating a list of the ballerinas, you will try each of these methods with different ballerinas.

FIGURE 8-9: The *eight ballerinas* world

3. Click the **edit** button next to the *my first method* tile, and you will see `world.my first method` appear in the Editor area.

4. First, drag a copy of the **jump who** tile from the methods tab into `world.my first method` in the Editor area. When the menus appear, select **Bronwyn, the entire Bronwyn.**

5. Next, drag a copy of the **armsUp who** tile into `world.my first method` and drop it below the *world.jump who = Bronwyn* instruction tile. When the menus appear, select **Ava, the entire Ava**.

6. Now, drag a copy of the **armsDown who** tile and drop it below the *world.armsUp who = Ava* instruction tile in `world.my first method`. When the menus appear again, select **Ava, the entire Ava**.

7. Drag a copy of the **spin who** tile into `world.my first method` and drop it below the *world.armsDown who = Ava* instruction tile. When the menus appear, select **Addie, the entire Addie**.

8. Drag a copy of the **jumpMove who direction** tile into `world.my first method` and drop it below the *world.spin who = Addie* instruction tile. When the menus appear, select **Daphne, the entire Daphne**, and **left** as the direction.

9. Drag another copy of the **jumpMove who direction** tile into `world.my first method` and drop it below the first *world.jumpMove* instruction tile. When the menus appear again, select **Daphne, the entire Daphne**, but this time choose **right** as the direction.

10. Finally, drag a copy of the **bow who** tile into `world.my first method` and drop it below all of the other instruction tiles. When the menus appear, select **Mardi, the entire Mardi**.

11. Now `world.my first method` contains an example of each of the instructions for the individual movements for a ballerina. Save the world with the name **ballerina movements**, and then play it to see what each of the movements looks like. You may want to try it a few times or to experiment with the various instructions for the ballerinas before continuing.

Creating a List of the Ballerinas

Your next task is to create a list containing the eight ballerinas so that you can try the *For all in order* and *For all together* instructions. You won't need the sample instructions you just tried, so they can be discarded. It's actually easier to restart the *eight ballerinas* world than to delete each of the instructions in `world.my first method`. You will begin by reopening the *eight ballerinas* world and creating a list of the ballerinas.

1. Close and reopen the Alice software. This will ensure that memory is clear before creating the new world. If the system warns you that the world has been modified and asks you if you want to save it, select **no**.

2. Reopen the original **eight ballerinas** world from the student data files for this book.

3. Save the world with the name **ballerina company** so that your changes will not affect the original *eight ballerinas* world.

4. Select the **world** tile in the Object tree and the **properties** tab in the Details area.

5. Click the **create new variable** button on the properties tab; the create new variable dialog box should appear. Type **company** as the name, select **Object** as the type, and make sure that the **make a** option is checked and that **list** is selected in the Values section of the window. Do not click the OK button at this time.

6. Next, you will add the ballerinas to the new list. Click the **new item** button in the create new variable dialog box, and a line for *item 0* should appear just above the button, as shown in Figure 8-10.

FIGURE 8-10: The create new variable dialog window

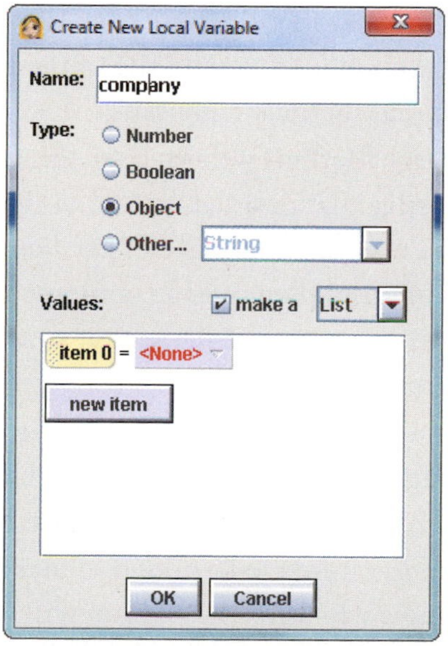

7. Click the word **None** next to *item 0*, and select **Bronwyn**, and then **the entire Bronwyn** from the menus that appear.

8. Click the **new item** button again, and a line for *item 1* will appear. This time, click the word **None** next to item1, and select **Ava**, and then **the entire Ava** from the menus that appear.

9. In a similar manner, add **Addie** as **item 2**, **Mardi** as **item 3**, **Evelyn** as **item 4**, **Daphne** as **item 5**, **Kristen** as **item 6**, and **Meagan** as **item 7**.

10. When you are finished, click the **OK** button in the create new variable dialog box. A new tile for the company list should appear in the properties tab. You now have a list containing the eight ballerinas.

11. Save the world before continuing.

Creating a Dance Routine for the Ballerinas

Now that you have a list with the eight ballerinas in the list, you can place some instructions in `world.my first method` to create a routine for the ballerina company. The routine will be a fairly simple one, just enough for you to learn how to use the *For all in order* and *For all together* instructions.

One at a time, each of the ballerinas will spin while saying her name, and then the ballerinas will perform a few movements together. When they are finished, each will bow, and then the entire company will bow together.

1. Click the **methods** tab in the Details area, and the blank `world.my first method` should appear in the Editor area. If it does not appear, click the **edit** button next to the *my first method* tile in the Details area. If it is not blank, then delete any instructions it contains.

2. First, each of the ballerinas will do something one at time, so drag a copy of the **For all in order** tile from the bottom of the Editor area and drop it into `world.my first method` in place of *Do Nothing*. When the menus appear, select **expressions** and then **world.company**. An instruction tile will appear in `world.my first method` that says *For all world.company, one item_from_company at a time*.

3. Each ballerina will do two things together—say her name and spin—so drag a copy of the **Do together** tile from the bottom of the Editor area and drop it in the *For all* instruction tile in place of *Do Nothing*.

4. Now an instruction needs to be added to make the ballerina say her name. Figure 8-11 shows what this instruction will look like when it is complete. Drag the **item_from_company** object tile from the *For all world.company, [obj] one item_from_company at a time* tile, and drop it into the *Do together* tile in place of *Do Nothing*.

FIGURE 8-11: Instructing a ballerina to say her name

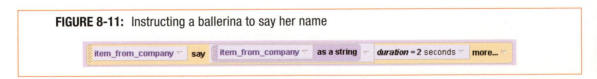

5. A menu will appear allowing you to select which of the primitive methods you want to have the *item_from_company* perform. Select **item_from_company say**, and then **hello**.

6. However, *item_from_company* should say its own name, not *hello.* You must use a function to do this. Select the **functions** tab in the Details area, find **what as a string**, and then drag and drop a copy of it in the *item_from_company say hello* instruction in place of the word *hello.*

7. When the menu appears, select **expressions**, and then **item_from_company**. Now the instruction looks as it should.

8. Save the world again and test it before continuing. Each ballerina should say her own name in turn.

If everything works okay so far, then you can continue. If not, then you need to find and fix any errors before continuing. Once everything is okay, you can proceed with creating the dance routine. To do this, you need to add the spin instruction to the *Do together* tile; then you can start adding the dance routine.

1. Click the **methods** tab in the Details area so that you can again see the list of generic methods in the world.

2. Drag a copy of the **spin who** tile from the methods tab and drop it below the *item_from_company say* instruction in the *Do together* tile in `world.my first method`. When the menu appears, select **expressions**, and then **item_from_company**.

3. A spin takes two seconds to complete, so, to synchronize the spin and say instructions, click the word **more** in the *item_from_company say* instruction tile and set the **duration** to **2 seconds**.

4. Test the world again, and this time each ballerina should say her name while spinning. If it looks correct, then save the world again.

Next you will add instructions to `world.my first method` to create the dance routine. All of the ballerinas will perform the routine together, so the instructions will be contained in a *For all together* tile. The ballerinas will jump, spin, jump left, jump right, and then spin again. After they are finished, they will each bow while saying their names, and then the company will bow together.

1. Drag a copy of the **For all together** tile from the bottom of the Editor area and drop it into `world.my first method` below the *For all world.company, one item_from_company at a time* tile. When the menus appear, select **expressions,** and then **world.company**. An instruction tile will appear in

`world.my first method` that says *For all world.company, every item_from_company together.*

2. Drag a copy of the **jump who** tile from the methods tab and drop it in the *For all world.company, every item_from_company together* tile in place of *Do nothing*. When the menu appears, select **expressions**, and then **item_from_company**.

3. Drag a copy of the **spin who** tile from the methods tab and drop it in the *For all world.company, every item_from_company together* tile below the *world.jump who = item_from_company* instruction. Again select **expressions**, and then **item_from_company** when the menu appears.

4. In a similar manner, add instructions to **jump move left**, **jump move right**, and then **spin** again.

5. Save the world before continuing.

Now you can add the instructions to make the ballerinas each say their names and bow at the end of the routine. They will drop their arms after bowing, and then all bow together.

1. Drag a **For all in order** tile from the bottom of the Editor area and drop it into the bottom of `world.my first method` after all of the other instruction tiles in the method. When the menu appears, select **expressions** and **world.company**.

2. Drag the second object tile that says *one item_from_company* from the top of the new *For all world.company, one item_from_company at a time* tile, and drop it into the tile in place of *Do Nothing*.

3. Select **item_from_company say**, and then **hello** from the menus that appear.

4. Select the **functions** tab in the Details area, and then scroll through the functions until you find the **what as a string** function. Drag a copy of it from the functions tab and drop it in the *item_from_company say hello* instruction in place of the word *hello*. When the menu appears, select **expressions**, and then **item_from_company**. The *say* instruction is now complete.

5. Select the **methods** tab in the Details area, and drag a copy of the **bow who** instruction from the methods tab and drop it just below the *item_from_company say* instruction tile. When the menu appears, select **expressions**, and then **item_from_company**.

6. Drag a copy of the **armsDown who** instruction from the methods tab and drop it below the *world.bow who item_from_company* instruction tile. When the menu appears, select **expressions**, and then **item_from_company**.

Finally, the last movement that needs to be added to the routine is the company bowing together.

1. Drag a copy of the **For all together** tile from the bottom of the Editor area and drop it into `world.my first method` below all of the other instructions. When the menus appear, select **expressions**, and then **world.company**.

2. Drag a copy of the **bow who** instruction from the methods tab and drop it in the new *For all world.company* tile in place of *Do Nothing*. When the menu appears, select **expressions**, and then **item_from_company**.

3. That's it! Save the method, and then play the world to see what happens. If everything is correct, the ballerinas should each say their name while spinning, complete several moves together, bow individually while saying their names, and then bow together. If they do not, then find and fix the error before continuing.

You now know how to create a list and how to use the *For all in order* and *For all together* instructions to perform operations on lists.

TUTORIAL 8B—MARCHING TOY SOLDIERS

In this tutorial, you will work with a list of toy soldiers to make them complete a marching drill routine. You will use the *For all in order* and *For all together* instructions to make the soldiers complete marching maneuvers sequentially and concurrently in the routine.

The Toy Soldiers World

In the student data files for this book, there is a *toy soldier* world containing a list of four toy soldiers with methods to make each of them march. You probably could create such a world on your own, but in the interest of time, you will start with a world in which this has already been done. You will start by exploring the existing world to become familiar with its features.

1. Start the Alice software and open the **toy soldiers** world from the student data files for this book. When the world loads, you should see a squad of four toy soldiers on the screen, as in Figure 8-12. The first toy soldier has black pants, and the rest have blue pants. You should also notice that there are tiles for four toy soldiers in the Object tree, named *toySoldier1* through *toySoldier4*.

FIGURE 8-12: The *toy soldiers* world

2. Before doing anything else, save the world with the name **toy soldiers marching** so that your changes do not affect the original *toy soldiers* world.

3. Click the **properties** tab in the Details area, and you will see that there are two variables: a list of objects named *squad*, and a Boolean variable named *marching*, which is initialized to *true*, as in Figure 8-13.

FIGURE 8-13: A list variable and a Boolean variable for the *toy soldiers* world

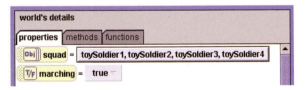

4. Click the button after the equals sign following the *squad* tile on the properties tab, and you will see the Collection Editor window open, as shown in Figure 8-14. The Collection Editor window shows that the list contains the four toy soldiers, with *toy soldier1* as the first element, and so on up to *toy soldier4* as the last element in the list. Click the **OK** button to close the Collection Editor window.

FIGURE 8-14: The Collection Editor window

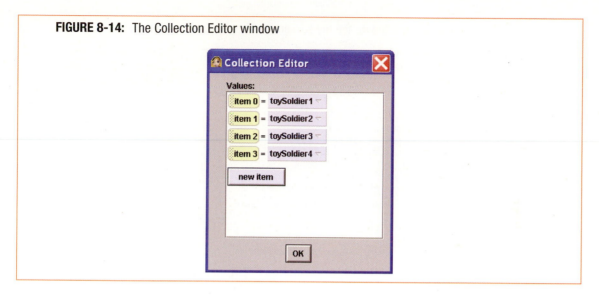

5. Look in the Events area and you will see that there is an event to run the method `world.squadMarch` while the world is running.

6. Click the **methods** tab in the Editor area and then the **edit** button next to `squadMarch` to see what this method does. If you look at the method in the Editor area, you will see that if the Boolean variable *world.marching* is true, then each of the four toy soldiers will march, and if it is not true, then nothing happens—in other words, they will not march. The *world.marching* variable is a state control variable, which controls the status of the toy soldiers. When it is true, they will be marching; when it is false, they will not be marching.

7. Because the Boolean variable *marching* is initialized to *true*, the squad should march if the world is played. Play the world and you should see the soldiers march off the screen. Once they have marched away, you can stop the world.

8. From now on, you do not want the soldiers to march away when the world starts, so click the **true** button next to the *marching* tile on the world's properties tab in the Details area, and change it to **false**.

Creating a Marching Routine

You are now ready to create a method to make all of the soldiers complete a marching drill routine. They will start marching, then after two seconds they will turn right one at a time, and then after another two seconds, they will turn right all at once. This process will be repeated four times, which should create an interesting marching routine using only a few simple instructions. Figure 8-15 shows what this method will look like when it is finished.

FIGURE 8-15: A marching routine for the toy soldiers

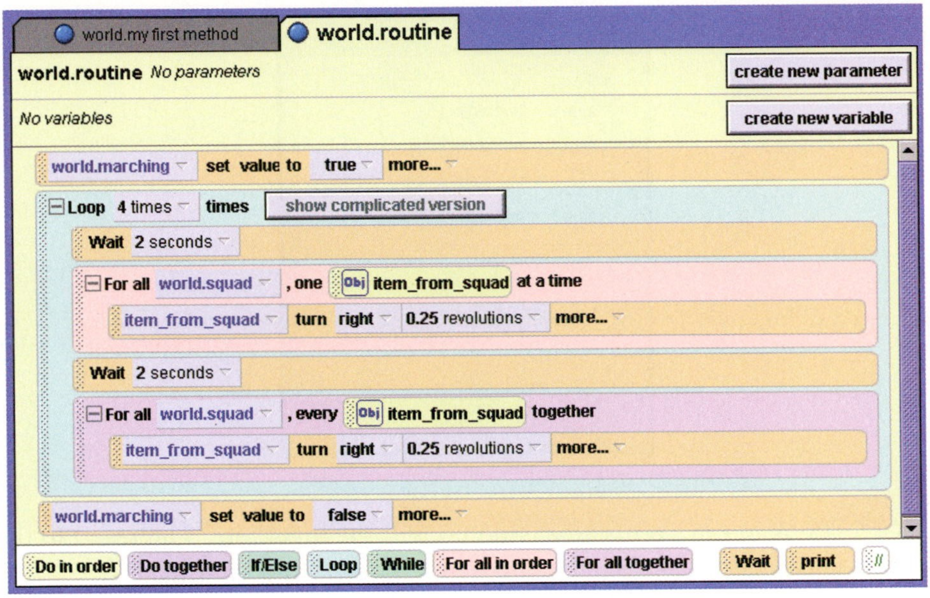

1. Click the **world** tile in the Object tree, and then the **methods** tab in the Details area.

2. Click the **create new method** button on the methods tab, type the name **routine** in the new method dialog window that appears, and then click the **OK** button.

3. Click the **properties** tab and drag a copy of the **marching** Boolean variable tile from the properties tab and drop it into the world.routine method in place of *Do Nothing*. Select **true** from the menu that appears. Setting the *marching* variable to *true* will have the affect of a "Forward, march!" command and will start the soldiers marching when the routine is run.

4. The routine will contain a process to be repeated four times, so drag a copy of the **loop** instruction from the bottom of the Editor area and drop it in the world.routine method below the *world.marching set value to true* instruction. Select **other** from the menu that appears, enter the value **4** using the calculator style keypad that appears, and then click the **Okay** button.

5. Drag a copy of the **Wait** instruction from the bottom of the Editor area and drop it into the *loop* instruction in place of *Do Nothing*. Set the duration for the *wait* to **2 seconds**.

6. Drag a copy of the **For all in order** tile from the bottom of the Editor area and drop it into the *loop* instruction below the *wait* instruction. When the menus appear, select **expressions**, and then **world.squad**.

7. The new instruction now says *For all world.squad one [obj] item_from_squad at a time*. Drag a copy of the **item_from_squad** parameter in this instruction and drop it in the same instruction in place of *Do Nothing*.

8. When the menus appear, select **item_from_squad turn,** then **right**, and then **¼ revolution**.

9. Next, right-click the **wait** tile in the `world.routine` method and select **make copy**. Move the copy of the **wait** instruction to the end of the *loop* instruction, inside the *Loop* tile but below the *For all* tile.

10. Drag a copy of the **For all together** tile from the bottom of the Editor area and drop it into the *loop* instruction below the second *wait* instruction. When the menus appear, select **expressions**, and then **world.squad**.

11. The new instruction now says *For all world.squad every [obj] item_from_squad together*. Drag a copy of the **item_from_squad** parameter in this instruction and drop it in the same instruction in place of *Do Nothing*.

12. When the menus appear, select **item_from_squad turn,** then **right**, and then **¼ revolution**.

13. Finally, drag a copy of the **marching** Boolean variable tile from the properties tab and drop it into the `world.routine` method at the very bottom, below the *loop* instruction tile. Select **false** from the menu that appears. This will have the effect of a "Halt" command and will stop the soldiers from marching.

14. Your new method is now complete. Save the world again before continuing.

Finally, to make the soldiers carry out the routine when the world starts, you need to put a *routine* instruction in `world.my first method`.

1. Click the **world.my first method** tab in the Editor area and the method should become visible. It should be blank except for *Do Nothing*.

2. Drag a copy of the **routine** tile from the methods tab in the Details area and drop it into `world.my first method` in place of *Do Nothing*.

3. Save the world again before continuing.

4. Play the world and watch what happens. The soldiers should complete two circuits of their routine before stopping. Each iteration through the loop in the `routine` method is only one-half of the routine's circuit, which is why they will complete two circuits when the loop is set to repeat four times. If the method does not perform as expected, then find and fix any errors before continuing.

TUTORIAL 8C—SALUTING TOY SOLDIERS

In this tutorial, you will create a method to make the toy soldiers from the previous tutorial salute, which will provide you with practice in manipulating the parts of objects that are contained in a list. Manipulating the parts of an object can be the most tedious part of programming objects in three-dimensional virtual worlds like Alice, but the result is that the objects function more like similar items in the real world.

You will actually create two methods. First, you will create a generic salute method to make any soldier salute; then you will the use the *For all together* instruction to create a method to make the entire squad salute. It is necessary to use several *move* and *turn* instructions to manipulate the right arms of the toy soldiers to make them salute.

Creating a Generic Salute Method

To salute, a soldier needs to raise its arm into a saluting position, and then drop the arm back to its original position. You will first create a generic method with a *who* parameter to enable any soldier to salute.

1. If necessary, start the Alice software and open the **toy soldiers marching** world that you saved in the previous tutorial, or open the world from the student data files for this book. When the world loads, you should see a squad of four toy soldiers on the screen, as shown in Figure 8-12.

2. Save the world with the name **toy soldiers salute** before continuing so that you do not change the existing *toy soldiers marching* world.

3. Click the **create new method** button on the methods tab in the world's Details area, type the name **salute** in the New Method dialog window that opens, and then click the **OK** button. A new method named `world.salute` will appear in the Editor area.

4. Click the **create new parameter** button at the top of the new method in the Editor area, and the Create New Parameter window will open. Type the name **who**, make sure that **Object** is selected as the parameter type, and then click the **OK** button.

Figure 8-16 shows what the first part of the `salute` method will look like. This is the part that will cause the soldier to raise his arm into a saluting position.

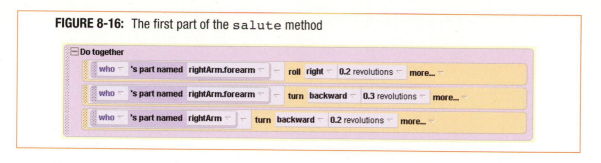

FIGURE 8-16: The first part of the `salute` method

You can see that three things need to happen to make the soldier salute:

- The right forearm needs to roll right .2 revolutions.
- The right forearm needs to turn backward .3 revolutions.
- The entire right arm needs to turn backward .2 revolutions.

The numeric values for the amounts of these movements were determined through calculation combined with trial and error. All three of these instructions need to be carried out at the same time, so they will be placed inside a *Do together* tile. Because the method will be a generic method to make any soldier salute, you will also need to use an object parameter in the method to indicate which soldier should salute.

There is one complication that you will encounter in creating the `salute` method. To manipulate parts of an object in a generic method, such as a soldier's arm or forearm, it is often necessary to use a function that points to the object's part by name. The two parts you need to manipulate are the *rightArm* and the *rightArm.forearm*. When the time comes below to use these, you will need to type in their names, so be careful: the capitalization and spelling are important.

1. Drag a **Do together** tile from the bottom of the Editor area and drop it into the `world.salute` method in place of *Do nothing*.

2. Drag a copy of the **who** parameter tile from the top line of the `world.salute` method and drop it in the *Do together* tile in place of *Do Nothing*.

3. When the menus appear, select **world.salute who roll**, then **right**, and then **other**. Use the calculator style keypad to enter **.2**, and then click the **Okay** button.

4. The last instruction in the method now reads *who roll right .2 revolutions*. This needs to be modified, because you do not actually want *who* to roll, but *who's forearm* to roll.

You will now need to use the function that points to an object's part. To get to this function, you will need to look at the functions tab for one of the toy soldiers.

1. Click the **toySoldier1** tile in the Object tree and then the **functions** tab in the Editor area.

2. Scroll through the functions until you find the **toySoldier1's part named key** function tile. It is near the bottom of the functions tab. Drag the tile into the Editor area and drop it in the *who roll right .2 revolutions* instruction in place of *who*.

3. Now click the **toy soldier1** parameter just before the words *part named*, and select **expressions**, and then **who** from the menu that appears.

4. Finally, click the **empty white box** just after *part named* in the same instruction, select **other** from the menu that appears, and the Enter a string dialog window will appear. Carefully type **rightArm.forearm** in the box, and then click the **OK** button. The instruction should now look like the roll instruction in Figure 8-17.

FIGURE 8-17: The instruction to move a soldier's right forearm

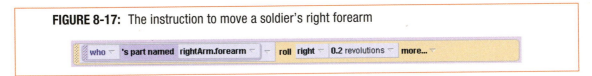

Now you will add the instruction to make the forearm turn backward .3 revolutions.

1. Drag a copy of the **who parameter** tile from the top of the `world.salute` method, and drop it in the *Do together* tile just below the *roll* instruction.

2. When the menus appear, select **world.salute who turn,** then **backward,** and then **other.** Use the calculator style keypad to enter **.3**, and then click the **Okay** button.

3. You need to again use the part name function, but this time you can copy it from the previous instruction. Drag a copy of the purple box that says *who's part named rightArm.forearm* from the *roll* instruction and drop it on the Clipboard; then drag it from the Clipboard and drop it into the *who turn* instruction at the bottom of the *Do together* tile in place of *who*. Your turn instruction should now look like the turn instruction in Figure 8-18.

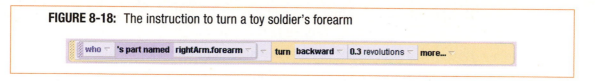

FIGURE 8-18: The instruction to turn a toy soldier's forearm

Next, you will add the instruction to make the entire arm turn backward 0.2 revolutions. You will do this by copying and modifying the instruction that you just completed.

1. Drag a copy of the **who's part named rightArm.forearm turn backward .3 revolutions** instruction to the Clipboard; then drag it from the Clipboard and drop it into the bottom of the *Do together* tile as the last instruction in the tile.

2. Click the **rightArm.forearm** box in the last instruction and select **other** from the menu that appears. Carefully type **rightArm** in the Enter a string dialog window that appears, and then click **OK**.

3. Click the **.3 revolutions** box in the last instruction and select **.2 revolutions** from the menu that appears. Your method should now look like Figure 8-19.

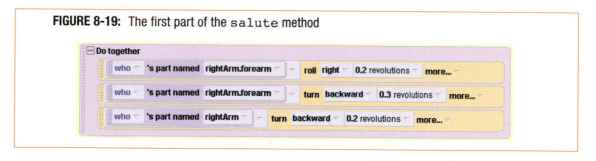

FIGURE 8-19: The first part of the `salute` method

The `salute` method is not finished yet, but you can unit test it to see what it does so far. It should cause a soldier to raise its arm into a saluting position. To test the method, you will need to modify `world.my first method`, and then play the world. `World.my first method` currently contains the *routine* instruction, which the soldiers carry out in their marching routine. You will temporarily disable the *routine* instruction to unit test the `salute` method.

1. Click the **world** tile in the object tree and then the **methods** tab in the details area.

2. Click the **world.my first method** tab in the Editor area, and the method should become visible.

3. Right-click the **world.routine** instruction tile and select **disable** from the menu that appears.

4. Drag a copy of the **salute who** method tile from the methods tab and drop it into `world.my first method` in the Editor area above the *routine* instruction so that it becomes the first instruction in the method.

5. Select **toySoldier1**, **the entire toySoldier1**, from the menus that appear.

6. Now play the world. The first soldier should raise his arm into a saluting position. If it does not, then check your work and fix the problem in the `salute` method. If the method runs but the salute looks funny, then you should check the direction and amount of the parameters in the *turn* and *roll* instructions in the `salute` method. If you get a "*subject must not be null*" error message, then the name of one of the parts you typed as the *part named* parameters in the *turn* and *roll* instructions may be wrong.

7. Save the world again before continuing.

The method makes the toy soldier raise its arm into a saluting position, but it also needs to make it drop its arm. To add this to the method, you will simply make a copy of the *Do together* tile in the `salute` method, and then reverse the direction of each of the arm movements.

1. Click the **world.salute** tab in the Editor area.

2. Drag a copy of the **Do together tile** from the `world.salute` method and drop it on the Clipboard, and then drag it from the Clipboard and drop it into the `world.salute` method below the original *Do together* tile.

3. Now, one at a time, click each of the direction parameters in the three instruction tiles inside the bottom *Do together* tile and reverse the direction. Change **right** to **left** in the first tile, and **backward** to **forward** in each of the other two tiles. When you are finished, the second *Do together* instruction should look like Figure 8-20.

FIGURE 8-20: The second part of the `salute` method

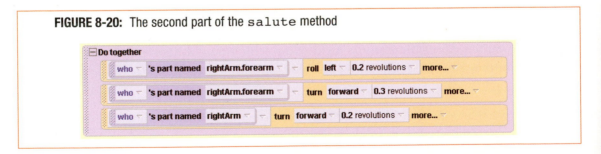

4. Now the soldier should raise its salute, and then drop its salute. Play the world again to see if it works, fix any errors you encounter, and then save the world again before proceeding.

Making All of the Soldiers Salute

Now that you have a generic method to make any soldier salute, you need to create a method to make the entire squad of soldiers salute together. To do this, you will create a `squadSalute` method that contains the generic `salute` method inside a *For all together* instruction for the squad of soldiers. Your finished method should look like Figure 8-21.

FIGURE 8-21: A method to make all of the toy soldiers salute

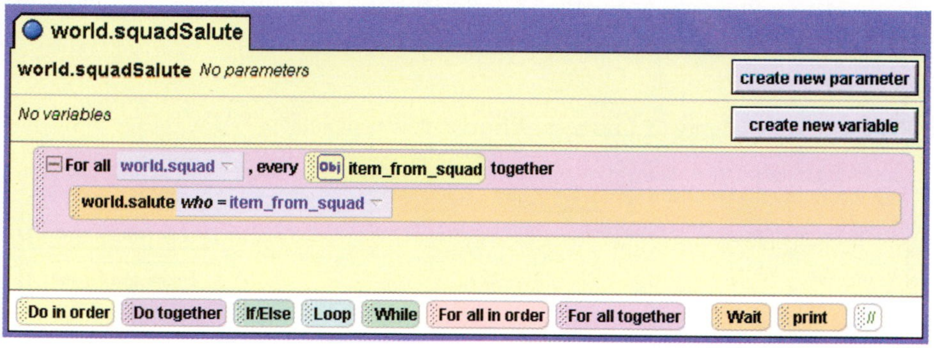

1. Click the **create new method** button on the **methods** tab in the world's Details area.
2. Type the name **squadSalute** in the New Method dialog window that opens, and then click the **OK** button. A new method named `world.squadSalute` will open in the Editor area.
3. You will use a *For all together* instruction to have the soldiers all salute at the same time. Drag a copy of the **For all together** tile from the bottom of the Editor area and drop it in the `squadSalute` method in place of *Do Nothing*.
4. When the menus appear, select **expressions,** and then **world.squad**.
5. Drag a copy of the **salute who** tile from the methods tab and drop it into the *For all* tile in place of *Do Nothing*.
6. When the menus appear, select **expressions,** and then **item_from_squad**.
7. The `squadSalute` method is finished and should resemble Figure 8-21. Save your world before continuing.

You are now ready to test the `world.squadSalute` method.

1. Click the **world.my first method** tab in the Editor area to see the method. The method still contains the instruction *world.salute who = toySoldier1* and the disabled *routine* instruction.

2. Drag a copy of the **squadSalute** method from the Editor area and drop it into `world.my first` method between the two instructions.

3. Now play the world to see if it works as expected. If it does, then the first soldier should salute, followed by all of the soldiers saluting together.

Finally, you need to enable the disabled `routine` instruction in `world.my first` method.

1. Right-click the disabled **world.routine** instruction and select **enable** from the menu that appears. The `world.my first` method is now complete and should resemble Figure 8-22.

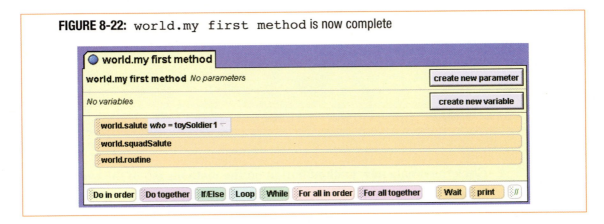

FIGURE 8-22: `world.my first` method is now complete

2. Save the world again, and then play the world to see if it performs as expected. The first soldier salutes, all soldiers salute, and then they complete their routine. If the world does not perform as expected, then find and fix any errors before continuing.

If you like, you can copy and paste from the existing instructions in `world.my first` `method` to make the soldiers turn and salute again when they are finished with their marching routine.

TUTORIAL 8D—SORTING AN ARRAY OF SIXTEEN BALLERINAS

This tutorial is a little different from the others because you will not create any new worlds but simply examine a world from the student data files for this book. The world, named *sixteen ballerinas,* has an array that contains sixteen ballerinas. The array exists as an Array Visualization Object, which will let you see the array as a set of adjacent boxes in the Alice world, much like the way an array would be stored as a set of consecutive locations in a computer's memory.

The array has room for sixteen elements, with one ballerina stored in each spot in the array. The ballerinas are different sizes, and the world contains a method to sort the ballerinas in the array according to their height. The sorting method uses the bubble sort technique, which is not the most efficient sort, but it is fairly easy to understand.

1. Start the Alice software and open the world named **sixteen ballerinas** that is in the student data files for this book.

2. You will see that the world has a set of sixteen ballerinas, all lined up in separate "boxes" in an array. The ballerinas are all different heights, as seen in Figure 8-23.

FIGURE 8-23: The *sixteen ballerinas* world

3. Play the world, and you will see that the ballerinas are sorted in order according to their heights.

4. Click the **array** tile in the Object tree and the **methods** tab in the Details area. You will see that there are two different user-created methods for the array—swap and bubbleSort.

5. Click the **edit** button next to the swap method; the method becomes visible in the Editor area. There are two spots in the method where the *duration* is set to .1 seconds. Changing these to a larger number will slow down the sort.

6. Click the **edit** button next to the bubbleSort method; the method becomes visible in the Editor area.

Notice that there are two loops in the bubbleSort method, a WHILE loop and a *count-controlled* loop. The count-controlled loop goes through the array once, comparing each element in the array to the next element. This is done by using the index variable from the loop to refer to the element in the array. The elements *array[index]* and *array[index +1]* are adjacent elements in the array. If *index* is 2, for example, then *index +1* will be 3, and the two elements being compared will be *array[2]* and *array[3]*. If the two elements are out of order, then they are swapped. Each time through the loop, comparing each item to its adjacent item, is called a pass though the loop.

The method continues to make passes through the loop until no more swaps occur. The Boolean variable called *changed* is used to keep track of when a swap occurs. It is set to *false* at the beginning of the WHILE loop, and is only reset to *true* if a swap occurs when going through the inner count-controlled loop. This will cause the program to keep repeating passes through the list until no swap occurs; then the program stops.

In other words, in a bubble sort, the computer goes through the array, comparing each value to the one that follows it. If they are out of order, then they are swapped; otherwise, they are left in place. The computer continues to make passes through the array until it makes one pass in which no swaps occur. Once it can do this, the list is in the correct order, and the sorting stops. As stated earlier, this is not the most efficient way to sort an array, but it is a reasonably easy-to-understand technique that correctly sorts an array.

If you look through the various parts of this world, you will see that it contains both an array and a list. The world is really just included for demonstration purposes so that you can see a program that operates on an array.

Close the Alice software when you are finished examining the *sixteen ballerinas* world.

Chapter Summary

This chapter consisted of a discussion of data structures, followed by four tutorials. The discussion of data structures included the following:

- ☐ A data structure is a scheme for organizing data in the memory of a computer. Some of the more commonly used data structures include lists, arrays, stacks, queues, heaps, trees, and graphs.

- ☐ Alice has instructions that will allow you to manipulate two of the most basic data structures—lists and arrays.

- ☐ Computer programmers decide which data structures to use based on the nature of the data and the processes that need to be performed on that data because the way in which the data is organized affects the performance of a program for different tasks.

- ☐ A queue is a set of data items with a beginning and end, called the front and back of the queue. Data enters the queue at one end and leaves it at the other. Because of this, data exits the queue in the same order in which it entered the queue, like people in a checkout line at a supermarket.

- ☐ A binary tree is a data structure that looks like an upside-down tree. Each spot on the tree, called a node, holds an item of data along with a left pointer and a right pointer. The pointers are lined up so that the structure forms the upside-down tree, with a single node at the top, called the root node, and branches increasing on the left and right as you go down the tree.

- ☐ By comparing the queue with the binary tree, you can see how the structure of the data affects what can be done efficiently with the data.

- ☐ One of the simplest of all data structures is a list, which is an ordered set of data. It is often used to store objects that are to be processed sequentially.

- ☐ Alice has a number of instructions that can be used to manipulate lists, including *For all in order* and *For all together*.

- ☐ *For all in order* will perform an instruction on each item in a list one at a time, beginning with the first item in the list and going through the list in order. This is known as iterating the list.

- ☐ *For all together* will perform an operation on all of the items in a list at the same time.

- ☐ An array is a set of indexed variables, each containing objects of the same data type.

- ☐ Each variable in the array is identified by its unique index value.

- ☐ A list is a set of objects, while an array is a set of variables that hold objects. It is as if a list were a collection of things, and an array were a collection of boxes that hold things.

- ☐ A list is linear, while an array may be multidimensional. A two-dimensional array, for example, could be thought of as having rows and columns, with one subscript for the row and one for the column. A two-dimensional array is sometimes called a table, or a two-dimensional matrix. A simple one-dimensional array is sometimes called a vector.

- ☐ Alice has a special object called an Array Visualization Object, which is used to show us an array in an Alice world, rather than just creating it in the memory of the computer.

In Tutorial 8A, you created a list of ballerinas and used the *For all in order* and *For all together* instructions to perform operations on the list.

In Tutorial 8B, you again used the *For all in order* and *For all together* instructions to perform operations on a list of toy soldiers so they would complete a marching routine.

In Tutorial 8C, you created a generic method that performs operations on the parts of objects contained in a list to make the toy soldiers salute.

Tutorial 8D demonstrated the use of an Array Visualization Object in a method that uses the bubble sort technique to sort a set of objects stored as an array.

Review Questions

1. Define the following terms:

☐ array	☐ index value	☐ node
☐ Array Visualization Object	☐ iterate a list	☐ queue
☐ binary tree	☐ list	☐ root node
☐ data structure	☐ matrix	☐ vector

2. How do programmers decide what data structures to use for different programs?

3. Why is a queue a good data structure to use for keeping track of documents to be printed on a network printer?

4. Why would a binary tree be a good data structure to use for storing a dictionary on a computer?

5. What is the difference between a list and an array?

6. What is the role of index values in an array?

7. What does it mean to say that an array can be multidimensional?

8. What is the difference between using the *Do together* and the *For all together* instructions in an Alice world?

9. The swap method in Tutorial 8D contains an object variable called *temp*. Why is it needed in this method?

10. An encapsulated data structure is one that includes functions, such as adding an element to the data structure, but the details of those methods are hidden from the user. In other words, they can use the methods, but they cannot see inside them. List several encapsulated methods that would be useful for all of the following data structures: a queue, a binary tree, a list, and an array. List several methods that would each be useful for one of the data structures but not necessarily the others.

Exercises

1. Create an Alice world with four helicopters and a list containing the helicopters. Program the world to make the helicopters each lift off from the ground one at a time, and then all turn and fly away together.

2. The Animals folder in the Alice Local Gallery contains several different kinds of fish, including a goldfish and a shark. The Ocean folder contains an ocean floor background. Using these items, create an Alice world with a school of goldfish that swim around together, and then scatter when a shark appears. You may be tempted to use the Lilfish in the Ocean folder instead of the goldfish, but be careful—each instance of the Lilfish requires more than 2 megabytes of memory, while each Goldfish requires only 30 kilobytes.

3. Create a drill routine of your own for the *toy soldiers* world from Tutorial 8B that demonstrates the use of the *For all in order* and *For all together* instructions, along with good modular programming techniques.

4. Create an Alice world with several objects from the People gallery. Place some of the objects in one list and some of the objects in another list. Create a method to make each object in the first list say hello to each object in the second list, and vice versa.

5. Create several new generic movement methods for the *eight ballerinas* world, and then demonstrate their use in methods that use the *For all in order* and *For all together* instructions.

6. Create a series of keyboard and mouse events for either the *eight ballerinas* world that will allow the user to control a ballet routine, or for the *toy soldiers* world that will allow the user to control a marching drill routine while the world is running.

7. Open the generic triple jump world from the student data files for this book and add a set of five different heights to the world as a list of numbers. Create a method to iterate through the list and have the three characters jump each of the heights contained in the list.

8. Create a search method for the *sixteen ballerinas* world that will do all of the following:
   a. Allow the user to input a ballerina's name.
   b. Go through the list to find the ballerina in the list that has the name from Step 8a.
   c. Have the ballerina respond by performing a dance maneuver.

   If the list does not contain a ballerina with the name that the user entered, then one of the ballerinas should tell the user that this is the case.

9. The Bugs folder inside the Animals folder in the Alice Local Gallery contains a Butterfly class of objects. Complete the following:

    a. Create an Alice world with six butterflies in the world.
    b. Create a generic method to make any butterfly flap its wings.
    c. Create a generic random movement method that will use random numbers to pick a direction and an amount, and then cause a butterfly to move accordingly.
    d. Place the six butterflies in a list, and create methods and events to make all of the butterflies fly around gently in an Alice world, flapping their wings and moving about randomly.

10. The National Institute for Standards and Technology has a Dictionary of Algorithms and Data Structures on the Web at *http://www.nist.gov/dads/*. Look up the definitions for the data structures stack and queue, and then describe the differences between a stack and a queue.

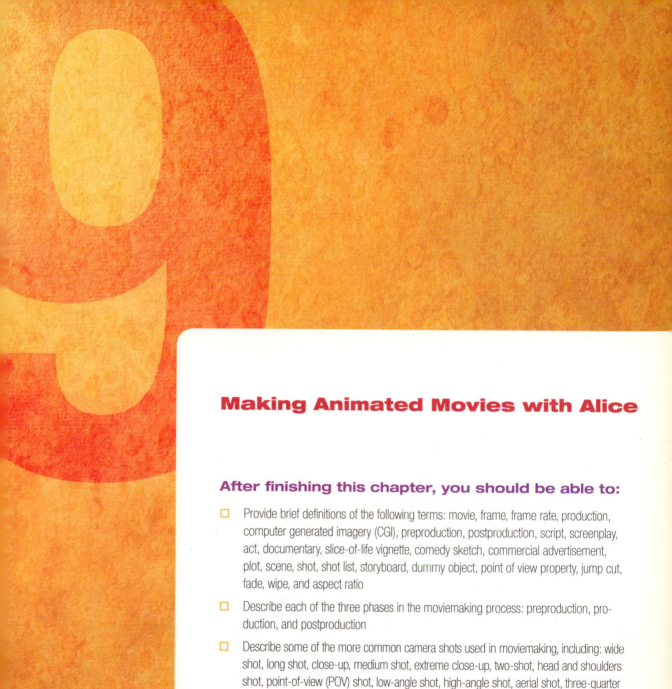

Making Animated Movies with Alice

After finishing this chapter, you should be able to:

☐ Provide brief definitions of the following terms: movie, frame, frame rate, production, computer generated imagery (CGI), preproduction, postproduction, script, screenplay, act, documentary, slice-of-life vignette, comedy sketch, commercial advertisement, plot, scene, shot, shot list, storyboard, dummy object, point of view property, jump cut, fade, wipe, and aspect ratio

☐ Describe each of the three phases in the moviemaking process: preproduction, production, and postproduction

☐ Describe some of the more common camera shots used in moviemaking, including: wide shot, long shot, close-up, medium shot, extreme close-up, two-shot, head and shoulders shot, point-of-view (POV) shot, low-angle shot, high-angle shot, aerial shot, three-quarter shot, over-the-shoulder shot, profile shot, moving shot, and following shot

☐ Outline the plot and visual flow of a movie using storyboards and shot lists

☐ Position the camera in an Alice world to match shots described in a storyboard and shot list

☐ Use dummy objects to simulate the use of multiple cameras in an Alice world

☐ Make a movie with multiple camera shots from an Alice world

INTRODUCTION

In this chapter, you will use Alice to make short animated movies. The chapter includes some background information on the nature of movies, a look at the process of moviemaking, and several tutorials that show you how to plan and set up camera shots for recording an Alice world as a movie.

This chapter focuses on the visual aspects of moviemaking. The sound techniques discussed in Chapter 6 can be used in conjunction with the techniques in this chapter.

NOTE □ □ □ Animated moviemaking is both processor and memory intensive. Recording movies from Alice worlds works best on computers with more memory, a good processor, and a good video card. See Appendix A for more specific information on hardware requirements.

A **movie** is a flat two-dimensional picture that moves. Actually, when we view a movie, we are watching a rapidly changing series of still images, each slightly different from the previous image. Instead of seeing many still images, we experience them as a moving picture. See Figure 9-1.

FIGURE 9-1: Video-editing software showing several frames from a movie

Each still image in a movie is called a **frame**, and the number of frames per second (fps) in a movie is called the **frame rate**. The frame rate for films in a movie theatre is 24 fps, while the frame for broadcast television is roughly 30 fps. Anything slower than around 16 fps might look a bit choppy.

Most computer monitors refresh their displays 60 or 72 times per second, so when you are viewing an Alice world, you are seeing images that are changing faster than the frame rates for television or film. The moviemaking option in Alice captures a series of still pictures many times a second while an Alice world is playing, and then combines the still images into a movie.

In the late 1800s, pioneering inventors like Thomas Edison in the United States and the Lumiere brothers in France developed cameras and projectors that could record and project movies using photographic film, giving rise to the motion picture film industry. The development of electronics in the 20th century, including television and computer technology, has taken us to the 21st century age of digital video, in which video cameras and display screens are everywhere, and film-based recording is mostly a thing of the past.

Yet, despite the movie industry's change to digital technology, the fundamental principles of moviemaking remain the same. For example, movies don't need to be long to be interesting. The Lumiere brothers' first films, which were each less than a minute long, were a big hit because of the novelty of moving pictures, and because of the human aspect of filmmaking: people are captivated by movies that tell a story. Their most popular films were those that told a story.

Your experience making movies with Alice will, in some ways, be like that of the Lumiere brothers. You won't start by making feature-length films; you will create short movies—most less than a minute in length. And, like the Lumiere brothers, you should keep in mind that the most interesting movies tell a story.

THE MOVIEMAKING PROCESS

The moviemaking process has three phases: preproduction, production, and postproduction, as shown in Figure 9-2.

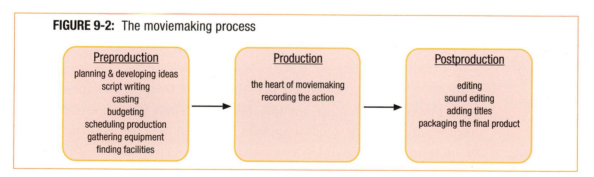

FIGURE 9-2: The moviemaking process

Preproduction
planning & developing ideas
script writing
casting
budgeting
scheduling production
gathering equipment
finding facilities

Production
the heart of moviemaking
recording the action

Postproduction
editing
sound editing
adding titles
packaging the final product

Production is the heart of the moviemaking process, the actual recording of the movie. In traditional filmmaking, it is when the cameras are rolling and action is captured on film. The production phase for an animated movie includes creating the animations and recording them. Today most animations are **computer generated imagery (CGI)**. In fact, many traditional movies often include some CGI, and, of course, Alice movies are produced entirely with CGI.

Yet, as important as it is, production takes up only a small part of the time needed to make a movie. **Preproduction**, the planning and preparation required before production can begin, usually takes much longer than production. Preproduction includes developing ideas for the movie, writing the script, casting, scheduling production, and gathering all of the resources for production—including people, equipment, and facilities.

Postproduction includes all of the tasks that take place after a movie is recorded, such as editing, adding titles, and packaging the final product.

If you are going to make movies, then you need to allow enough time to do so—good moviemaking takes time. Creating short animated movies using Alice is a lot like producing a single scene from a feature-length movie, yet the development of an Alice movie still includes preproduction, production, and postproduction. The rest of this chapter will take you through the process, but first, let's review the mechanism for recording movies in Alice.

TUTORIAL 9A—RECORDING A MOVIE FROM ALICE

Tutorial 1E showed you how to record your first Alice world, *Hello World!*, as a movie file that was about four seconds long. For review, we'll go through the recording process again, but this time you will record Alice's *lakeSkater* example world, which is about 55 seconds long.

You may recall from Chapter 1 that Alice allows you to export a world as a video file using the QuickTime *.mov* format. You can then view the world, post it to a Web page as an embedded or streaming video, or you can use Adobe Premiere, Windows Live Movie Maker, Apple's iMovie, or other software to edit the movie or save it in another format.

To save the *lakeSkater* example world as a movie file:

1. Start Alice, and open the **lakeSkater** Alice world from the examples tab.
2. Click **File** on the menu bar, and then click the **Export Video** option. The Save World As dialog window appears. You must save the world as a part of the recording process, and you may save it in a new location with a new name if you would like to do so. Save the world before continuing. Alice's Export video window will appear next. See Figure 9-3.

FIGURE 9-3: Alice's Export video window with controls for recording a movie

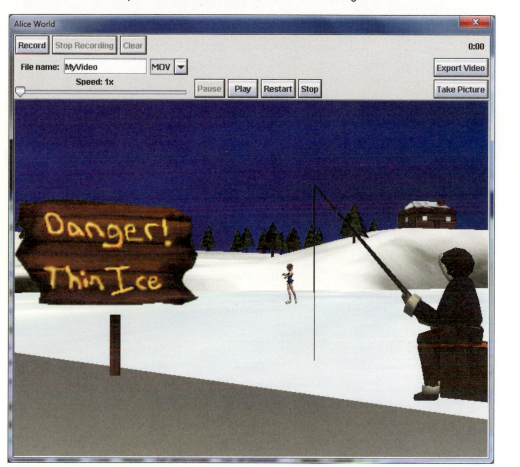

3. Type the name of your movie file in the **File name** text box before recording the video. The name of the movie file does not need to be the same as the name of the Alice world.

4. Click the **Record** button to start recording your movie. The world will start playing *and* recording at the same time. As the world plays, Alice is rendering and capturing about 30 frames a second. The world takes about 55 seconds to play all the way through. At the end, the skater winks, then blinks, and then the camera pulls back. When this happens, the world is finished playing.

5. Press the **Stop Recording** button to finish recording. The recording does not stop automatically so you will you need to pay attention and watch for the end of the action. You may want to play the world first without recording so that you will recognize when the action is complete.

 If you stop during recording and wish to restart recording, press the **Clear** button first to clear the frames that have already been recorded. Also, note that you do not need to record your Alice world from the beginning. You could play the world, pause it, and then record from that point forward only.

6. Click the **Export Video** button to save the recording as a movie file. The file will be saved in the same folder that you used to save the Alice world file (*.a2w) in Step 2. Alice will first encode the video and then the audio; then Alice merges the video and audio together. Alice records the movie file frame by frame. This process takes longer on computers that have less memory or a less sophisticated video card, so be patient. When the information boxes stop appearing, the video has been saved.

PREPRODUCTION

It works best to have a design for something before building it. This is just as true for movies as it is for computer programs. So, the first part of preproduction is designing your movie. The primary design document for a movie is a **script**, which is a scene-by-scene description of the movie, with dialog and descriptions of the critical action. See Figure 9-4 for an example. You need to decide the type and topic of your movie, outline the plot, pick the setting and characters, and then write the script.

FIGURE 9-4: Sample script

> **CLASSROOM – AFTERNOON**
>
> There is a desk or table and blackboard in the front of the room. A door is to the right of the desk, MARIE stands to the left of the desk, looking toward the back of the room.
>
> **JOE COOL opens the door and enters.**
>
> **JOE COOL**
> (waving to MARIE)
> Ehhhh... Mom ami.
>
> **MARIE turns to face JOE COOL, shakes her head, and sighs.**
>
> **JOE COOL**
> Je t'dore.
>
> **Marie raises her arms in confusion.**
>
> **MARIE**
> Shut the door? Shut it yourself.
>
> **MARIE turns and walks away.**
> JOE COOL's eyes follow her.

Yet, even in carefully scripted movies things change during the actual production process, so no script is really carved in stone. In some cases, experimental moviemakers start a production without any script—making things up as they go along. However, it is probably best to spend some time developing a script before attempting to produce a movie, even a very short one.

Once the script is written, the next step is to gather the necessary resources to make it into a movie. This includes things like casting (selecting the actors), finding locations for scenes in the movie, creating any additional scenery, gathering costumes and props, putting together a crew, making sure you have the right equipment, preparing any special effects, dealing with any legal issues, budgeting the project, and scheduling production. Often, the script is shaped to fit the available resources. For example, students making a two-minute movie as a project for a drama class would likely use easily accessible locations, rather than spending hundreds of thousands of dollars on a travel budget or for extensive scenery.

Making animated films is a little different from making live-action movies, mainly because artists create the characters, costumes, props, and scenery. However, there is still a lot of work to do before the movie can be recorded. As an Alice moviemaker, you will pick your characters (complete with costumes), props, and scenery from a gallery. You can shape your script to fit the characters in the gallery and the programming techniques that you know how to use to animate those characters.

A full discussion of planning a movie would be a whole book in itself, so here we will just take a brief look at some of the more important elements of making a movie.

Movie Types

Most movies fit into one of several types, and the type a moviemaker chooses will determine a lot about the structure of the movie. The most important thing about the type of a movie is whether the work is a screenplay or a documentary.

A **screenplay** is the video equivalent of a play in a theatre. A screenplay unfolds over a series of scenes, and the plot determines the structure of the story. It could be fictional, or it could tell a true story. The most common arrangement for a screenplay is a three-act structure. Even short movies can fit the three-act format. Each **act** is a dramatic component of the story. In the first act, the characters and story are introduced to the audience. Usually there is a hero (or set of heroes), called the protagonist, who has an objective in mind.

At the end of the first act or near the beginning of the second act a problem is introduced, in the form of an obstacle or a villain, called the antagonist. As the second act progresses, the hero moves toward solving the problem and reaching his or her objective, but usually by the end of the second act something has gone wrong and the hero is in trouble.

The third act is the conclusion in which the trouble is resolved. As a moviemaker, you need to decide if you want your story to have a happy ending. Many stories, whether three-act screenplays or five-act theatrical dramas, do have happy endings, but some very good stories, such as Shakespeare's *Hamlet* or Eric Segal's *Love Story,* do not. In any case, the final act brings the story to a close.

A **documentary** is an expository movie, which either teaches a lesson, or presents someone's opinion on an issue. Some documentaries, such as Michael Moore's *Roger & Me,* are done in the form of a screenplay, but most are more like the structure of a simple five-paragraph essay. The first "paragraph" is a thesis, which states what you intend to teach, or your position on an issue. The second, third, and fourth paragraphs each provide more detailed information about what you intend to teach, or evidence for your position. The fifth paragraph is the conclusion, which ties everything together and wraps up the documentary.

Figure 9-5 shows the structure of a three-act screenplay and the structure of an essay-like documentary side-by-side. For our purposes, this is a simplification of the complex structures of many movies, but even most complex movies fit one of these two general patterns fairly well.

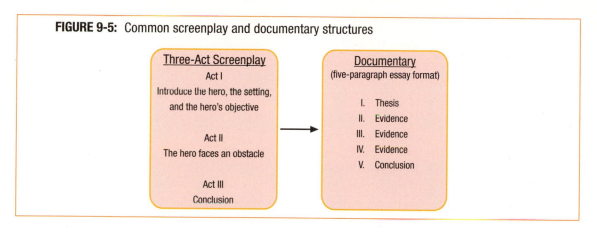

FIGURE 9-5: Common screenplay and documentary structures

Some shorter movies are simply a **slice-of-life vignette**, showing an everyday event, such as a boy riding by on a bicycle, or a flock of geese flying overhead. Slice-of-life vignettes might tell a story, but they also may just be intended to show the subject in action. The purpose of a vignette might be to show the viewer something about the subject, or to demonstrate that the moviemaker has mastered some new moviemaking techniques or technology, as Edison and the Lumiere brothers did.

Shorter movies may also be a **comedy sketch**—the visual equivalent of telling a joke—like a skit that Boy Scouts or Girl Scouts might act out around a campfire. A short movie could also be a **commercial advertisement**, which attempts to convince someone about the merits of a particular product or service, or to expose them to something in a positive way that they will remember.

To summarize, common movie types include screenplays, documentaries, slice-of-life vignettes, comedy sketches, and commercial advertisements. When making a movie, you need to decide which of these types best fits the purpose of your movie.

Movie Topics

At first glance, the idea of a topic seems pretty simple: what is your movie about? Is it a screenplay about a particular person or an incident in a person's life? Is it a documentary about how to do something? Is it an essay telling you why the moviemaker thinks you should do something, such as voting for a particular candidate?

Movie topics can be simple elements of everyday life, or they can be complex ideas deeply rooted in the cultural traditions of a society. It's really up to you as a moviemaker to decide what your movie will be about, but one thing is certain, before you start making a movie, you should have a topic and know your topic well. Many novice writers are told to *write what you know*. The same is good advice for novice moviemakers: make movies about things that you understand.

Outlining the Plot: Scenes, Shots, and Storyboarding

Once you determine the type and topic for your movie, then you can develop an overall structure for the plot. The **plot** is the storyline or plan for the dramatic flow of the movie. It is tied to the visual flow of the movie—how the movie progresses from scene to scene. Before actually writing a complete script you can start by outlining the main ideas for your plot. How does the movie open? What action comes first? What comes after that, and so on, and finally, how are things wrapped up?

A **scene** is part of a movie that takes place in a single location at a particular time. A movie is a sequence of scenes, and the scene outline for a movie should describe the location, characters, and action for each scene. The 1939 film *Gone with the Wind,* for example, has 67 scenes that take place in about 20 different locations. (Links to a description of the plot and an outline of the scenes in *Gone with the Wind* are at the *History in Film* Web site, online at: *www.historyinfilm.com/gwtw/index.htm.*)

Each scene is a collection of shots. A **shot** is a particular view of the action from a specific camera, set up in a specific way. A **shot list** is a list of the shots needed for each scene, describing the kind of shot, the characters involved, roughly what happens in the shot, and the length of time the shot stays on the screen. See Figure 9-6. Other details, such as lighting and special effects, could also be included.

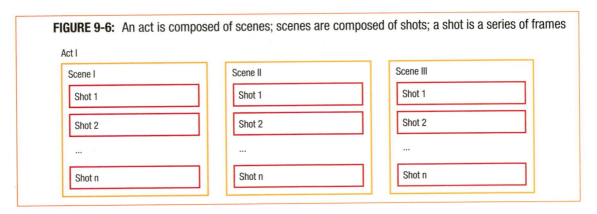

FIGURE 9-6: An act is composed of scenes; scenes are composed of shots; a shot is a series of frames

There are many characteristics of shots, such as the distance from the camera to the subject of the shot, the angle of the camera, how the subject is lit, what colors predominate, and so on. Many different kinds of shots are used to make movies, but here are some of the most common, described in terms of the subject's apparent distance from the camera, and the camera angle:

- Wide shot: a shot that shows a broad view of a scene from a distance
- Long shot: a shot of a person, object, or action from a long way away, focusing on the subject in an overall context

- Close-up: a tightly framed shot showing the details of a subject, such as an image of a person's face

- Extreme close-up: a close-up showing a very close or intimate view of a subject, which can sometimes be uncomfortable; it is often used for emotional impact.

- Two-shot: a shot that shows two people together, usually talking or interacting with one another

- Head and shoulders shot: a shot showing the head and shoulders of a person, usually someone speaking or reacting to something

- Point-of-view (POV) shot: a shot taken from the point of view of a subject showing what the subject sees

- Low-angle shot: a shot looking up at a subject from a position below most people's normal line of sight; it can make the subject seem more powerful or threatening. In the movie *Star Wars*, for example, Darth Vader is often shown from a low-angle shot.

- Aerial shot: a long shot of a subject seen from well above the subject, often from directly above the subject; aerial shots and very high-angle shots are sometimes called *bird's-eye view* shots.

- Three-quarter shot: a shot that shows a subject from an angle rather than straight on; three-quarter shots usually seem more natural than head-on shots, which can seem staged.

- Over-the-shoulder shot: a shot taken from behind the head and shoulders of a person, showing that person's head and shoulders in part of the frame and the subject the person is looking at in the rest of the frame

- Profile shot: a shot showing the subject directly from the side; profile shots often don't work well, but some advanced moviemakers can use them to great effect.

- Zoom-in and Zoom-out shots: shots in which the camera appears to move closer to the subject or farther away from a subject; many live-action cameras can zoom without moving. In Alice, this is most often done by actually moving the camera, although the camera's *lens angle* property can be used to create a zoom effect. The speed of a zoom can be adjusted for dramatic effect. Many professional moviemakers criticize novices for overusing zoom effects.

- Moving shot: a shot taken by a camera that is moving; early films rarely used moving shots, but today they are common.

- Following shot: a shot taken by a camera that is following a moving subject; in Alice this can be achieved by making the subject a *vehicle* for the camera.

NOTE □ □ □ Lighting can be an important aspect of a camera shot, but it is not covered in this chapter because it is a more advanced skill that takes time to learn. Beginning filmmakers should simply make sure that their subjects are well lit so they can be seen clearly, which should not be a problem in Alice virtual worlds. If necessary, additional lights can be added to an Alice world from the Lights folder in the Alice local object gallery. Exercise 9-6 deals with lighting.

Storyboards can help describe the shots in a movie as well as its plot. A **storyboard** is a collection of rough sketches of particular shots showing both the visual flow of the movie from scene to scene and the progression of the movie's plot. They are called storyboards because the sketches for the shots in a single scene are usually pasted on a single large board so they can be viewed together. Many people find storyboards very helpful in preproduction and production. Storyboards can be an important tool in developing a movie. See Figure 9-7.

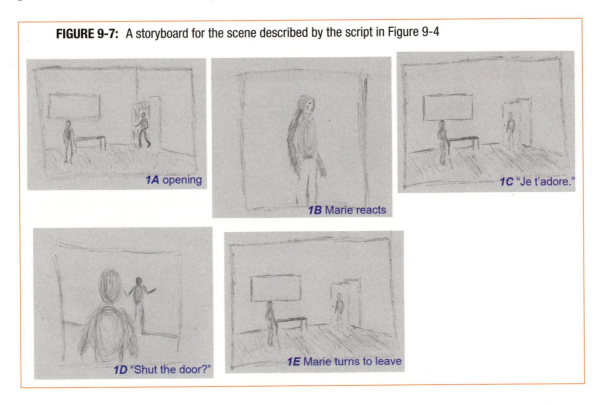

FIGURE 9-7: A storyboard for the scene described by the script in Figure 9-4

1A opening

1B Marie reacts

1C "Je t'adore."

1D "Shut the door?"

1E Marie turns to leave

Even in today's modern world of technology, storyboards are still often drawn by hand. Yet, you do not need to be a great artist to draw a storyboard; each image in a storyboard is just a rough sketch of what a particular shot should look like.

The tools for describing a movie—plot and scene outlines, storyboards, scripts, and shot lists—are often developed together in preproduction. More visually oriented people may prefer to start with a storyboard, while more verbally oriented people might start by writing a script, but eventually all of these tools together will serve as the documentation to define the movie for the production staff.

TUTORIAL 9B—STORYBOARDING

In this tutorial, you will develop a storyboard and shot list for an existing video before you try to plan a new video with these techniques. In this case, you will develop a storyboard and shot list for Alice's *lakeSkater* example world.

You can do this by yourself, or by working with others. Most video projects are developed by a team, and this exercise works quite well with a group of two to four people.

To document the *lakeSkater* world with a storyboard and shot list:

1. Prepare for the exercise by getting lined paper for note taking, blank paper for sketching, and pens or pencils for writing and sketching. Pencils usually work best for sketching.

2. If you are working in a team, decide who will take which roles for this exercise—you will need someone to create the shot list, someone to sketch the shots, someone to work the buttons, and someone to direct the exercise. The director will decide when to stop, pause, and restart the action, and he or she will coordinate everyone else's work. You don't need to say "*cut*" and "*action*," but the director should call the shots and should be clearly understood by the person pushing the buttons. It is important in a team for the director to listen to the team members, and for the team members to respect the director's decisions so that things run smoothly. Of course, if you are working by yourself you will fill all the roles.

3. Find and play the **lakeSkater** movie file **lakeSkater.mov** that you saved in Tutorial 9A, or copy it from the student data files for this book. The movie file works better for this exercise than the Alice world because you can stop, start, and rewind the movie file more easily.

4. Play the movie, and then practice pausing, rewinding, and starting the movie to freeze the screen when a shot changes. For our purposes here, a shot changes when the camera position changes, not when the skater moves into a different position. You are trying to document the different shots in the movie, not the details of the skater's routine.

5. When you are ready, play the world, pausing when the shot changes. Each time you pause, you should make a rough sketch of the shot, and make an

entry in the shot list describing the kind of shot, the characters, roughly what happens in the shot, and the length of time the shot stays on the screen.

6. Compare your sketches and shot list to those in the file **lakeSkaterShots.docx** that comes with the student data files for this book. It is a Word document that integrates a storyboard and shot list for the movie.

CAMERA PLACEMENT AND SHOT TRANSITIONS

Camera placement in Alice is different from the real world for two reasons: first, in Alice, the moviemaker programs the camera to move, and second, Alice only has one camera. However, as you will discover while completing the next tutorial, it's not that hard to manipulate the camera to simulate multiple cameras capturing a scene.

Alice uses dummy objects to mark spots in an Alice world. A **dummy object** is an invisible object that occupies a single point in an Alice world. Alice has commands to drop a dummy where a camera is, and to drop a dummy where an object is. An Alice moviemaker can play around with camera angles and placement within a scene using dummy objects to mark key spots, and then program the camera to move to those spots as a scene progresses. You will do so in the following tutorials.

Dummy objects can also be used to set marks for where objects should be in a scene, similar to the way movie directors set marks for actors and props in a scene. Exercise 9-8 at the end of this chapter deals with this process, called *blocking*.

You can use many different effects when transitioning from shot to shot. In the upcoming tutorials you will use simple jump cuts for shot transitions. A **jump cut**, sometimes called simply a cut, is a sudden transition from one shot to another. The last frame of one shot is followed immediately by the first frame of the following shot, without any transition effects. A jump cut is the most sudden and most commonly used transition from one shot to another.

A video **fade** occurs when the viewer's image lightens or darkens to or from a solid color. For example, a script may contain the direction *slow fade to black* at the end of a scene, meaning that the image the viewer sees would slowly fade to black, as if someone were turning down the lights on a scene. Fades can be to or from any color, but black is the most common, followed by white. A transition from one shot to another could also *fade through black*, with one scene fading to black and the next then fading from black.

A **wipe** occurs when a still image or another shot moves to cover the current shot like a curtain coming down. Wipes can occur from any direction. A curtain coming down would be a *wipe from above*, for example. Exercise 9-9 at the end of this chapter deals with fades and wipes.

TUTORIAL 9C—SIMULATING MULTIPLE CAMERAS

In this tutorial, you will take the role of a director who must place cameras for recording a scene that has already been prepared. You will start with a script, a storyboard, and an Alice world that follows that script, but which is seen by a single fixed camera. Your task will be to simulate multiple cameras to record the scene as shown in the storyboards. In this tutorial, you will complete a short exercise to simulate multiple cameras.

The secret to simulating multiple cameras in Alice is to move the camera using a duration of zero seconds for the move. This will look like a jump cut in a movie. However, you can't just move the camera—you need to move and aim the camera. Each Alice object has a **point of view**—a property marking the object's location and orientation. Setting a camera's point of view to that of another object will move and reorient the camera. So, you can best simulate multiple cameras by setting the camera's point of view to that of another object with a duration of 0 seconds for the instruction. In this part of the tutorial, you will move preplaced dummy objects to change the camera's point of view, simulating a director switching from one camera to another.

To use dummy objects to simulate multiple cameras:

1. Open the Alice world **wonderland** that comes with the student data files for this book.
2. Play the world and watch what happens. Notice that the entire world is a single shot from a high angle. The scene is complete when Alice says "Oh dear!"
3. Click the **plus sign** next to Dummy Objects in the Object tree, and you will see that there are three dummy objects: first position, second position, and opening position, as shown in Figure 9-8. If necessary, scroll down in the Object tree window to see them. The three dummy objects have been arranged to mark positions and points of view for the camera so you can turn this single-shot scene into a three-shot scene.

FIGURE 9-8: Dummy objects in the Object tree

4. Select the **camera tile** in the Object tree, and then the **methods** tab in the Details area. Drag a **camera set point of view to** method tile from the methods tab and drop it in `World.my first method` as the first instruction, above the *Wait 2 seconds* tile.

5. From the menu that appears, select **Dummy Objects**, and then **opening position** as the target object.

6. Select **more...** in the newly placed *camera set point of view* instruction tile, and set the duration to **0 seconds**.

7. Drag the new **camera set point of view to** instruction tile and drop it on the Clipboard to make a copy of it; then drag the tile from the Clipboard and drop it in `World.my first method` after the *Wait 2 seconds* instruction tile.

8. Change the target parameter for this copy of the instruction to **first position**.

9. Drag another copy of the **camera set point of view to** instruction tile from the Clipboard, and drop it in `World.my first method` after *cheshireCat say Touch the yellow flower*.

10. Change the target parameter for this copy of the instruction to **second position**. `World.my first method` should now look like Figure 9-9, which indicates where the three *camera set point of view* instruction tiles should be.

FIGURE 9-9: Code for `world.my first method` showing the camera moves

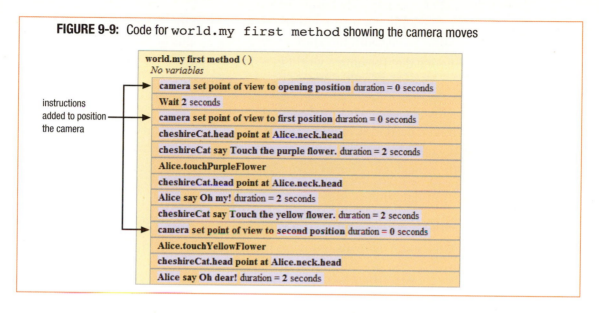

instructions
added to position
the camera

```
world.my first method ( )
  No variables
    camera set point of view to opening position duration = 0 seconds
    Wait 2 seconds
    camera set point of view to first position duration = 0 seconds
    cheshireCat.head point at Alice.neck.head
    cheshireCat say Touch the purple flower. duration = 2 seconds
    Alice.touchPurpleFlower
    cheshireCat.head point at Alice.neck.head
    Alice say Oh my! duration = 2 seconds
    cheshireCat say Touch the yellow flower. duration = 2 seconds
    camera set point of view to second position duration = 0 seconds
    Alice.touchYellowFlower
    cheshireCat.head point at Alice.neck.head
    Alice say Oh dear! duration = 2 seconds
```

11. Save the world with the name **Wonderland revised**, and then play the world to see the difference the new instructions make. You should notice that there are now two jump cuts, and that the scene now is composed of three shots instead of one—the high-angle opening shot, a two shot of the Cheshire Cat and Alice, followed by a high-angle medium shot. It looks as if the scene is being recorded by more than one camera.

12. Save the world as a movie file with the name **Magic Flowers** by using the **Export Video** option on the File menu.

TUTORIAL 9D—RECORDING CAMERA POSITIONS FOR A MULTI-SHOT SCENE

In this tutorial, you will line up camera locations for the shots in a scene according to what's shown in a storyboard, and then use dummy objects to record the camera positions. You will actually record the camera's point of view, which includes location and orientation, and then position the camera in the recorded points of view as the world plays.

The script in Figure 9-4 describes a scene to be recorded as a part of a movie. The scene is an interaction between two characters, *Marie* and *Joe Cool*. The storyboard in Figure 9-7 describes the shots that will be used for the scene. The scene has been prepared as the Alice world *Shut the Door*, but you must line up the camera locations to match the shots described in the storyboard.

1. After reviewing the script and storyboard, open the Alice world **Shut the Door** that comes with the student data files for this book. Play the world, and notice that the entire world is a single shot.

2. Save the world with the name **Shut the Door complete.**

The storyboard shows that the camera's initial point of view will be used in three of the shots—1A, 1C, and 1E. You need to save the camera's initial point of view before manipulating the camera to set up the other shots. This can be done by dropping a dummy at the camera location, and then setting the dummy object's point of view to match that of the camera.

To record the camera's initial point of view:

1. Click the green **ADD OBJECTS** button to enter Alice's Scene Editor mode.

2. Click the **more controls** button to the right of the World window. Advanced controls will appear as shown in Figure 9-10.

FIGURE 9-10: Advanced controls in Scene Editor mode

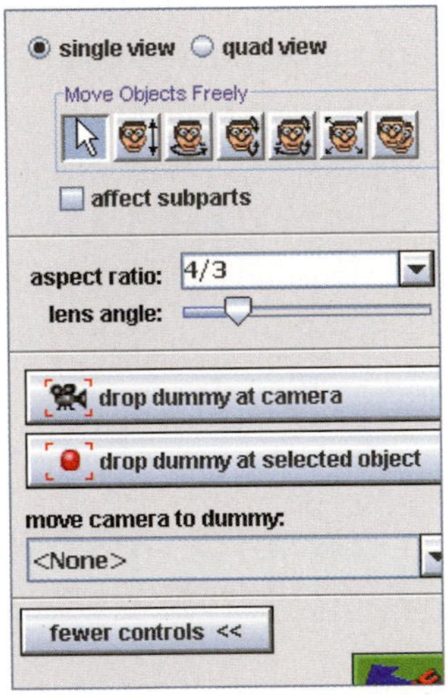

● single view ○ quad view	
Move Objects Freely	
affect subparts	
aspect ratio: 4/3	
lens angle:	
🎥 drop dummy at camera	
🔴 drop dummy at selected object	
move camera to dummy:	
<None>	
fewer controls <<	

NOTE Notice in Figure 9-10 that the aspect ratio of the Alice world window can be changed using the advanced controls in Alice's Scene Editor mode. The **aspect ratio** is the ratio of an image's width to its height. Ratios in Alice include 4/3 (1.33), 1.85, and 2.35. The 4/3 ratio is the standard television ratio, while the other two are wider cinema formats. An Alice world is recorded as video using the aspect ratio set for the World window at the time of recording.

3. Click the **drop dummy at camera** button. A *Dummy Objects* tile will appear in the Object tree.

4. Click the **plus sign** next to the *Dummy Objects* tile and a tile for the dummy object named *dummy* will appear, as shown in Figure 9-11.

FIGURE 9-11: A new dummy object appears in the Object tree as *dummy*

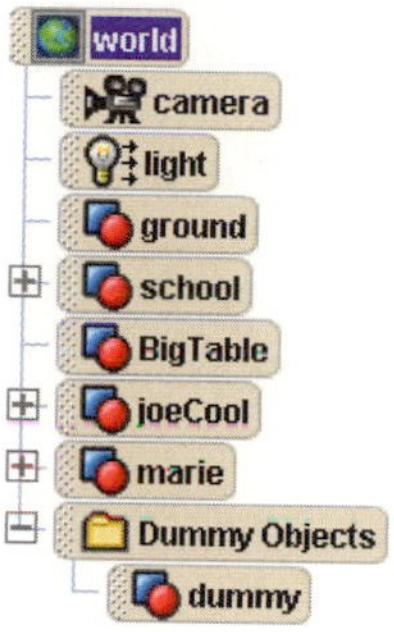

5. Right-click the **dummy** tile, and rename the object **opening**.
6. Right-click the **opening** tile again, and then select **methods**, **opening set point of view to**, and **camera** from the menus that appear.
7. Save the world again before continuing.

The opening point of view of the camera is now recorded. Next, you will line up and record the camera's point of view for the second shot, which according to the storyboard is a three-quarter shot of Marie reacting to Joe Cool's greeting.

To record the camera's second point of view:

1. Using the **blue camera control arrows** below the World window, manipulate the camera until a shot is lined up similar to the one shown in shot 1B in the storyboard in Figure 9-7. Notice that when you line up the shot, Marie will be in position, but will still be facing the back of the room, not Joe Cool.
2. Click the **drop dummy at camera** button. A new dummy object will appear in the Object tree.
3. Right-click the **dummy** tile and rename the object **marieThreeQuarters**.
4. Right-click the **marieThreeQuarters** tile again, and then select **methods**, **marieThreeQuarters set point of view to**, and **camera** from the menus that appear.
5. Save the world again before continuing.

The second point of view of the camera is now recorded. The point of view for the third shot will be the same as for the opening, but the fourth shot will be an over-the-shoulder shot showing Marie from behind Joe Cool. Joe Cool is currently out of the room, behind the door. An examination of the code for the *Shut the Door* world would show that Joe Cool will move three meters forward when he enters, so you will move Joe Cool three meters forward, line up the shot, and then move him backward three meters to his original position.

To line up and record the point of view for the fourth shot:

1. Right-click the **joeCool** tile in the Object tree, and then select **methods, JoeCool move**, and **forward** from the menus that appear. Set the distance for the move to **3 meters**.

2. Using the **blue camera control arrows** below the World window, manipulate the camera until a shot is lined up with the camera behind Joe Cool, similar to that shown in shot 1D in the storyboard in Figure 9-7.

3. Click the **drop dummy at camera** button. A new dummy object will appear in the Object tree.

4. Right-click the **dummy** tile and rename the object **behindJoe**.

5. Right-click the **behindJoe** tile again, and then select **methods, behindJoe set point of view to**, and **camera** from the menus that appear.

6. Right-click the **joeCool** tile in the Object tree, and then select **methods, JoeCool move**, and **backward** from the menus that appear. Set the distance for the move to **3 meters**.

7. Save the world again before continuing.

Now all three camera points of view are saved, so you can add instructions to World.my first method to position the camera for each of the five shots. The transitions between shots will be simple jump cuts, similar to those in the previous tutorial.

To add instructions to move the camera while the world is playing:

1. Click the green **DONE** button to exit Scene Editor mode.

2. Select the **camera** tile in the Object tree, and then the **methods** tab in the Details area. Drag a **camera set point of view to** instruction tile from the methods tab and drop it in World.my first method as the first instruction, above the *marie.stand* tile.

3. From menu that appears, select **Dummy Objects**, and then **opening** as the target object.

4. Select **more...** in the *camera set point of view* instruction tile and set the **duration** to 0 seconds.

5. Drag the **camera set point of view to** instruction tile and drop it on the Clipboard; then drag the tile from the Clipboard and drop it in `World.my first method` above the *marie.no* instruction tile. Change the instruction tile's target to **marieThreeQuarters**.

6. Drag another **camera set point of view** instruction tile from the Clipboard and drop it in `World.my first method` above the *joeCool say Je t'dore* instruction tile; leave its target as **opening**.

7. In a similar manner, insert a fourth **camera set point of view** tile immediately below the *joeCool say Je t'dore* instruction tile with **behind.Joe** as the target, and then a fifth **camera set point of view** tile immediately below the *Marie Shut the Door?* instruction tile with **opening** as the target. Figure 9-12 shows these last three *camera set point of view* instruction tiles in place.

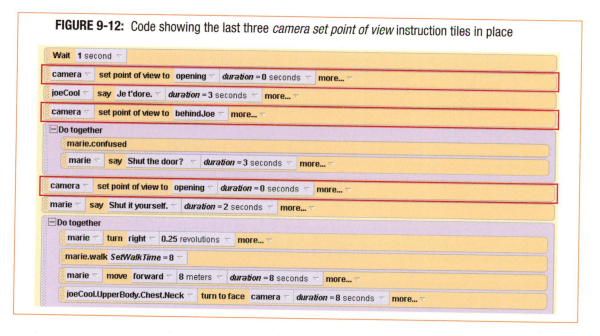

FIGURE 9-12: Code showing the last three *camera set point of view* instruction tiles in place

8. Save the world before continuing.

The world is now ready. It is not necessary to realign the camera before beginning because the first instruction in `World.my first method` will do so. Play the worlds, and you should see the five shots as in the storyboard.

POSTPRODUCTION

The postproduction process includes editing recorded scenes to form a complete movie, adding titles to the movie, refining the movie's soundtrack, making a master copy of the movie, and preparing it for distribution. This chapter will not cover most of the postproduction process; however, the following is a list of postproduction tips you should keep in mind when creating a movie in Alice:

- Alice movies can either stand on their own as complete movies, or they can be edited using video-editing or moviemaking software. Alice movie files can be imported into most common video-editing software, such as Adobe Premiere, Windows Live Movie Maker, or Apple's iMovie, for postproduction work. You can download Windows Live Movie Maker for free from Microsoft at *http://windowslive.com/desktop/moviemaker.*

- Titles and sound can be added to your movie using video-editing software, or from within Alice, using some of the techniques described in Chapter 6.

- The movie files that Alice outputs are QuickTime movie files. Sometimes Windows Media Player has trouble playing QuickTime files. You can view the movies using the QuickTime viewer, which can be downloaded for free from Apple at *www.apple.com/quicktime/download.*

- Uploading your movie files to social networking and media sharing sites, such as YouTube, might be easier if you first convert them to Adobe's Flash movie format (*.flv*). This can be done with Flash, or with many other free movie file conversion programs available on the Web. Simply use a search engine, such as Google, to look for "free *.mov* to *.flv*" software. Most conversion programs are easy to use. The directions for uploading movies to social networking and media sharing sites vary from one site to another, but are generally easy to follow.

- The file size for an Alice movie depends on the length of the movie and the size of the World window when the movie is recorded as video. If your file is too large, try shrinking the World window by clicking and dragging its perimeter and then recording it again.

Chapter Summary

This chapter consisted of a discussion of the technical nature and history of movies, the moviemaking process, camera placement and shot transitions during production, and a brief look at postproduction, followed by four hands-on tutorials involving making movies with Alice.

The discussions in the chapter included:

- ☐ A movie is a flat two-dimensional picture that moves. When we view a movie we are watching a rapidly changing series of still pictures that creates the illusion that something is moving.

- ☐ Each of the still images in a movie is called a frame, and the number of frames per second (fps) in a movie is called the frame rate. The frame rate for films is 24 fps, while the frame for broadcast television is roughly 30 fps. Alice renders and saves each frame when it exports a movie into the QuickTime movie file format.

- ☐ The motion picture film industry began with pioneers like the Lumiere Brothers in France and Thomas Edison in the United States in the late nineteenth century. Film-based movie recording is largely a thing of the past, due to the rise of digital moviemaking.

- ☐ The moviemaking process has three phases: preproduction, production, and postproduction. Production is the heart of the moviemaking process, the actual recording of the movie when cameras are set up and rolling and action is recorded. Preproduction encompasses all of the planning and preparation that is necessary before production can begin. Postproduction includes all of the tasks required after a movie is recorded, such as editing, adding titles, and packaging the final product.

- ☐ The production phase for an animated movie includes creating the animations and recording them. Today most animations are computer generated imagery (CGI). Many traditional movies often include some CGI. Alice movies are produced entirely in CGI.

- ☐ Common movie types include screenplays, documentaries, slice-of-life vignettes, comedy sketches, and commercial advertisements. Many screenplays follow a three-act format. A documentary is an expository movie that teaches a lesson or presents an opinion, much like an essay, with a thesis, points of evidence, and a conclusion. Documentaries can also be used as teaching tools.

- ☐ The primary design document for a movie is called a script, which is a scene-by-scene description of the movie with dialog and descriptions of the critical action.

- ☐ A shot is a particular view of the action in a movie from a specific camera set up in a specific way. A shot list is a list of the shots needed for each scene, describing the kind of shot, the characters involved, roughly what happens in the shot, and the length of time the shot stays on the screen. Other details, such as lighting and special effects, could also be included.

❑ A storyboard is a collection of rough sketches of particular shots showing both the visual flow of the movie from scene to scene and the progression of the movie's plot.

❑ Many different kinds of shots are used to make movies. The most common were described in terms of the subject's apparent distance from the camera and the camera angle.

In Tutorial 9A, you reviewed the process of recording a movie from an Alice world.

In Tutorial 9B, you created a storyboard for an existing movie.

In Tutorial 9C, you learned to simulate multiple cameras in an Alice world, using dummy objects and jump cuts.

In Tutorial 9D, you learned to line up and record camera positions using dummy objects, and then program the camera's point of view using the dummy objects as the camera is recording.

A brief discussion at the end of the chapter summarized some tips for postproduction.

Review Questions

1. Define each of the following:

❑ act	❑ frame rate	❑ screenplay
❑ aspect ratio	❑ jump cut	❑ script
❑ CGI	❑ movie	❑ shot
❑ comedy sketch	❑ plot	❑ shot list
❑ commercial advertisement	❑ point of view property	❑ slice-of-life vignette
❑ documentary	❑ postproduction	❑ storyboard
❑ dummy object	❑ preproduction	❑ wipe
❑ fade	❑ production	
❑ frame	❑ scene	

2. List and describe the three phases in the moviemaking process.

3. How are preproduction and production processes different for animated movies compared to live-action movies?

4. List and describe several commonly used moviemaking design documents.

5. List and briefly describe five common types of movies.

6. How are the terms *act, scene, shot,* and *frame* related to one another?

7. The chapter contains a list of camera shots described in terms of the subject's apparent distance from the camera and the camera angle. Explain which types of shot would be appropriate for each of the following, and why (more than one type of shot may be appropriate for each situation):

   a. Establishing where a character is in relation to the surrounding environment, such as at a football game, or walking through a park

   b. Showing the relative position of two characters as they talk with one another

c. Revealing a person's emotional reaction to bad news

d. Conveying that a powerful character is menacing or threatening

e. Presenting the outfit a person is wearing for a commercial advertisement

8. What is meant by the term *point of view?* How can points of view be recorded and used for camera positions in an Alice world?

9. How can jump cuts from one camera to another be simulated in Alice with a single camera?

10. What movie file format does Alice use to record movies, and what software is best used to view movies of this type? Which format works better for posting movies to social networking and media sharing sites, and how can Alice movie files be converted to this format?

Exercises

1. Create a plot outline, shot list, and storyboard for a scene for an animated version of a short nursery rhyme or children's story, such as *The Three Little Pigs*. Keep in mind the scope of your project and try to keep your scene relatively short, with fewer than a dozen camera shots.

2. Videos of the first short films by Thomas Edison and the Lumiere Brothers are widely available on the Internet. View some of these films and describe how they are different from modern movies. In particular, how does camera placement and shot selection seem to be different from that used in making modern movies?

3. The student data files for this book contain the Alice world *The Letter P*. The world is similar to a scene from the children's television show *Sesame Street*, in which a letter of the alphabet sponsors part of the show. View the world as it is, and then do the following:

a. Develop a shot list for the world that includes multiple camera points of view for multiple shots in the scene instead of a single shot.

b. Modify *The Letter P* world to include the shots you described. Save the finished world as a movie file.

The student data files for this book include a *ballerinas dancing* Alice world, a Japanese *fan dancer* Alice world, and a *toy soldiers marching* Alice world. You will use these worlds for Exercises 4, 5, and 6.

4. Open each of the three worlds mentioned above, view the world, and then create a shot list or storyboard describing how the world could be recorded using three different camera points of view. Explain why you chose the three points of view that you did for each world.

5. Modify one of the three worlds from Exercise 4, using the three camera points of view that you described. Save the finished world as an Alice world and as a movie file.

6. Adjusting the lighting in a scene can create different dramatic effects in a movie. Alice has several different lights in the *lights* folder in the Local Alice Object Gallery. You can darken a scene by adjusting the *ambient light brightness* and *fog* properties of an Alice world. Open one of the three Alice worlds mentioned above, or a version of the world that you modified in Exercise 5. Darken the scene, and then add lights, using them to illuminate different characters as the world plays. Save the file as an Alice world and as a movie file when you are done.

7. The aspect ratio and lens angle for an Alice world can be changed using the advanced Scene Editor controls. Pick an Alice world that you have created or modified and view it with different settings for the aspect ratio and lens angle.

    a. Which looks best for the world you have chosen?
    b. How can you modify the world to make it look better in a wide-angle shot?
    c. What are the advantages and disadvantages of recording a movie in a wider format compared to a 4/3 screen format?
    d. How does changing the lens angle affect what the viewer sees?
    e. How does changing the lens angle compare to moving the camera in and out?

8. Dummy objects in Alice can be used for blocking a scene—marking the positions for object placement and movement, similar to the way dummy objects were used in this chapter for camera positioning. The *move to*, *turn to face*, and *point at* instructions can be used to make objects move in relation to the dummy objects. Create a simple Alice world with two characters who engage in a dialog. Have the characters enter the scene, greet each other, and then have one character tell the other character a joke. Use dummy objects for blocking the scene and for camera placement.

9. Billboard objects, which were discussed in Chapter 6, can be used in Alice to create curtains for fade effects and wipes. An image of a black rectangle, for example, could be used to *fade to black*, or *fade from black*. The opacity property of a billboard can be changed to achieve a fade effect, or a billboard can be moved in front of the camera to achieve a wipe effect. Using a drawing or painting program, create a black rectangle and then use the saved rectangle to do the following:

    a. Add opening and closing *fade from black* and *fade to black* effects to a copy of Alice's *lakeSkater* example world. Save the finished world as a movie file.
    b. Add a wipe effect between two shots in the *Shut the Door complete* Alice world that resulted from Tutorial 9D. A copy of the world is included with the student data files for this book. (*Hint*: This is harder than it appears.) You will need to move the rectangle in front of the camera before changing the camera point of view, and may need a second copy of the rectangle to finish the wipe after the change.

10. Two advanced camera techniques are the *Hitchcock Zoom* and *the Ken Burns Effect*. Using the Internet, find out who Alfred Hitchcock and Ken Burns are, and what these two effects are. Try to create each of these two effects in Alice. (*Hint*: Alfred Hitchcock was a master at manipulating camera properties.)

Video Game Programming

After finishing this chapter, you should be able to:

☐ Provide a brief definition of the following terms: video game, Massive Multiplayer Online Role-Playing Game (MMORPG), game engine, HCI (Human-Computer Interaction), Artificial Intelligence (AI), Application Program Interface (API), graphics engine, physics engine, collision detection, and ballistics

☐ List and describe several common genres of modern video games

☐ Describe at least five different roles, other than programming, in the video game industry

☐ Describe four different roles for computer programmers in the creation of video games

☐ Describe the importance of a physics engine in video games and simulations

☐ Demonstrate the ability to do each of the following in Alice:

   ■ Create a scorekeeping mechanism for a game

   ■ Create a timekeeping mechanism for a game

   ■ Use collision detection in building a simple video game

   ■ Use a physics engine to make an object fly through the air in a simple video game

WHAT IS A VIDEO GAME?

In this chapter, you will explore video game programming, starting with a look at what video games are, then moving on to a discussion of careers in the video game industry. The chapter describes the roles that programmers play in video game development, including some of the features of video games that programmers need to build. The chapter includes hands-on tutorials in Alice that will introduce you to video game programming.

A **video game** is a game played on a video screen, controlled electronically using computer software. It is an interactive combination of hardware and software that allows the user to play a game against another person or against a computer. A few electrical engineers and computer pioneers experimented with games on cathode ray tubes in the 1950s and 1960s, but the first commercial video games from Magnavox and Atari appeared in the 1970s. They were instant hits, and as the personal computer industry grew, so did the video game industry.

Today, millions of copies of the most popular video games sell each year for systems like Nintendo's Wii and Microsoft Xbox. Many more games are available for personal computers, from simple games like minesweeper and solitaire, which come with the Microsoft Windows operating system, to Massive Multiplayer Online Role-Playing Games. A **Massive Multiplayer Online Role-Playing Game (MMORPG)** is played online with hundreds or thousands of people, each playing the role of a character in a virtual environment at the same time. One of the most popular MMORPGs, *World of Warcraft*, has more than 10 million subscribers.

The great variety of video games fit into several different genres. The most popular include:

- Adventure games: An adventure game is a game in which the player is on a quest or adventure to solve a mystery, find a lost object, or complete some other goal that involves exploration and overcoming obstacles. Text-based adventure games such as *Colossal Cave* and *Zork* first appeared in the 1970s. Adventure games with graphics, such as the *Myst* series of games, emerged as the graphics capabilities of computers developed starting in the 1980s. Today, adventure games include features of other games, and have evolved into role-playing games, interactive fiction, and action adventure games.

- Casino games: Traditional casino games like blackjack, poker, and roulette are popular as computer games, especially the Texas Hold 'Em variation of poker.

- Board games: A board game involves moving pieces on a board, which is usually marked with squares. Simple board games like tic-tac-toe, checkers, and chess continue to be among the most commonly played of all games. Many computer versions of these exist, along with more sophisticated board games like *Monopoly* and *Risk*.

- Shooter games: Shooter games require the player to hit a target, as if shooting a gun. *Asteroids* and *Spacewar* were early two-dimensional shooter games that were popular as arcade games and as computer games. First-person shooter games, such as *Doom, Halo,* and *Quake,* place the player in the role of a character in a virtual environment—like an adventure game—in which they shoot as they move through the environment.

- Platform games and maze games: Platform games like *Donkey Kong* and the *Mario Brothers* games require the user to move through a virtual world by climbing and jumping from one platform to another while avoiding obstacles. Maze games are similar but require the player to move through a maze while avoiding obstacles. *Pacman* and its variations are the most popular maze games.

- Role-playing games: In a role-playing game, the player plays the role of a particular character, usually the hero of an adventure. Role-playing games often combine features of many other games.

- Driving and racing games: There are a variety of games in which the player drives a race car, skis down a hill, or is involved in some other form of racing, either against the computer or another player.

- Sports games: Many video games are based on sports, such as baseball, football, and basketball. Some require the player to develop keyboard and mouse skills to play the game, while others are strategy games in which the player plays the role of a coach making decisions.

- Puzzles: Puzzle games require the player to complete a puzzle by either manipulating objects on the screen, or solving a word puzzle. Puzzle games, such as Tetris, can be more fast-paced and more sophisticated than actual physical puzzles.

- Simulations: Real-world environments can be simulated on a computer as the basis of a game. Some, such as *Flight Simulator*, require the player to carry out tasks, such as flying a plane, while others are strategy games. Military strategy and management strategy games, like the *Tycoon* series of games and *SimCity*, are very popular and can take many hours to play. Some simulations are purely for entertainment, while others are intended to teach players real-world skills.

- Music and dance games: Games based on music and dancing, such as *Dance Dance Revolution* and *Guitar Hero,* are among the most popular games for game consoles, such as Wii and PlayStation. In most of these games, the players must perform, either against or with other players.

Many of the most popular games are not limited to a similar genre, but are a combination of two or more, such as an adventure game that is also a shooter game. The characteristics of a good game vary depending on the type of game, but most of the more popular games are fast paced, have different levels of play, and include sophisticated graphics. They are easy to learn to play, but are challenging to the user and, in general, have some sort of intellectual component that occupies the player's mind.

VIDEO GAME CAREERS

Many people are attracted to careers in video game development because they like video games and think it would be fun to build games as a career, but what is it really like to work in the video game industry? In some ways it is similar to the rest of the creative entertainment industries, which include the music and motion picture industries, while in other ways it is more like traditional book publishing—with a software development component. Most commercially successful video games are developed by teams of professionals with specialized skills working on large development projects. Many work for large software and entertainment companies like Electronic Arts, Microsoft, and Nintendo, but some work for small startup companies that might have only one or two very successful games. Industry experts estimate that less than five percent of all professional video game development projects actually make money, largely because of the enormous investment needed to build a commercial quality video game. Employment in the video game industry can be volatile, as many smaller video game companies come and go.

There are always opportunities for talented newcomers who can build video games, but most of the people who make a living in the industry have spent years developing and perfecting their skills. Primary jobs in the video game industry include game design, game development project management, script writing, graphics arts, music and sound engineering, programming, and quality assurance. Secondary support is provided by business managers, office staff, and technical professionals, including computer and network support personnel.

Game Development Project Management

In the video game industry, a producer is in charge of a game development project; this role is similar to the role of a movie producer or a general contractor for a construction project. A video game producer should have a solid business background and excellent management skills, especially the ability to manage a large team of diverse people. Of course, it helps if the person is familiar with video games, but often video game producers are people with similar experience in related industries, such as the film or television industry.

The producer has overall responsibility for the development team and reports to a company's senior management, who may be the owner or representatives of the entity financing the game development project. On a larger project, assistant producers may be in charge of specific areas, such as the sound team or project finances.

Game Design

A game designer is a person who takes a concept or idea for a game and develops it into a plan for the overall play of a game, including the game's general theme, setting or environment, objectives, rules of play, structure, and so on. Game designers are to the video game industry what architects are to the construction industry.

Often a team of designers works together, with one senior person serving as the lead designer who coordinates the work of other designers and associated skilled professionals, such as graphic artists. Many game designers focus on specific aspects of a game. For example, a level designer may develop the levels of play within a game while the interface designer works with graphic artists and human-computer interaction (HCI) programmers to build the game's user interface.

Game designers, especially lead designers, work closely with producers to manage the game development project. Game designers must be aware of constraints imposed by the budget, the technology available, and the skills of the team, and should have an awareness of available resources. Many game designers are programmers or other skilled professionals who developed their design skills while working on previous projects. Others earned specialized college degrees with the specific intent of becoming a game designer.

The job market for game designers is very volatile, with many designers working on a project-by-project basis for different companies.

Script Writing

In many modern video game genres, writers are responsible for developing a script for a game, much like a script for a movie, describing the action or flow of a game, along with dialog for characters in the game. The characters themselves may be developed by game designers and graphic artists working together with a writer.

Writers are also responsible for developing and editing any text that appears in a game, including instructions and help screen text. Some writers specialize in translating game text from one language to another. All writers need to have a cultural awareness of the game's target audience.

Graphics Arts

Graphic artists with special skills, often called *game artists*, create the artwork for a video game. Some fill traditional roles, such as package design, or text layout, while others have special skills for creating three-dimensional objects and characters using tools such as 3D Studio Max and Maya. Many artists specialize in specific game elements, such as characters, vehicles, or natural terrain.

Often one graphic artist with exceptional artistic and management skill serves as a project's art director, coordinating other artists and making sure their work fits the overall artistic vision for the project.

Music and Sound Engineering

Composers, musicians, voice-over artists, and sound engineers all play a role in the development of modern video games, just as they do in the movie industry. The amount of music, and thus the need for people with musical talent, depends on the type of video game.

Often a game company hires outside musical talent to create original music for a video game, but sometimes they use in-house personnel. Sound engineers who are responsible for the recording process and for integrating the recorded sounds into a video game are most likely to be in-house personnel, as are sound engineers who specialize in creating and recording special effects, which are most often computer generated. Often the same person is in charge of sound engineering and special sound effects.

Programming

At its heart, a video game development project is a software development project requiring people with software engineering and programming skills. Often, a lead programmer with good management skills will supervise many people with specialized programming skills working on different aspects of game programming. Many game programmers will use existing software as the basis for their work, including game engines. A **game engine** is a software tool that allows developers to assemble video games from existing objects and methods, much like the way a person can build an Alice world from existing objects and methods. Larger and older companies have their own in-house game engines, but some firms use commercially available general purpose games engines. Game Maker, for example, is an easy-to-use game engine from Yoyo Games, which will host games created with Game Maker on their Web site, *www.yoyogames.com*.

Sophisticated games still require specialized custom programming, and someone needs to build the game engines and other software tools used by game developers. Here is a look at some of the programming specialists who work on video game development:

- Human-Computer Interaction programmers develop the game's user interface. **Human Computer-Interaction (HCI)** is a specialized area of computing dealing with the development of user interface hardware and software. Most video games are developed to run on existing hardware, so HCI hardware engineers are not commonly used on game projects, but HCI programmers are employed to customize existing interface software and develop new interface software for video games. For example, HCI programmers develop software for Nintendo's Wii game system that takes advantage of things like the Wii Wheel, The Wii Balance Board, or the Wii MotionPlus Controller. (See *www.nintendo.com/wii/console/accessories*.)

- Artificial Intelligence programmers develop the logic in a game, especially for strategy games in which a user may play against the computer. **Artificial Intelligence (AI)** is a branch of computer science devoted to developing software that can mimic human intelligence in a computer, especially human perception and decision making.

- Graphics programmers work with graphic artists to create new graphical elements for games and to implement the graphics created by the artists.

- Physics programmers implement software that simulates the movement of objects in the real world, which are affected by things like gravity and the collision of one object with another. Physics programmers generally need to have an understanding of physics as well as advanced math skills.

- Data Communications programmers create and maintain the software used for networked versions of video games, particularly for MMORPGs played over the Internet.

Whatever their specialty, game programmers need to have good general software development skills and a firm knowledge of more advanced programming topics, such as data structures and the mathematics of computer programming. Game programmers often also need specialized knowledge and experience in their particular programming area.

Quality Assurance

Quality assurance specialists in the video game industry are responsible for the overall quality of video games and the correctness of the underlying software. Software quality assurance specialists test video game software under all possible circumstances to make sure that it works properly, testing the overall software and components of the software as they are developed. Software testing typically requires special training—usually a degree in computer science, with courses in software testing and validation.

Video game testers are also employed to examine games for both correctness and playability. They are not only concerned with whether or not a game works properly, but also with how well it works. Is it interesting and fun to play? Will it be a marketable commercial product? What can be done to make the game better?

Most video game testers are people with advanced game playing skills, the ability to recognize which features of a game could be problematic, and the ability to identify and communicate things that could improve the game. Video game testers should have in-depth knowledge of video games and a good understanding of how the potential audience for a video game will react to various aspects of game play.

VIDEO GAME PROGRAMMING FEATURES

There are several features of video games that must be built by programmers or imported into a video game from somewhere else, including a user interface, scorekeeping, artificial intelligence, graphics, and a physics engine. Entire semesters, or even a series of courses, can be spent examining each of these. We will look at each briefly and see how some are implemented in Alice.

A User Interface

A user interface provides controls for a game so that the user can play the game. The most common user interfaces are a command-driven interface and a Graphical User Interface (GUI). With a command-driven interface, users communicate with the computer by giving it individual commands, usually by typing them on a keyboard, similar to the Windows command prompt. Very few video games use a command-driven interface.

As discussed in Chapter 3, GUIs use a computer's graphics capabilities to enable users to communicate with the computer by manipulating what they see on the computer screen. The mouse, the keyboard, or special hardware can be used to pick commands from menus or directly manipulate objects in a game. Windows is an example of a graphical user interface, as are most common video game consoles, such as Microsoft Xbox 360 or Sony's PlayStation 3.

Event-driven programming, which was covered in Chapter 3, is essential for building a GUI. The nature of the interface depends on the type of game being played. In first-person shooter games the user moves a camera or pointer with the mouse or keyboard controls, while in other games, such as a chess game, the keyboard or mouse control game objects that move while the camera stays fixed.

Most programming environments include Application Programmer Interfaces for creating a GUI. An **Application Programmer Interface (API)** is software that provides expanded capabilities for computer programmers. In Java, for example, the Abstract Windowing Toolkit (AWT) and Swing are two APIs that provide programmers with the ability to create their own GUIs for Java programs. GUI events are included in Alice, so no API is needed to build graphical controls in Alice. Some of the Alice events used for building a game interface for an Alice world are shown in Figure 10-1. See Chapter 3 for more details about using Alice events to create keyboard and mouse controls.

FIGURE 10-1: Alice events that can be used to build a game interface

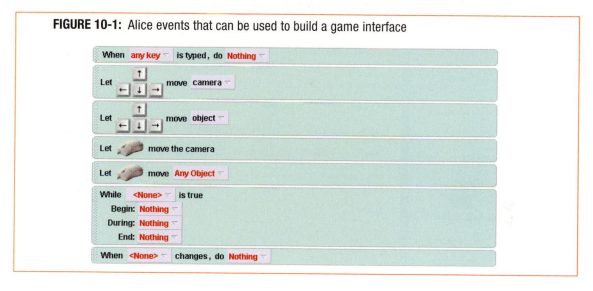

Scorekeeping

Scorekeeping is an important part of most video games, and can be accomplished through the use of simple numeric variables. Someone with basic programming skills should be able to build scorekeeping methods for a game.

In positive scorekeeping, a player accumulates a number of points while playing a game, similar to the way score is kept in basketball or baseball. Typically, the person with the highest number of points wins, although in some games, such as golf, the low score wins. Sometimes, time is used as a scoring mechanism, often with the lowest time winning, such as in a race.

In negative scorekeeping, players start with a certain number of points and lose points as they make errors, or as time goes by. Sometimes both are used together, with positive scorekeeping for things a player accomplishes and negative scorekeeping—usually in the form of penalty points subtracted from the total score—for things a player does wrong.

In Alice, there are two primary ways to keep track of scores—through method variables and through properties of objects. Both can be manipulated by Alice methods and events. Figure 10-2 shows examples of both in an Alice world. Method variables are best used to keep track of the time or points for a person playing a game. Such points are not attached to any object in the game.

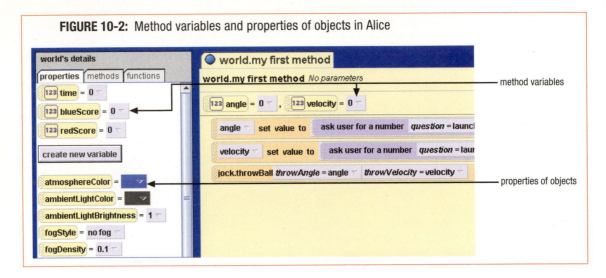

FIGURE 10-2: Method variables and properties of objects in Alice

Properties of objects can be used to keep track of scores associated with objects, such as characters, in a game. They can also be used to keep track of characteristics of an object that could change as a game is played. One technique used in some video games is aging—in which properties of an object are reduced over time, affecting the ability of an object. For example, in a game with a frog who hops, the distance the frog is able to hop could be decreased as the game progresses, simulating the frog growing more tired.

Graphics

Graphics are the visual images that people see when they play a video game. They are the *video* part of video gaming. The graphics for video games vary widely, from the simple two-dimensional block graphics of Nolan Bushnell's *Pong* or the first versions of *Tetris,* to modern role-playing games with three-dimensional graphics that mimic the look of the real world.

Ultimately, the graphics for video games need to be developed using rather sophisticated mathematics, which will be beyond the reach of most people and are the domain of a few highly trained professionals. Many three-dimensional virtual world environments, like Alice or the Sims, for example, use quaternions, which can be described as four-dimensional imaginary numbers that are used to keep track of rigid bodies in three-dimensional space as they move and rotate. Matrix algebra, Euler angles, hyperbolic geometry, fractals, and other advanced math are also used to program graphics for video games and simulations that look like the real physical world in which we live.

Fortunately, experts in these areas have developed graphics engines and APIs, which can be used by people with more ordinary math skills to create video games and simulations. A **graphics engine** is a set of encapsulated software components that perform the necessary math and render objects for video games, simulations, and other software. Graphics engines often provide a software toolkit which includes objects and functions that game developers can use to work with graphics in two-dimensional or three-dimensional environments, without doing all the math.

Graphics APIs allow programmers to include instructions for graphics programming in their software. Two of the most common graphics APIs are OpenGL and DirectX, which interface with the operating system and software built into a computer's graphics hardware to provide a library of graphics commands in various computer programming languages. Java OpenGL or JOGL, for example, is a cross-platform API that provides graphics commands for the Java programming language. It was used in the development of Alice. DirectX is a graphics API from Microsoft for use with the Windows operating system. It includes Microsoft Direct3D, which is the base for all graphics programming on the Microsoft Xbox series of video game consoles.

Users of graphics APIs need to be programmers who have some facility with mathematics, such as a grasp of standard high school level algebra and geometry. However, many video game engines include a graphics engine that provides even more simplified graphics commands than a graphics API, allowing people with very little knowledge of mathematics to create and move objects.

The three-dimensional graphics needed for Alice have all been incorporated into the system, so Alice will handle the graphics when you use commands, such as move or turn, to manipulate objects.

Physics Engines

Rendering objects so that they look like objects in the real world is only part of what is needed for video games and simulations that mimic the real world. The physics of moving objects, including the effects of gravity, friction, objects bumping into one another, wind resistance and fluid dynamics, need to be addressed so that objects will act like objects in the real world. Fortunately, just as graphics programmers have created graphics engines for others to use, physics programmers have created **physics engines** which have objects and methods to address these issues. Physics APIs also exist.

Yet, even when using a physics engine or a gaming engine with a built-in physics engine, keeping track of moving objects and the interactions between them can be rather complicated, especially in 3D virtual worlds. In fact, it can become so complicated that it can take up most of the processing power of a good modern computer. Fortunately, video game programmers don't have to account for every interaction between objects in virtual worlds, just enough to make the game somewhat realistic and believable, especially in video games, which don't need to be as realistic as simulations. Games only need to be entertaining so that people will want to play them, while at least some elements of simulations may need to be very realistic.

Often gaming software only attempts to implement the minimum amount of physics needed for a particular game. Large game development companies have their own libraries of physics routines with just enough physics software for certain games or families of games. Physics engines and APIs for certain types of physics programming are available to the public. For example, Box2d is a popular physics engine for two-dimensional games, while the Nvidia PhysX Software Development Kit, Newton Game Dynamics, and Bullet are all 3D physics engines used by game developers to make their games behave more realistically. Bullet is an open source physics engine used for many gaming platforms including Xbox, Wii, Windows, the iPhone, and others. It has been used for many popular games, including some of the *Grand Theft Auto* games, and to create virtual worlds for Hollywood movies, including several by Disney and Sony.

Alice does not have a built-in physics engine, so you must build your own software for realistic object interaction or get the software from someone else. Two of the simpler things that can be done with physics engines are **collision detection** (detecting when objects in a virtual world collide with one another) and **ballistics** (determining the paths of objects, such as baseballs, as they fly through the air).

The following tutorials explore game programming. In Tutorial 10A, you will learn how to add a scorekeeping mechanism to a video game. Tutorial 10B will show you how to include simple collision detection in a video game. Tutorial 10C allows you to examine ballistics software for throwing a ball though the air.

TUTORIAL 10A—WHERE'S ALICE?

In this tutorial, you will add a scorekeeping mechanism to a video game. Both the scorekeeping mechanism and the game are simple—the game is a guessing game. The scorekeeping mechanism will keep track of the number of guesses.

The game, called *Where's Alice?*, is shown in Figure 10-3. Alice is hiding behind one of three doors. The user must guess which door. However, things are a bit complicated because if the user picks the wrong door, then Alice can move to a different door.

FIGURE 10-3: A scene from the game *Where's Alice?*

Scorekeeping usually involves using a variable to keep track of the user's score and instructions in methods or events to add or subtract points, depending on what happens in the game. Scorekeeping points are related to the object of the game. The object of *Where's Alice?* is to find Alice in as few guesses as possible, so one point will be added each time the user picks a door. At the end of the game, the program will display the number of guesses it took to find Alice.

Some games have more complicated scorekeeping mechanisms, some of which use more than one variable. Some role-playing games and adventure games, for example, have variables for an overall score and additional variables for things such as the strength of a character. As the game progresses, the character's power strengthens or weakens, with the game ending if the character's power drops too low. Points, in this case strength points, are added to or subtracted from the strength variable depending on what happens in the game. In this example, the character would be an object, and strength would be a property of the object, possibly along with other similar properties, such as hunger and health.

In this tutorial, the scorekeeping mechanism is simple, and only one action, picking a door, will add a point to the user's score. You will start by playing the game without a scorekeeping mechanism. Then, you will add scorekeeping, and you can try the game again.

To play *Where's Alice?*:

1. Open the Alice world **where's Alice.a2w** that is included in the student data files for this chapter. Notice that the world contains a billboard with directions for the game, shown in Figure 10-4. Also, notice that this world has a wider window—the window's aspect ratio is 2.35 to 1, which was set using the advanced controls in scene editor mode.

FIGURE 10-4: The directions for *Where's Alice?* as an Alice billboard

2. Play the game a few times to become familiar with how it works.

You may examine the code for the game, if you would like to see how it works. The main method in the game is `world.game`, shown in Figure 10-5.

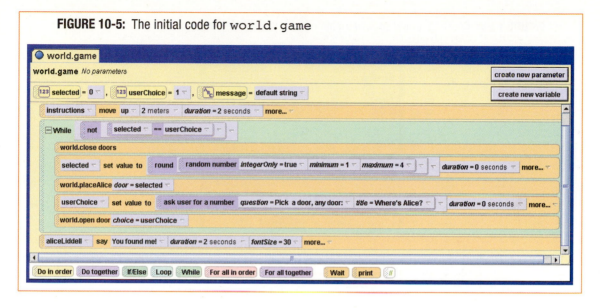

FIGURE 10-5: The initial code for `world.game`

The method first moves the directions for the game off-screen, and then it plays a loop in which the computer picks an integer between 1 and 3, places Alice behind the corresponding door, and then asks the user to guess which door. The loop will repeat as long as the guess and the door that Alice is behind are not the same. When the guess is the same as the correct door, the loop ends and Alice says "You found me!"

After you play the game a few times, you can add scorekeeping to the game. You will add a scorekeeping variable, an instruction to increment the score each time the user guesses, and instructions to build and display a message showing the score at the end of the game.

To add a scorekeeping variable to the game:

1. Click the **create new variable** button on the *world.game* tab in the Editor area.
2. Name the new variable **score**, make sure that **Number** is selected as the variable type, that its initial Value is zero, as shown in Figure 10-6, and then click the **OK** button.

FIGURE 10-6: Creating a new *score* variable with an initial value of zero

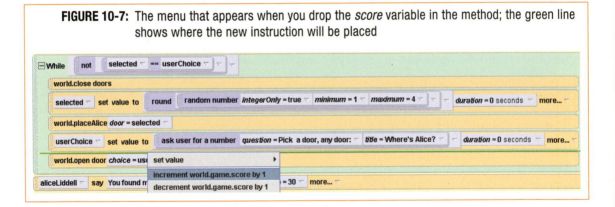

3. Drag a copy of the **score** variable tile from the top of the method and drop it just below *the userChoice...* instruction inside the While loop. A menu will appear, as shown in Figure 10-7.

FIGURE 10-7: The menu that appears when you drop the *score* variable in the method; the green line shows where the new instruction will be placed

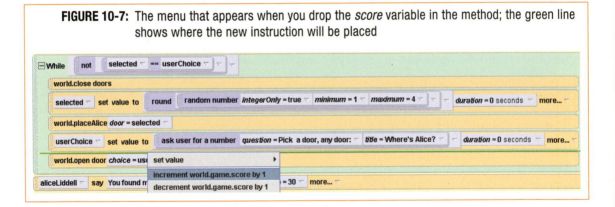

4. Select **increment world.game.score by 1** from the menu. An instruction to increment the score will appear in the method. This is the equivalent of *score = score +1*, or *score++*, from languages like Java or C++.

Now you need to add instructions to build a message to display the score and to show this message. An unused string variable called *message* is already in the method, as you can see in Figure 10-7. You will add an instruction to build the message by concatenating three parts of the message—"It took you " + score + " guesses." To concatenate strings means to put strings together to build a larger string. Alice has a string function *[[A] joined with [B]]* that does this.

To add an instruction to build a scorekeeping message in the game:

1. Drag a copy of the **message** variable tile from the top of the method and drop it in the method as the last instruction in the method, after the *Alice say "You found me!"* instruction. A *set value* menu will appear.

2. Select **set value**, then **other**, and enter **It took you**, with a blank space after *you*, as the string.

3. Next, drag a copy of the **[[A] joined with [B]]** function tile from the world's details tab in the Details area and drop it in the new instruction in place of *[It took you]*. A *b* menu will appear, asking you for the next part of the string.

4. Select **default string** from the menu that appears.

5. Now you will replace the default string with the variable *score*. Drag a copy of the **[[what] as a string]** function tile from the world's details tab and drop it in the new instruction in place of *default string.* A *what* menu will appear, as shown in Figure 10-8.

FIGURE 10-8: The menu that appears when you use the *[[what] as a string]* function to put a numeric value in a string

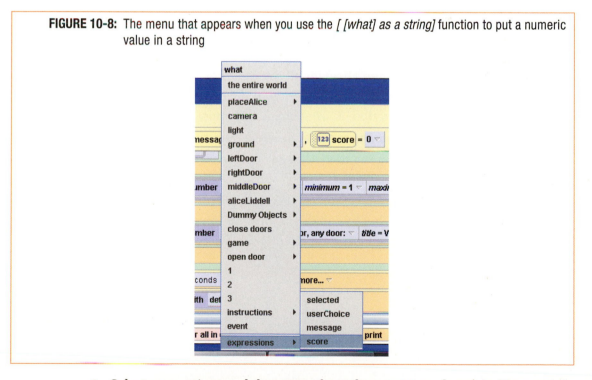

6. Select **expressions** and then **score** from the menus, as shown in Figure 10-8.

7. Drag another copy of the **[[A] joined with [B]]** function tile from the world's details tab and drop this copy in the new instruction in place of the word *joined* in *[[It took you] joined with [score]]*. A *b* menu will appear, asking you for the last part of the string.

8. Select **other** from the menu, then enter **guesses!** as the string. Be sure to include a blank space before the "g" in guesses as well as an exclamation point at the end of the word. The new instruction is complete and should look like the one shown in Figure 10-9.

FIGURE 10-9: The instruction to create the scorekeeping message

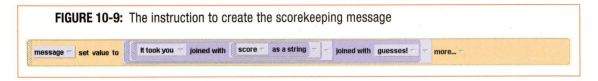

Finally, you will add an instruction to display the score, and then save the new copy of the game. Alice will say the scorekeeping message.

To add an instruction to make Alice say the scorekeeping message:

1. Select the **aliceLiddell** tile in the object tree and the **methods** tab in the Details area.

2. Drag a copy of the **aliceLiddell say** tile from the methods tab and drop it in the method as the last instruction in the method, after the *message set value ...* instruction. A *what* menu will appear.

3. Select **expressions**, and then **message** from the menus that appear.

4. Click **more...** in the new *Alice say [message]* instruction and change the duration to **2 seconds**.

5. The `world.game` method should match Figure 10-10. Save the world as **where's Alice**, but in a different location from the data files for this chapter so that you won't wipe out the original *where's Alice* world.

FIGURE 10-10: The complete `world.game` method for the *Where's Alice?* Game

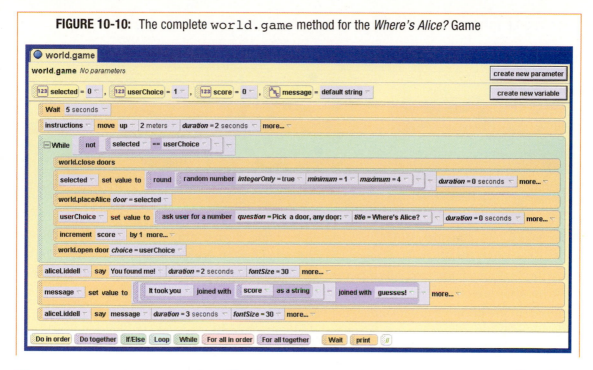

Your new world is now complete. Try the new version of the game a few times and see how scorekeeping makes it more interesting.

TUTORIAL 10B—DON'T SPLASH THE PENGUIN!

In this tutorial, you will create an exciting new video game called *Don't Splash the Penguin!* The game contains an ice skating rink with a penguin at one end and a flag at the other. There are holes in the ice, and the player's goal is to get the penguin to the flag as quickly as possible without falling through the holes in the ice. Figure 10-11 shows the penguin in the starting position, an overhead view of the skating rink full of holes, and the flag the penguin must reach.

FIGURE 10-11: Several views of the Alice world for the *Don't Splash the Penguin!* game

It can take a long time to build a complete video game, even a simple game like this one, so an Alice world with the objects needed for the game has been created and saved with the data files for this chapter as *Splash setup.a2w*. The objects in the world include the frozen lake from the *lakeSkater* demo world, a snowbank around the skating rink on the lake, the penguin, the flagpole, and, of course, the holes in the ice. There are also some hidden objects, including the camera, a directional light attached to the camera to help make the scene more visible, and dummy objects to keep track of camera and object positions. All of these are in the world in their correct starting positions.

The world also contains two Alice billboards—one with a victory message to be displayed when the penguin reaches the flagpole and one with a *game over* message to be displayed if the penguin falls through one of the holes in the ice. These are off camera.

Your main tasks will be to add simple user controls for the penguin and to add collision detection to the world. Both will be implemented using events. The penguin controls are very easy, but the collision detection is a bit more complicated. You will also add code to show the victory or game over billboards at the appropriate times and to display the time it took to reach the flagpole from the start of the game.

You will start by opening the world and exploring it, then you will add user controls for the penguin.

To explore the world:

1. Open the Alice world **Splash setup.a2w** that is included in the student data files for this chapter.
2. Save the world as **penguin splash.a2w.**
3. Notice that the world contains an event to keep the camera pointed at the penguin. This is the only code in the setup world. Play the world and you will see the camera turn to point at the penguin. Later, as you play the game, the camera will stay pointed at the penguin because of this event.

4. Click **Stop** to go back to the Alice interface.

5. Explore the world by using the camera control arrows to move the camera around. You may want to move the camera overhead and tilt it down so that you can see the rink from above. You should also look at the objects in the Object tree and the world's properties tab to see some things that have been added to this world. The two billboards, named splash and victory, are located at the camera, with the camera set as their vehicle, so you will not be able to see them. Look around, but don't change anything in the world.

6. When you are finished exploring the world, you need to put the camera back in its starting position. Right-click the **camera** tile in the Object tree, and then select **methods**, **Camera set point of view to**, and **starting position**, as shown in Figure 10-12.

FIGURE 10-12: Menus for returning the camera to its starting position

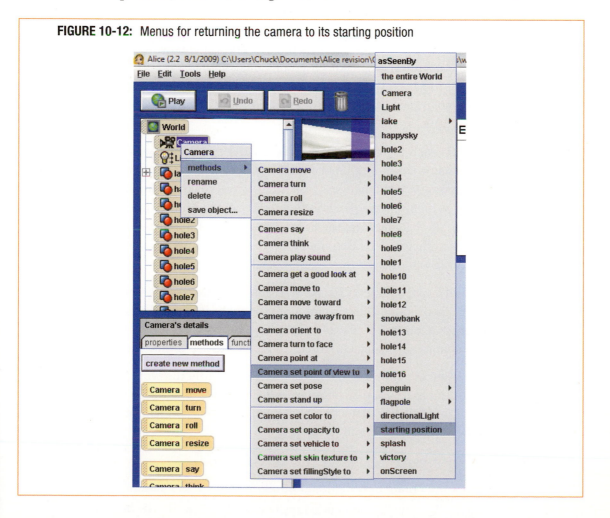

To add user controls to the penguin:

1. Click the **create new event** button in the Events area.
2. Select **Let the arrow keys move <subject>** from the menu that appears.
3. An event will appear that will allow the arrow keys to move the camera. Click the **camera** parameter in this event tile and use the menus that appear to change the parameter to **penguin, the entire penguin.**
4. Save the world before continuing.

Next, you will add collision detection to the world. Collision detection works by checking to see if one object overlaps another in a virtual space, like the world of Alice. This can be very complicated, as you must check each part of each object that is moving to see if it overlaps with any part of any other object. The shapes of objects in a virtual world can be approximated by a collection of geometric shapes, such as circles, rectangles, and triangles on a two-dimensional flat plane, or with spheres, rectangular solids, and cylinders in a three-dimensional world. The mathematics for this are complicated, and collision detection software can be time consuming to create. Often physics engines with built-in collision detection are included in gaming engines. In this case, you will create your own simple collision detection software, checking to see if the penguin hits a hole, hits the snowbank that surrounds the skating rink, or reaches the flagpole.

The holes in the ice are each flat circles, with a radius of 1 meter, on the surface of the ice. Every object in Alice has a point of reference marking its location on the world. For 3D objects that are characters, like the penguin, the point of reference is usually at the center of the base of the object, which, for the penguin, would be on the ground halfway between the penguin's feet. For the circles that form the holes, the point of reference is at the center of the circle. This makes collision detection much easier—you simply need to see if the penguin is within 1 meter (the radius) of the center of each hole.

The holes are stored in a list, which will make it easier to check all of the holes at once using Alice's *for all together* instruction. This is similar to the technique used in sophisticated collision detection engines. Objects are placed in an array or a list, and the collision detection software checks the shapes of the objects stored in the lists to see if they are overlapping.

You are going to build an event that will continuously run while the world is playing, with an event handler method that will react whenever the penguin is within 1 meter of the center of a hole. There it is—collision detection made simple. First you will build the event handler method, and then you will add the event.

To build a collision detection event handler:

1. Click the **create new method** button on the world's methods tab.
2. Name the new method **collisionCheck**, and click the **OK** button.

3. Drag a **For all together** tile from the bottom of the Editor area and drop it into the `collisionCheck` method in place of *Do Nothing.* Select **expressions**, **World.holes** from the menus that appear.

4. Drag an **IF/ELSE** tile from the bottom of the Editor area and drop it into the *For all together* tile in place of *Do Nothing.* Select **true** as the condition.

5. Select the **penguin** tile in the Object tree and the **functions** tab in the penguin's Details area. Drag a copy of the **penguin is within [threshold] of [object]** tile from the functions tab and drop it in the *IF/ELSE* tile in place of the *true* parameter. Select **1 meter**, **expressions**, **item_from_holes**, from the menus that appear, as shown in Figure 10-13.

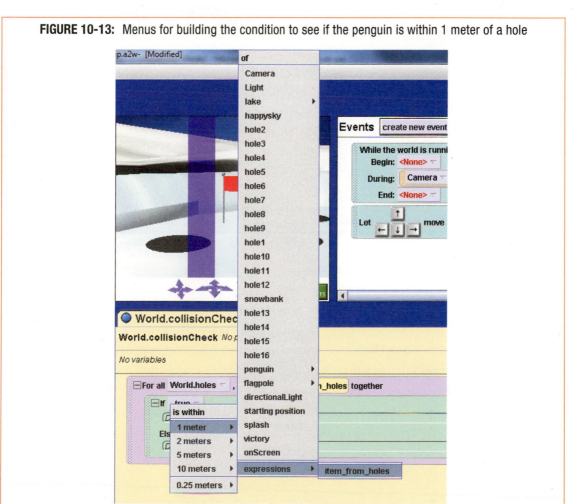

FIGURE 10-13: Menus for building the condition to see if the penguin is within 1 meter of a hole

6. Select the **methods** tab in the penguin's Details area. Drag a copy of the **penguin move** tile and drop it in the *IF/ELSE* tile in place of *Do Nothing*. Select **down** and **5 meters** as the parameters for the move instruction.

7. Select **[more...]** on the *move* instruction tile, and set the duration to **.25 seconds**.

8. Your method should now look like Figure 10-14. Save the world before continuing.

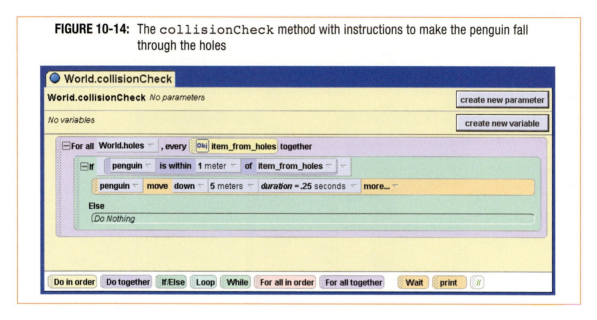

FIGURE 10-14: The `collisionCheck` method with instructions to make the penguin fall through the holes

Next, you will create the event to go with this event handler.

To build a collision detection event:

1. Click the **create new event** button in the Events area.

2. Select **When the world starts** from the menu that appears.

3. Right-click the new **When the world starts** event tile and change it to a **While the world is running** event.

4. Drag the **collisionCheck** method tile from the methods tab in the world's Details area and drop it in the new event in place of the **None** parameter following *During*.

5. Save the world before continuing.

Now the penguin will fall through the holes. Play the world and try it. The arrow keys should control the penguin's movements. Whenever the penguin gets within 1 meter of the center of a hole, it should fall through the ice. However, something is still missing. You need to show the splash billboard with the *game over* message when the penguin falls through a hole.

A dummy object named *onScreen* has been set up in front of the camera. To show the billboard, you simply need to set the billboard's point of view to that of the onScreen object with a duration of zero for the instruction. This will be similar to a jump cut in a movie, as discussed in Chapter 9.

To add code to show the splash billboard:

1. Select the **splash** tile in the Object tree and the **methods** tab in splash's Details area.

2. Drag a **splash set point of view to** tile from the methods tab and drop it into the *IF/ELSE* tile in the `collisionCheck` method just below the *penguin move down* tile. Select **onScreen** from the menu that appears.

3. Click **[more...]** on the *splash set point of view to onScreen* instruction tile and set the duration to **0 seconds**.

4. You will also add a *Wait* instruction to include a delay between the penguin falling through the ice and the end of game message appearing. Drag a **Wait** instruction from the bottom of the editor area and drop it between the *penguin move down* tile and the *[splash] set point of view to [onScreen]* tile in the *IF/ELSE* tile in the `World.collisionCheck` method. Set the duration to **1 second**.

5. Your method should now look like Figure 10-15. Save the world before continuing.

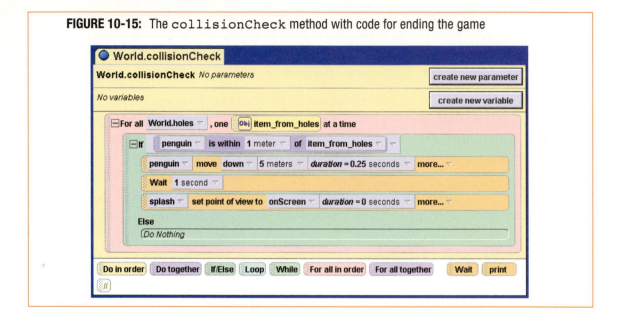

FIGURE 10-15: The collisionCheck method with code for ending the game

Play the world a few times and see what happens when the penguin hits a hole. The collision detection for the holes is now complete, but the penguin can still go through the snowbank around the skating rink, so next you will add collision detection for the snowbank. The perimeter snowbank is actually a doughnut-shaped object called a *torus*. The point of reference for the snowbank object is in the center of the circle formed by the torus, much like the reference point for a circle is in the center of the circle. The snowbank has an inner radius—the distance from the center point to the inside edge of the snowbank, and an outer radius—the distance from the center point to the outside edge of the snowbank. The inner radius is 10.5 meters. This means that if the penguin reaches any point 10.5 meters from the center of the torus-shaped snowbank, it hits the snowbank. You will add code to the collisionCheck method to detect this collision with the snowbank.

Physics engines have software that will react to a collision when it occurs. Objects could bounce off of other objects, break into pieces, and so on. In the case of the penguin hitting a hole in the ice, the penguin falls though the hole. In the case of the penguin hitting the snowbank, you will simply make the penguin move back a quarter meter toward the center of the torus, as if it is bouncing off of the snowbank.

To add snowbank collision to the collision detection event handler:

1. Drag an **IF/ELSE** tile from the bottom of the Editor area and drop it into the collisionCheck method just below the *For all together* tile. Select **true** as the condition.

2. Select the **penguin** tile in the Object tree and the **functions** tab in the penguin's Details area. Drag a copy of the **penguin is at least [threshold] away from [object]** tile from the functions tab and drop it in the new *IF/ELSE* tile in place of the *true* parameter. Select **1 meter, expressions, snowBank**, from the menus that appear.

3. Select the **1 meter** parameter in the *penguin is at least [1 meter] away from [snowBank]* tile and change it to **10.5 meters**.

4. Drag a copy of the **penguin move toward** tile from the methods tab in the penguin's Details area and drop it in the new *IF/ELSE* tile in place of *Do Nothing*. Select **1 meter** and **snowBank** as the parameters for the *move toward* instruction. This instruction will make the penguin move back toward the center point of the torus.

5. Change the **amount = 1 meter** parameter in the new *penguin move toward* instruction tile to **.25 meters**.

6. Select **[more…]** on the *penguin move toward* instruction tile and set the **duration** to **0 seconds**. Save the world before continuing.

Your method should now look like Figure 10-16.

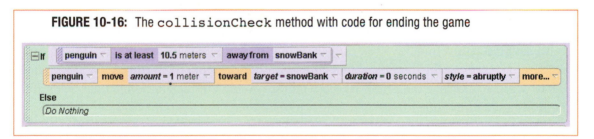

FIGURE 10-16: The collisionCheck method with code for ending the game

Next, you will add instructions to the collisionCheck method to detect and react when the penguin reaches the flagpole. When this happens, the victory message should appear.

To add instructions to react when the penguin reaches the flagpole:

1. Drag an **IF/Else** tile from the bottom of the Editor area and drop it into the bottom of the *collisionCheck* method tile. Select **true** as the condition.

2. Select the **penguin** tile in the Object tree and the **functions** tab in the penguin's Details area. Drag a copy of the **penguin distance to** tile from the functions tab and drop it in the *IF/ELSE* tile in place of the *true* parameter. Select **1 meter, expressions, flagpole** from the menus that appear.

3. Select the **victory** tile in the Object tree and the properties tab in victory's Details area.

4. Drag the opacity tile from the properties tab and drop it into the new IF/ELSE tile in the `collisionCheck` method in place of *Do Nothing*. Select **1 (100%: fully opaque)** from the menu that appears.

5. Click **[more...]** on the *[victory] set opacity to 1 (100%)* instruction tile and set the duration to **2 seconds**.

6. Figure 10-17 shows what the code you just added should look like. Save the world before continuing, and then play the game to see what happens when the penguin reaches the flagpole.

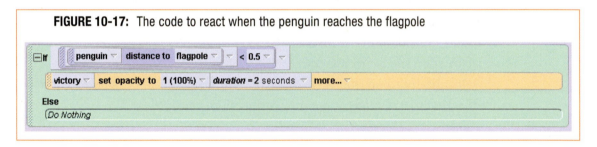

FIGURE 10-17: The code to react when the penguin reaches the flagpole

The last thing you need to do is to add timekeeping to the world. Alice has a world-level function to capture the *time elapsed*, which is the time since the Alice software was most recently started. Unfortunately, this value does not reset when someone plays a world, but instead keeps track of the total time since the world was last opened. You will add instructions to capture and save the *time elapsed* when the world starts, and then subtract the start time from the ending time to see how long it took to reach the flagpole. You will add an instruction to display this time when the victory message appears. Two numeric variables, *time* and *startTime,* have already been added to the world to use for timekeeping. You will add an event to capture the *startTime* when the world starts playing, and then add instructions to the `collisionCheck` method to calculate and display the *time* when the penguin reaches the flagpole.

To add an event to capture the starting time:

1. Click the **create new event** button in the Events area.

2. Select **When the world starts** from the menu that appears.

3. Drag the **startTime** tile from the properties tab in the world's Details area and drop it in the new event in place of *Do Nothing*. Select **1** as the value from the menu that appears.

4. Find the **time elapsed** tile on the functions tab in the world's Details area. Drag and drop a copy of it into the *[World.startTime] set value to [1]* tile in place of the value 1, so that the instruction looks as shown in Figure 10-18.

FIGURE 10-18: An event to capture a world's starting time

To add instructions to calculate and print the ending time:

1. Drag the **Time** tile from the properties tab in the world's Details area and drop it in the `collisionCheck` method in the *If [penguin] distance to flagpole < 0.5* tile above the *victory set opacity to 1(100%)* instruction tile. Select **1** as the value from the menu that appears.

2. Drag the **time elapsed** tile on the functions tab in the world's Details area. Drag and drop a copy of it into the *World.time set value to [1]* tile in place of the value 1.

3. Click the down arrow next to the **time elapsed** parameter in the *World.time set value to [elapsed time]* instruction tile and select **math**, **[time elapsed –]**, **expressions**, and **World.startTime** from the menus that appear, as shown in Figure 10-19.

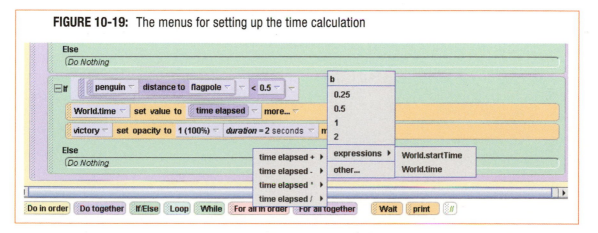

FIGURE 10-19: The menus for setting up the time calculation

4. Drag a **print** tile from the bottom of the Editor area and drop it in the *If [penguin] distance to flagpole < 0.5* tile as the last instruction in the tile, just above *Else*. Select **object**, **expressions**, and **World.time** from the menus that appear.

5. Congratulations, *Don't Splash the Penguin!* is now complete. Save the world, and then see how quickly you can get the penguin to the flagpole.

TUTORIAL 10C—VIDEO GAME BALLISTICS

In this tutorial, you will examine a ballistics routine from a physics engine for Alice, similar to that found in other physics engines. Ballistics is the science of projectiles, which are objects flying through the air after they have been thrown or launched by some force. Projectiles include balls in a sporting event, such as baseballs, basketballs, or footballs, bullets, arrows, darts, horseshoes, or any object that is flying through the air without some power of its own. A rocket becomes a projectile once its engine runs out of fuel. Projectiles are an important part of many video games. A person jumping freely through the air is, in terms of physics, a projectile.

You will examine an Alice world in which an athlete (the jock character from the Alice galleries) throws a ball at a target object, shown in Figure 10-20.

FIGURE 10-20: An Alice world with an athlete throwing a ball

The path that the ball takes is a curve called a parabola. The shape of the parabola is affected by the force of gravity, air resistance, the angle at which the ball is thrown, and the ball's initial velocity. Simulations need to match the real world as closely as possible, but video games don't need to match the real world exactly, as long as they are real enough for game play. In this case, we will ignore the air resistance because it complicates the math for the problem and because a game can still appear realistic without it. Figure 10-21 shows what the path of the ball would look like if the athlete threw the ball at an angle of 45 degrees with an initial velocity of 8 meters per second.

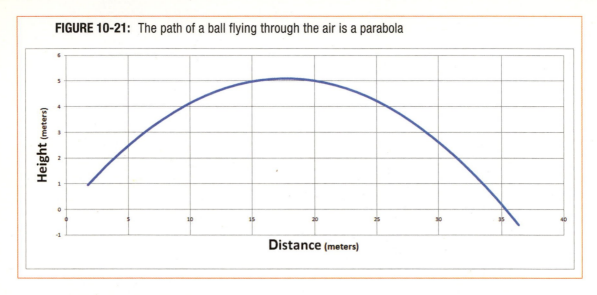

FIGURE 10-21: The path of a ball flying through the air is a parabola

Once the ball leaves the athlete's hand, it moves forward and up, with the forward velocity and upward velocity determined by how hard the ball was thrown and at what angle. The ball's forward velocity doesn't change if we leave out air resistance, but its upward velocity is slowed down by gravity, until finally the force of gravity pulls it downward and it hits the ground. For every second the ball is in the air, the force of gravity will first slow down the ball's upward velocity by 9.8 meters per second, and then after it starts coming down will increase its downward velocity by 9.8 meters per second. The equations shown in Figure 10-22 show how to use this information to figure out the position of the ball at any time after it was thrown.

FIGURE 10-22: Equations for both the x and y positions of a ball in flight

$$X = V_{0x}\, t$$

$$Y = V_{0y}\, t - \frac{1}{2} g\, t^2$$

V_{0x} and V_{0y} are the initial velocity in the x and y directions

t is the time since the ball was thrown

g is the downward acceleration due to the force of gravity

In the Alice ballistics routine, a loop is set up to figure out the position at each 1/100 of a second after the ball is thrown, and then, using that data, to move the ball from its old location to the new location. The Alice method to do all of this is shown in Figure 10-23.

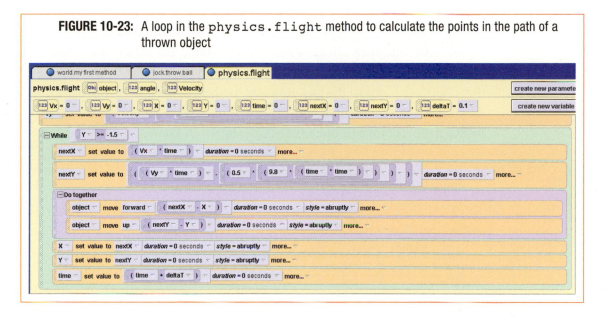

FIGURE 10-23: A loop in the `physics.flight` method to calculate the points in the path of a thrown object

Obviously, to write the method you would need to know the math and physics for all of this, which most people don't. That's why we need physics engines created by people with advanced math and physics skills. When the ball hits the ground, it might bounce, it might break open, or it might just stick in the soft earth. What actually happens depends on many factors that are, like air resistance, too complicated for us to consider in this example, so we will assume that the ball stops where it lands. In fact, the math for a complete and accurate physics engine requires knowledge of matrix algebra, trigonometry, calculus, and differential equations. You've heard the expression, "It isn't rocket science"? Well, without a physics engine, the knowledge of math and physics needed to create a realistic video game, even for simple things like a person throwing a ball, is, literally, rocket science.

In the remainder of this tutorial, you will load and play the Alice world with the ballistics routine discussed above, and then you will change the world so that user can input the angle and velocity with which the ball was thrown.

To explore the world:

1. Open the Alice world **Ball.a2w** that is included in the student data files for this chapter. Notice that `world.my first method` contains two events which are disabled. You will work with these later.

2. Notice that `world.my first` method also contains an instruction to run the method `jock.throw ball`. Play the world to see what this method does. Try it a few times and watch the path of the ball as it flies through the air.

3. Click the **jock** tile in the Object tree, and then the **methods** tab in the jock's Details area, and then click the **edit** button next to the *throwBall* method tile to see the code for this method in the Editor area. Most of the instructions here are to make the jock move as he throws the ball. If you scroll down through the method, you will find the *physics.flight* instruction that makes the ball move through the air, as shown in Figure 10-24.

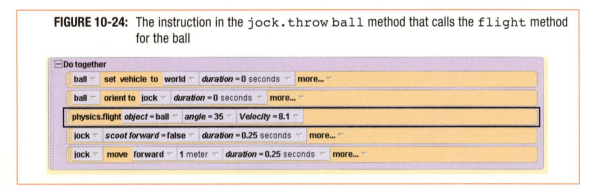

FIGURE 10-24: The instruction in the `jock.throw ball` method that calls the `flight` method for the ball

4. Click the **Physics** tile in the Object tree and then the **edit** button next to the flight method. This is the ballistics method discussed earlier in this chapter. Notice that it has three input parameters—*object,* which is the object being thrown, *angle,* and *velocity.* The *angle* and *velocity* are the initial angle and velocity with which the object is thrown.

You are going to modify the `jock.throw ball` method to make the initial velocity and angle input parameters for the method. You will then activate the input instructions in `world.my first method` to let the user input the initial velocity and angle.

To make the initial velocity and angle input parameters for the method:

1. Save the world as **throw ball with user input** before continuing.

2. Click the tab for the `jock.throw ball` method in the Editor area.

3. Click the **create new parameter** button in the method to create a new parameter. Name the parameter **throwAngle** and make sure it is a Number parameter, and then click **OK**. The new parameter will appear at the top of the method.

4. Click the **create new parameter** button again. Name this parameter **throwVelocity,** make sure it is a Number parameter, and then click **OK**. This parameter will also appear at the top of the method, as shown in Figure 10-25.

FIGURE 10-25: The two new input parameters in the `jock.throw ball` method

5. Scroll down in the method and find the *physics.flight* instruction. Click the **angle = 35** parameter in the instruction tile, and, using the menus that appear, change it by selecting **expressions** and **throwAngle.**

6. In a similar manner, click the **velocity = 8.1** parameter and change it by selecting **expressions** and **throwVelocity** from the menus that appear.

7. Save the world before continuing.

Now you will activate the input instructions in `World.my first method` and use their values for method parameters.

To modify `World.my first method` for user input:

1. Click the tab for `World.my first` method in the Editor area.

2. Right-click the first instruction tile, and select **enable** from the menu that appears.

3. Right-click the second instruction tile, and select **enable** from the menu that appears.

4. Click the **throwAngle = 1** parameter in the last instruction tile, and, using the menus that appear, change it by selecting **expressions** and **angle.**

5. Click the **throwVelocity = 1** parameter in the last instruction tile, and, using the menus that appear, change it by selecting **expressions** and **velocity.**

6. Save the world before continuing.

The new world is now complete. When you play the world, it will ask for the angle and velocity of the throw. The values that the user inputs are saved as *angle* and *velocity*, and are then passed to the `jock.throw ball` method, which in turn passes them on to the `physics.flight` method. Try it a few times and see what happens with different values. The pin will fall if the ball hits it. There are many different combinations of angles and velocities that will work, but one of them is an angle of *35* degrees and a velocity of *8.1* meters per second.

We have not examined all of the math in the `physics.flight` method. If you are familiar with the physics it uses, then you should be able to see what's happening in the method. If you are not familiar with the physics, then there is no need to examine the method.

There are two kinds of game programmers who deal with physics engines like this ballistics routine—those who use physics engines and those who program them. Someone needs to create physics engines, but, just as with graphics and other aspects of programming, most people use software created by specialists. However, all good programmers need to understand some math to be able to use physics engines and similar software. So, if you want to program video games, you should study some math, computer graphics, and software engineering, no matter what area of video game programming you choose as your specialty.

Chapter Summary

This chapter included brief discussions of different genres of video games, video game development careers, and some common video game programming features. It included two tutorials—one about collision detection and another about ballistics.

The discussions in the chapter included:

- ☐ A video game is a game that is played on a video screen controlled electronically using computer software. It is an interactive combination of hardware and software that allows the user to play a game against another person or against a computer.

- ☐ The great variety of video games fit into several different genres. The most popular include adventure games, casino games, board games, shooter games, platform games, maze games, role-playing games, driving and racing games, sports games, puzzles, simulations, and music and dance games.

- ☐ Many of the most popular games are not limited to a similar genre, but are a combination of two or more.

- ☐ A Massive Multiplayer Online Role-Playing Game (MMORPG) is played online with hundreds or thousands of people, each playing the role of a character at the same time over the Internet in a virtual environment.

- ☐ Most commercially successful video games are developed by teams of professionals with specialized skills working in large development projects.

- ☐ Primary jobs in the video game industry include game design, game development project management, script writing, graphics arts, music and sound engineering, programming, and quality assurance. Secondary support is provided by business managers, office staff, and technical professionals, including computer and network support personnel.

- ☐ A game designer is a person who takes a concept or idea for a game and develops it into a plan for the overall play of a game, including the game's general theme, setting or environment, objectives, rules of play, structure, and so on. Often a team of designers works together, with one senior person serving as the lead designer who coordinates the work of other designers and associated skilled professionals, such as graphic artists.

- ☐ The person in charge of a game development project is not a designer, but a game's producer, whose role is similar to that of a movie producer or a general contractor for a construction project.

- ☐ Writers are responsible for developing a script for a game, much like a script for a movie, and work with game designers and graphic artists to create storylines and characters for a game.

- ☐ Graphic artists with special skills, often called *game artists*, create the artwork for a video game. Many artists specialize in specific game elements. A graphic artist with exceptional artistic and management skill will often serve as a game development project's art director.

- ☐ Composers, musicians, voice-over artists, and sound engineers all play a role in the development of the sound for modern video games.

❑ A video game development project is a software development project requiring people with software engineering and programming skills. A lead programmer with good management skills will supervise many people with specialized programming skills working on different aspects of game programming.

❑ Human-Computer Interaction (HCI) programmers develop a game's user interface.

❑ Artificial Intelligence (AI) programmers develop the logic in a game, especially for strategy games in which a user may play against the computer.

❑ Graphics programmers work with graphic artists to create new graphical elements for games and to implement the graphics created by the artists.

❑ Physics programmers implement software that simulates the movement of objects in the real world, which are affected by things like gravity and the collision of one object with another.

❑ Data communications programmers create and maintain the software used for networked versions of video games.

❑ Video game software includes features that must be built by programmers or imported into a video game from somewhere else, including a user interface, scorekeeping, artificial intelligence, graphics, sound, and a physics engine.

❑ An Application Programmer Interface (API) is software that provides expanded capabilities for computer programmers.

❑ A graphics engine is a set of encapsulated software components that perform the necessary math and render objects for video games, simulations, and other software.

❑ Physics engines have objects and methods to address the physics of moving objects, including the effects of gravity, friction, objects bumping into one another, wind resistance, and fluid dynamics, so that objects in a video game will act like objects in the real world.

In Tutorial 10A, you added scorekeeping to the *Where's Alice?* game.

In Tutorial 10B, you created the *Don't Splash the Penguin!* video game with collision detection.

In Tutorial 10C, you examined an Alice world that uses a ballistics routine from a physics engine to make an athlete throw a ball like he would in the real world.

Review Questions

1.   Define each of the following:

❑ AI	❑ collision detection	❑ HCI
❑ API	❑ game engine	❑ MMORPG
❑ ballistics	❑ graphics engine	❑ physics engine
		❑ video game

2.	List and describe several common genres of video games.

3.	List five different jobs in the video game industry other than programming, and describe some of the responsibilities of each of the jobs. Using the Internet as a research tool, include in your answer the typical salaries and the type of education or training needed for each job.

4.	Describe four specialized kinds of programming needed in the video game industry.

5.	Create a table that has rows for eight different genres of video games and columns for five common video game programming features. Fill in the table with the value—*high*, *medium*, and *low*—indicating how important specific programming features are for each type of game.

6.	What is the difference between an API and a game engine?

7.	Why is a physics engine or equivalent software needed to develop many video games?

8.	Imagine that you are building an action-adventure video game with a character who could grow weaker or stronger. Describe how scorekeeping works in video games and how this is similar to scorekeeping.

9.	Describe what is meant by collision detection and how it generally works in a modern video game.

10.	What areas of mathematics does someone need to study to create the software for a physics engine?

Exercises

1.	Working alone or with other students, design a video game that has shopping in a supermarket as its major theme. This should be a general design for a game not necessarily based on Alice. You will design the game, but you will not build it. What genre will your game be? What are its objectives, rules of play, structure, and so on? What does the user interface look like? How will scorekeeping work? What other programming features are needed for the game?

2.	Create a development plan for the game you described in Exercise 1. What specialists are needed to create your game? What work will each of them need to do? How will your development team be organized?

The Alice world *penguin splash* included with the student data files for this chapter has the result of Tutorial 10A. It will be used for Exercises 3 through 6.

3.	Add sound to the *penguin splash* world. You could use events to initiate sound when the penguin hits the snowbank, falls into a hole, or reaches the flag.

4.	Using *Don't Splash the Penguin!* as the title, add an opening title in 3D to the *penguin splash* world, or create an opening billboard and add it to the world. The billboard could also include simple instructions for playing *Don't Splash the Penguin!*

5.	Add another character, perhaps a second penguin, to *penguin splash*, positioned near the flagpole. When the penguin reaches the flagpole, have this character tell the user how long it has been since the game started.

6. The Alice world *throw ball with user input* included with the student data files for this chapter has the result of Tutorial 10B. Add two characters. The data files *coach.a2w* and *cheerleader.a2w*, also included with the student data files for this chapter, have characters with methods for different behaviors that can be imported into an Alice world. Add the coach and the cheerleader to the *throw ball with user input* world. Position the coach a few feet behind the pin, in line with the pin and the athlete. Have the coach and cheerleader react when the ball hits the pin. Have the coach react if he is hit by the ball.

7. Using the techniques for collision detection found in the *Don't Splash the Penguin!* tutorial, create a *Don't Splash the Bunny!* world. Your world should start with a water template, using green circles as islands. The circles can be found in the Shapes folder in the Alice object gallery. Create a game that allows the user to move the bunny around on an island and then jump from one island to another. You will need to create a jump method and a triggering event. Pick an object to be the bunny's target, and create a game that requires the user to get the bunny to the target as quickly as possible.

8. The game *23 matches* is a simple game that could be turned into a video game. The game starts with 23 matches laid down on the ground or on a table. Players take turns picking 1, 2, or 3 matches. The player who picks up the last match wins the game. Create a version of this game using Alice. The user can play against the computer, or one person can play against another. Remember the six Ps of programming—*Proper Prior Planning Prevents Poor Programming.* Take the time to design your world before you build it.

9. Tic-tac-toe is a simple game that almost everyone knows how to play. An artificial intelligence engine for tic-tac-toe played against the computer would have to have the logic for the game in a series of *IF/ELSE* instructions telling the computer what moves to make. See if you can figure out or find a set of rules for how to win the game, and then write them as a series of *IF/ELSE* instructions. First, however, you will need to decide on a numbering scheme for the squares on the board.

10. An object can be saved in one Alice world and used in another. Save the physics object with the ballistics `flight` method from Tutorial 10B and then develop another simple Alice world that uses it. You don't need to know anything about the internal math of the method to use it, but you do need to know that it takes an initial angle and initial velocity as its parameters. You should keep your world simple; do not try to make a character look like it is throwing something, like the athlete in Tutorial 10B does, because that could take a lot of time to implement. The Alice local object gallery has a cannon that you could use. You might create a loop or event to keep something moving, and try to hit it with an object fired from the cannon.

Appendix A

Acquiring and Installing the Alice Software

In this appendix, you will learn the basics of acquiring and installing Alice.

Acquiring the Alice Software

Alice is available at no cost from Carnegie Mellon University. The software may be downloaded from the links found at *www.alice.org*.

At the time this book was published, versions of Alice 2.2 were available for IBM PC compatible computers running the Windows operating system and Apple MacIntosh computers running OSX.

System requirements for the PC version of Alice 2.2 are as follows:

- Windows 2000, Windows XP, Windows Vista, or Windows 7
- An Intel Pentium II or equivalent processor
- A VGA graphics card capable of 16-bit color and video resolution of 1024 × 768 pixels (A 3D video card is recommended.)
- 512MB of RAM (1GB recommended)
- A sound card to use Alice's sound features

System requirements for the Mac version of Alice are as follows:

- OSX 10.4 or higher
- A PowerPC or Intel processor
- 512MB of RAM (1GB recommended)
- A VGA graphics card capable of high (16-bit) color and 1024 × 768 resolution (A 3D video card is recommended.)
- A sound card to use Alice's sound features

Installing the Alice Software

Instructions for installing the Alice software on an Apple computer can be found at *www.alice.org*. To install the Alice software on a Windows system, simply unzip the software into the folder of your choice on your computer. A new folder named Alice will be created, containing two program icons named *Alice* and *SlowAndSteadyAlice* and a subfolder named *required*. You should not move or delete these three items, but you may copy the entire Alice folder from one place to another, such as onto a CD and then from the CD to another computer, and it will still work properly.

When the *Alice* program icon is clicked, the standard version of Alice will load and run on your computer. This is a hardware accelerated version of Alice that will use the circuitry in your computer's video card to render Alice on your computer screen.

The *SlowAndSteadyAlice* icon is for a special software rendering version of Alice that will run code through your machine's CPU to render Alice on the screen rather than trying to take advantage of the machine's video card. As the name implies, it is slower than the hardware accelerated version of Alice, but it is more reliable, especially on machines with older video cards. The developers of Alice recommend that you try the standard version of Alice first, and if it does not run well, then try the slow and steady version. The standard version of Alice should run well on almost any personal computer that is less than two years old.

The Alice software has been carefully designed so that it will not interfere with your system's registry, DLL files, or any other parts of your system software. However, to accomplish this, the Windows feature that allows you to run a program simply by clicking the icon for a saved file will not work for Alice worlds. You must run Alice first and then load saved worlds from inside Alice. You must also connect any storage devices that you want Alice to see, such as flash ROM drives, to your system before running Alice.

The Alice software was written with the assumption that it would be stored on a computer's C: disk drive. Instructions for changing this, such as for using Alice in a networked environment, can be found on the Alice download page at *www.Alice.org*.

One final tip: To make Alice easier to use, you can create a shortcut to either version of the Alice software and place the shortcut on your desktop. To do this, copy and paste the icon in the same Alice folder where the original resides, and then drag the new shortcut icon to your desktop. This is an easy way to keep the original Alice program in its folder so that it will run properly, while still being acessible from your desktop. The shortcut can also be placed on the taskbar at the bottom of your computer screen.

Appendix B

Although Alice does not contain a menu-driven set of commands like Microsoft Word, it is useful to be familiar with the features on the four Alice menus: File, Edit, Tools, and Help. The menus also show shortcut keys for various functions in Alice. This appendix contains a short summary of the options on the menus for Alice Version 2.2.

The File Menu

The File menu has the following submenus:

- **New World:** Starts a new Alice world. It will take you to the Templates tab of the Welcome to Alice! window, as described in Chapter 1.

- **Open World:** Opens an existing Alice world. It will take you to the Open a world tab of the Welcome to Alice! window, allowing you to navigate the system's directories, as described in Chapter 1.

- **Save World:** Saves the current Alice world. If used with a world that has not yet been saved, it will function like Save As; otherwise, it resaves the current world without further user interaction, as described in Chapter 1.

- **Save World As:** Saves the current Alice world with a new name or location. The Save World As window will appear, allowing you to select the location and enter the name of the file in which the world will be saved, as described in Chapter 1.

- **Export As a Web Page**: Exports the current Alice world as a folder with an HTML file, an a2w file, and an applet.jar file. A Save World for the Web window will open with options for the title of the Web page, the author's name, the size of the viewing window on the Web page, the location of the saved files, and whether or not to include code from the world on the page.

- **Export Video:** This option is discussed in Chapters 1 and 9.

- **Export Code for Printing**: Exports code from Alice methods and events to an HTML Web page for viewing or printing. A dialog box will appear allowing you to select which items to export and where to save the resulting HTML file, as described in Chapter 1.

- **Import:** Used to import external files into an Alice world. Most commonly, it is used to import objects saved from other worlds as a2c files. Right-clicking an object's tile in the Object tree will let you save an object, which can be imported into another world by using this option. Other files, including sound files and graphic image files, can also be imported, and they will show up as options on the appropriate menus.

- **Add 3D Text**: Creates 3D text objects in Alice, as described in Chapter 6.
- **Make Billboard**: Creates billboard objects from image files, as described in Chapter 6.

The Edit Menu

The only item on the Edit menu is Preferences, which will open a Preferences window with four tabs: General, Rendering, Screen Grab, and Seldom Used. A description of these tabs follows:

- **General**: Has options allowing you to change the number of worlds displayed on the Recent Worlds tab of the Open a World Window; choose whether to display Alice code in the Editor area as Alice style code, black-and-white Java style code (looks most like true Java programming), or color Java style code; set the default directory for opening and saving files; and choose the size of the font used to display code in the Editor area.

- **Rendering**: Has options for forcing software rendering that will cause Alice to run in the slow and steady mode, show the number of frames per second being rendered as an Alice world plays, numerically change the World window position and size, lock the window's aspect ratio, make sure the window is always visible, and select the rendering order for Alice so that it will try to render a world using either DirectX or Java3D rendering first.

- **Screen Grab**: Has options that affect the function of the Take Picture button on the playing world window, including which directory to use when saving an image, the base filename for the image file, how many digits to append to the base filename, whether to use the JPG or PNG image file format, and whether or not to show a dialog box when the *Take Picture* button is pressed while an Alice world is playing.

- **Seldom Used**: Has nine check boxes that affect different aspects of Alice and options to change the number of Clipboards available on the Alice interface, the number of minutes to wait before reminding a user that the current world has not been saved, and the number of backup copies of each world to maintain. The nine radio boxes allow you to turn features of Alice on or off, including showing the startup dialog box when Alice launches, showing warnings when browsing the Web Gallery, opening tabs that were previously open when a world loads, picking up tiles while dropping and dragging, using alpha blending in picked-up tiles, saving thumbnails with saved world files, showing world statistics on the bottom of the Alice interface, clearing text output each time a world is played, and enabling a special high-contrast video mode for use with projectors.

The Tools Menu

On the Tools menu, you will find the following submenus:

- **World Statistics**: Shows a variety of statistics about the current Alice world, such as the number of objects in a world, how much memory the texture maps in the world use, how many times a world has been run, how many times it's been saved, and the total amount of time the world has been open.

- **Text Output**: Shows a copy of the text log file for this world, including information about the version of Alice and the operating system in use, a record indicating each time the world was started or stopped, any messages that appeared in the print zone, and any error messages that were generated. The text in the window can be copied to the system's Clipboard and then pasted in Microsoft Word or other programs with an option to paste text from the Clipboard.

- **Error Console**: Functions the same as the Text Output option.

The Help Menu

On the Help menu, you will find the following submenus:

- **Example Worlds**: Opens the Examples tab on the Welcome to Alice! window.

- **Tutorial**: Opens the Tutorial tab on the Welcome to Alice! window.

- **About Alice**: Opens a window showing the version number of the Alice software being used, along with a reference to the Alice Web site.

Appendix C

Computer Programming Languages

Almost all modern high-speed digital electronic computers are based on the binary numbering system. At the heart of the computer, inside the central processing unit (CPU), there are one or more arithmetic logic units (ALUs) that process information by performing binary arithmetic. Everything associated with modern computers—audio, video, word processing, Internet access, and so on—is processed with binary arithmetic inside the CPU by these relatively simple electronic circuits. All data to be handled by the computer and all of its instructions must be processed in the CPU as streams of binary numbers.

The set of binary digits, or bits, that the CPU understands as an instruction set is called the computer's machine code. Eventually, everything that a computer does must be translated into its machine code. Each CPU, or each family of CPUs, such as the Intel Pentium family, has its own machine code. There are as many machine codes as there are families of processing units.

When a new processor is invented and manufactured, it only understands its machine code. Systems programmers work with these binary codes to create a new language called assembly language. They do this by using machine code to build an assembler, which is a program that translates assembly language into machine code. Assembly languages are made up of very primitive instructions, just like machine code, but they can be written using the following: numbers other than base two; mnemonics, or short words that sound like the instructions they represent, such as ADD for addition or SUB for subtraction; and symbolic names instead of numbers to refer to memory locations.

Writing sophisticated software, such as word processors and video games, is still rather difficult and very time-consuming in assembly language, so computer scientists and software engineers build translators that can handle high-level languages, which are closer to human languages. They are easier for people to understand, but harder to translate into a computer's machine code. Java, JavaScript, VB.net, C, C++, and Python are all examples of modern high-level computer programming languages. COBOL, FORTAN, BASIC, and Pascal are all examples of once-popular high-level languages that are now seldom used.

The translators that convert high-level languages into machine code fall into two categories: compilers and interpreters. Using a compiler, a programmer ends up with two stored copies of the program. The first, in the original high-level programming language, is called the source code. The second stored copy of the program, which is the same program after translation into a particular machine code, is called the object code. Even after translation into machine code, a program may still need to be processed so that it will run on a particular computer with a particular operating system. A program that has been translated into machine code and prepared to run on a particular system is called executable code or an executable file.

An interpreter is much simpler than a compiler. Rather than translating an entire source code program into object code all at once, the compiler translates each instruction one at a time and then immediately feeds it to the CPU to be processed before translating the next instruction. The only stored copy of the program is the original source code program. Scripting languages, such as JavaScript or Visual BASIC for Applications (VBA), often work this way. Scripting languages are simplified high-level programming languages that allow someone to program in a particular environment. JavaScript can be added to the HTML code for Web pages to provide them with some primitive data-processing capability. VBA allows someone to program features in Microsoft Office products, such as Microsoft Word or PowerPoint.

Interpreters are often used for teaching languages. Serious computer programming languages, such as Java and C++, that are used by professional programmers, are sometimes referred to as production languages. Teaching languages are languages that are not generally used in production environments but are instead used to teach someone the logic of computer programming or the processes used in creating computer software before attempting to teach them to use production languages. Alice is an example of a teaching language. Its primary purpose is to be used as a tool to introduce people to computer programming.

One of the first high-level languages in existence was the FORTRAN language, created in the 1950s by the U.S. Government in cooperation with IBM, which, at the time, was by far the world's largest computer company. FORTRAN was intended to be used by scientists and engineers working on large, primitive mainframe computers of the day—about 20 years before the first personal computers appeared—to program mathematical formulas and processes. In fact, the name FORTRAN comes from the two words "formula translator."

Before FORTRAN, all software had to be created using assembly language and machine code. Once FORTRAN appeared, people began to use it for much more than science and engineering. The increasing use of FORTRAN in the business world led to the development of the COBOL language in 1960. Like the name FORTRAN, COBOL is an acronym that comes from the words "common business-oriented language." It was based on work by Grace Hopper, who rose to become an admiral in the United States Navy before she retired more than 30 years later. It is estimated that as of the year 2000 there were more lines of code written in COBOL than in any other computer programming language. However, during the last five years, the use of COBOL has declined rapidly as other programming languages and applications software, such as electronic spreadsheets, have become more common.

Over the years, many high-level programming languages have evolved, each with different features that have changed the way people create and use computer software. Algol, BASIC (Beginner's All-purpose Instruction Code), Pascal, Smalltalk, ML, LISP, Prolog, and C are some of the most well known of these. Today, Java, C++, and VB.NET are probably the most important languages for professional programmers to know. New languages continue to emerge, such as the Python and Haskel languages that first appeared in the 1990s. The Association for Computing Machinery's Hello World! page, on the Web at *www2.latech.edu/~acm/HelloWorld.html*, has sample Hello World! programs in almost 200 different programming languages.

Glossary

absolute direction—A direction in relation to a scale of measurement.

act—A dramatic component of a story. The most common arrangement for a screenplay is a three-act structure. Acts are a collection of smaller units called scenes. In movies, scenes are composed of individual shots.

algorithm—A step-by-step process.

American Standard Code for Information Interchange (ASCII)—An 8-bit code used to represent characters in a computer. It includes letters, numeric digits, and some "hidden" control characters, such as the enter key and the escape key. Each character is given a numeric value, and the binary equivalents of those numeric values are used to store characters in the computer.

AND—A binary Boolean operation. Boolean means that it uses only true and false values, and binary means that it needs two operands. When two values are combined using the AND operation, the result is true only if both values are true. Otherwise, the result is false.

Application Program Interface (API)—Software that provides expanded capabilities for computer programmers. In Java, for example, the Abstract Windowing Toolkit (AWT) and Swing are two APIs that provide programmers with the ability to create their own GUIs for Java programs.

array—A set of indexed variables, each containing objects of the same data type. An array can be thought of as a set of numbered boxes each containing a value of a particular data type.

Array Visualization Object—A special object in Alice used to show an array in an Alice world, rather than just creating it in the memory of the computer. The name of the object in Alice is ArrayVisualization.

Artificial Intelligence (AI)—A branch of computer science devoted to developing software that can mimic human intelligence in a computer, especially human perception and decision making.

aspect ratio—The ratio of an image's width to its height. Aspect ratios in Alice include 4/3 (1.33), 1.85, and 2.35. The 4/3 ratio is the standard television ratio, while the other two are wider cinema formats. Newer HD televisions have a 16/9 ratio.

ballistics—The science of determining the paths of projectiles, which are objects flying through the air after they have been thrown or launched by some force. Projectiles include balls in a sporting event, bullets, arrows, darts, horseshoes, or any object that is flying through the air without some power of its own.

base case—The condition that stops a recursive algorithm from continuing, also called the base condition.

base condition—The condition that stops a recursive algorithm from continuing, also called the base case.

BDE event format—An event format in which the event's tile has places for three different event handlers. BDE stands for "Begins, During, and End." You can tell the world what methods to run when the event begins, during the time that the event is occurring, and when the event ends.

billboard—A picture file placed into an Alice world as a flat two-dimensional object with length and width, but no depth. Once placed in an Alice world, the image from the picture file will be seen on both the front and back of the billboard. Billboards are objects that can be manipulated with primitive methods, like move, turn, and roll, as well as with user-created methods.

binary branching—A branching routine in an algorithm in which the path or flow of the algorithm's sequential logic splits into exactly two possible paths.

binary bypass—A binary branching routine in which an instruction or set of instructions is either executed or bypassed.

binary choice—A binary branching routine in which one of two instructions (or one of two sets of instructions), but not both, is executed.

binary tree—A data structure in which each node on the tree holds an item of data along with a left pointer and a right pointer. The pointers are lined up so that the structure forms an upside down tree, with a single node at the top, called the root node, and branches increasing on the left and right as you go down the tree.

Boolean algebra—A formal language for a system of Boolean logic dealing with true and false values.

Boolean function—A function that returns a true or false value instead of a numeric value.

Boolean logic—A system of logic dealing with true and false values. It was first described by George Boole in 1854. The conditions that exist in branching and looping routines are a form of Boolean logic, which is the basis for all modern digital electronic technology.

branch—A path or flow of sequential logic in an algorithm.

branching routine—A set of instructions in an algorithm in which the path or flow of sequential logic splits into two or more paths. Branching routines are also known as selection sequences or selection structures.

breakpoint—A spot in a computer program just before or just after some action occurs. Breakpoints are often used in debugging.

CamelCase—The practice of writing compound names without using blank spaces, but capitalizing the first letter of each name that forms the compound name, like the name CamelCase itself. The very first letter in a CamelCase name may or may not be capitalized, such as CheshireCat or cheshireCat. CamelCase is used with most programming languages and is recommended by many software developers, such as Microsoft.

Cartesian coordinates—A system of quantification for two dimensions developed by the French mathematician Rene Descartes. Cartesian coordinates have an X-axis, and a Y-axis. The location of each point is referred to by an ordered pair of the form (x, y), in which x represents the point's location along the X-axis and y represents its location along the Y-axis.

CGI—Computer generated imagery, which includes both still images and movie frames generated by a computer. Alice is completely CGI.

class—A group of objects with the same properties and the same methods.

collate—To put a set of items in order according to a particular criteria.

collating sequence—A list that shows the correct order to be used when collating a set of items. The English language alphabet is commonly used as a collating sequence. The ASCII code and Unicode are often used as collating sequences in computers.

collision detection—The act of detecting when objects in a virtual world collide with one another. Often this is done by detecting when the parts that make up an object overlap or occupy the same space or are about to do so.

comedy sketch—The visual equivalent of telling or acting out a joke, like a skit that Boy Scouts or Girl Scouts might act out around a campfire.

command driven interface—A user interface through which people control a computer by typing in commands. Most modern software, such as word processing, electronic spreadsheets, Internet browsers, and computer games, use graphical user interfaces (GUIs), but older computers had only command-driven interfaces, in which it was often necessary to write or run a computer program in order to complete tasks that involved more than a few steps.

commercial advertisement—Any message that attempts to convince someone about the merits of a particular product or service, or to expose them to something in a positive and memorable way.

computer program—A step-by-step set of instructions telling a computer how to perform a specific task. Every computer program is an algorithm.

computer programming language—A particular set of instructions for programming a computer, along with the grammar and syntax for using those instructions.

concurrency—The process of running multiple threads of an algorithm at the same time. A thread is part of an algorithm that may be executed at the same time as other parts of an algorithm, or at the same time as another copy of itself. Algorithms that allow concurrency are known as parallel algorithms.

conditional recursion—Recursion that is not infinite.

control variable—A variable whose value controls whether or not a particular path in a selection sequence or in a repetition sequence will be executed.

counter—The control variable for a count-controlled loop. A counter needs to have an initial value, a final value, and an increment.

count-controlled loop—An element of logical structure in an algorithm in which a process is repeated a specific number of times.

data structure—A scheme for organizing data in the memory of a computer.

dialog balloon—A box with rounded corners that shows words that are supposed to have been spoken by an object, much like text appears in cartoons in a newspaper or magazine. Text created by the say method appears in a dialog balloon.

dimension—A value on a continuous scale applied to some property in a process called quantification. A dimension is a way of measuring something.

documentary—An expository movie that teaches a lesson or presents an opinion, much like an essay, with a thesis, points of evidence, and a conclusion.

dummy object—An invisible object, also called a dummy, that occupies a single point in an Alice world. Alice has commands to drop a dummy where a camera is, and to drop a dummy where an object is. Dummy objects have both a location and a point of view and can be used to mark key spots and program the camera or other objects to move to those spots as needed.

encapsulation—The concealment of the details of a method (or an object) from the user. Programmers may use an encapsulated method, but cannot see its inner workings. Alice primitive methods, such as move and turn, are examples of encapsulated methods.

Euclidean 3-space—A space measured in three dimensions by an X-axis, a Y-axis and a Z-axis that are each straight lines perpendicular to one another. The physical world around us can be thought of as a Euclidean 3-space.

event—An event trigger, and the name of a method, called an event handler. Whenever the event trigger occurs, the event handler is called into action.

event handler—A method that is activated when an event trigger occurs.

event listener—A combination of hardware and software that repeatedly checks the computer system for the event trigger.

event trigger—Any activity or condition selected by the programmer to initiate an event, such as someone pressing the enter key, or a bank account balance going below zero. When an event listener detects an event trigger, an event handler is called into action.

event-driven programming—The development of software that uses events to provide controls in computer systems. The use of a GUI on a modern personal computer requires event-driven programming.

exponential recursion—Recursion in which a method calls itself more than once in each pass through the recursive method. As a result, the number of copies of the world that are running grows exponentially.

fade—A transition that occurs when the viewer's image lightens or darkens to or from a solid color. For example, a script may contain the direction *slow fade to black* at the end of a scene, meaning that the image the viewer sees would slowly fade to black, as if someone were slowly turning down the lights on a scene. Fades can be to or from any color, but black is the most common, followed by white.

final value—The last value processed by a loop.

flowchart—A diagram showing the structure of an algorithm. Flowcharts are designed to show the possible paths through an algorithm.

font—A specification for a set of characters that includes typeface, size, style, and weight of the characters. Although the terms typeface and font are not synonymous, they are often used interchangeably. For example, Times New Roman is a typeface, whereas Times New Roman, 10 point, italics, bold is a complete specification for a font.

frame (n.)—Each still image in a movie.

frame (v.)—To position the camera so that a particular item fills the screen.

frame rate—The number of frames per second (fps) in a movie. The frame rate for films in a movie theatre is 24 fps, while the frame for broadcast television is roughly 30 fps. Anything slower than around 16 fps may look a bit choppy.

function—A method that returns a value, such as the distance between two objects.

game engine—A software tool that allows developers to assemble video games from existing objects and methods, much like the way a person can build an Alice world from existing objects and methods.

Graphical User Interface (GUI)—A user interface that has icons on the computer screen and a mouse to control a pointer that can be used to operate the computer by manipulating the icons. Most modern software, such as word processing, electronic spreadsheets, Internet browsers, and computer games, depends on the use of a GUI.

graphics engine—A set of encapsulated software components that perform the necessary math and render objects for video games, simulations, and other software. Graphics engines often provide a software tool kit which includes objects and functions that software developers can use to work with graphics in two-dimensional or three-dimensional environments, without doing all the math.

hardcode—To put a specific value in a program instead of a variable or parameter.

HSB—A color model for computer graphics in which the color of a pixel is expressed in terms of its hue, saturation, and brilliance.

Human Computer Interaction (HCI)—A specialized area of computing dealing with the development of user interface hardware and software.

IDE—*See* Integrated Development Environment

increment—The amount by which something is increased, such as the amount by which a counter in a loop in increased each time through the loop.

index value—A value, usually an integer, used to identify either an element in an array, or an iteration of a loop.

infinite recursion—Recursion that continues without ending on its own. It must be stopped by some external source, such as interrupting a program or turning off a computer.

initial value—The starting value for a counter in a loop.

instance—A copy of an object from a particular class.

instantiation—The act of adding an Instance of an object class to an Alice world.

Integrated Development Environment (IDE)—A computer program that is used to write other computer programs.

integration test—A test of a software method that checks to see if the method works when it is placed into a larger program in combination with other methods.

iterate a list—To go through the set of items in the list one at a time.

iteration—Each instance or occurrence of the body of instructions in a loop. The term iteration is also used to refer generally to looping as opposed to recursion.

iterative process—A process that uses a loop to repeat a set of instructions.

jump cut—A sudden transition from one shot to another. The last frame of one shot is followed immediately by the first frame of the following shot, without any transition effects. A jump cut, sometimes called simply a cut, is the most sudden and most commonly used transition from one shot to another.

linear recursion—Recursion in which a method calls itself only once each time through the method. Consequently, the number of copies of the method running grows linearly.

linear sequence—The simplest element of logical structure in an algorithm, in which one instruction follows another as if in a straight line. Linear sequences must have clearly stated entry and exit conditions, and they need to be complete, correct, and in the proper order.

list—An ordered set of data. In Alice, a list may be implemented as an object or as a variable.

logical comparison operators—Operators that compare two values according to either their numeric value or their value according to a collating sequence, depending on the data type of the values. They return a value of true or false.

loop—An element of logical structure in an algorithm in which the path of logic branches backward to a previous instruction, repeating part of the algorithm. A loop is also called a repetition sequence.

Massive Multiplayer Online Role-Playing Game (MMORPG)—A game played online with hundreds or thousands of people, each playing the role of a character in a virtual environment at the same time.

matrix—A matrix is an array, most commonly a two-dimensional array of numeric values.

method—A program that manipulates the properties of an object.

method header—The lines of text at the top of the method that provide information about how the method works, such as the full name of the method and the name and type of any parameters or variables used in the method.

method parameter—A piece of information that you must give to a method whenever you run the method.

module—A unit of software organization that is logically independent, performs a well-defined single task, and is compatible with other modules.

modular development—The process by which the parts, or modules, that make up a complete solution to a problem are developed individually and then combined to form that complete solution. Modular development is often used together with top-down design in which one concept or big idea, is broken down into several parts, and then those parts are further broken down. The end result is a collection of small solutions, called modules, which collectively contain the overall solution to the original problem.

movie—A flat two-dimensional picture that moves. When we view a movie we are watching a rapidly changing series of still images, each slightly different from the previous image. Instead of seeing many still images, we experience them as a moving picture.

multiple branching—The occurrence of a branching routine in an algorithm where the path or flow of the algorithm's sequential logic splits into more than two possible paths from a single point.

node—An organizational unit in a data structure, such as a graph or a tree, with a data element and one or more pointers to other nodes. In object-oriented programming, each node in a data structure is an object, and the data element is an object or a primitive data type.

NOT—A unary Boolean operation, Boolean means that it uses only true and false values, and unary means that it works on only one operand. It simply reverses the true or false value of its operand. In other words, NOT true yields false; NOT false yields true.

object—Something that can be represented by data in the computer's memory and manipulated by computer programs; a collection of properties and the methods used to manipulate those properties.

object-relative direction—A direction from the point of view of a particular object. It is determined by the object's position and orientation. In Alice's Euclidean 3-space, there are six major object-relative directions—forward, backward, left, right, up, and down.

object-relative position—The position of one object in relation to the position and orientation of another object. In Alice's Euclidean 3-space, there are six major object-relative positions—in front of, behind, to the left of, to the right of, above, and below.

off-camera—A term used to describe the location of an object in an Alice world that cannot be seen on the screen with the camera in its current position.

object-oriented programming (OOP)—A modern approach to computer programming focusing on objects as collections of properties and the methods that are used to manipulate those properties.

OR—A binary Boolean operation. Boolean means that it uses only true and false values, and binary means that it needs two operands. When two values are combined using the OR operation, if either value is true, then the result is true. Otherwise, the result is false.

ordered pair—Any pair of values of the form (x, y) in which one dimension is always listed first, and another dimension is always listed second.

orientation—The direction an object is facing. Location and orientation together are known as the point of view of an object.

overhead—The extra CPU time and space in a computer's memory needed to manage a method as it runs.

pan—To turn a camera left or right without moving the position of the camera, although it is possible that you could pan and move at the same time.

parallel algorithm—An algorithm in which multiple threads of sequential logic may be executed at the same time.

parameter—A variable whose value is passed from one method to another. Parameters have data types and they are stored in the memory of the computer, just like properties.

personification—The process of giving human qualities such as feelings, thoughts, speech, or human-like movements to inanimate objects.

physics engine—A set of software components addressing the physics of moving objects, including the effects of gravity, friction, objects bumping into one another, wind resistance and fluid dynamics that need to be addressed so that game and simulation objects will act like objects in the real world.

plot—A storyline or plan for the dramatic flow of the movie. It is tied to the visual flow of the movie—how the movie progresses from scene to scene.

point of view—A property marking an object's location and orientation. Each Alice object has a point of view property.

postproduction—The final phase of the moviemaking process. Postproduction includes all of the tasks that take place after a movie is recorded, such as editing, adding titles, and packaging the final product

posttest loop—A loop in which the test to determine whether or not to continue executing the loop comes after the body of instructions that are to be repeated. The body of instructions in a posttest loop must be executed at least once, since the test occurs after they are executed.

preproduction—The first phase of the moviemaking process. Preproduction is the planning and preparation that is necessary before production can begin. It includes developing ideas for the movie, writing the script, casting, scheduling production, and gathering all of the resources for production—including people, equipment, and facilities. It usually takes much longer than production.

pretest loop—A loop in which the test to determine whether or not to continue executing the loop comes before the body of instructions that are to be repeated. It is possible that the body of instructions in a pretest loop may not be executed, since the test occurs before they are to be executed.

primitive method—A built-in, predefined method that is part of each Alice object. Primitive methods provide simple basic behaviors, such as move, turn, and roll, and cannot be edited like user-defined methods can be.

production—The second phase of the moviemaking process. Production is the heart of the moviemaking process, the actual recording of the movie. In traditional filmmaking, it is when the cameras are rolling and action is captured on film. The production phase for an animated movie includes creating the animations and recording them.

property—Data that describes an object in some way.

proximity function—A function that returns a value based on the distance between two objects. A Boolean proximity function returns a true or false value. A numeric proximity function returns a numeric value.

pseudocode—A structured language used to describe algorithms. The term pseudocode comes from the fact that it looks something like the code in a computer programming language, but not quite.

quantification—The process of creating a dimension by assigning a value on a continuous scale to some property.

queue—A simple linear data structure with a beginning and end, called the front and back of the queue, in which data items enter the back of the queue and leave from the front of the queue in the same order in which they entered the queue. The front and back of the queue are also referred to as the queue's head and tail. A queue is a first in first out, or FIFO, data structure.

recursion—A design or pattern for part of something that repeats the structure of the whole thing itself. In computer programming, recursion occurs when an algorithm calls itself.

recursive method—A method that calls itself.

repetition sequence—An element of logical structure in an algorithm in which the path of logic branches backward to a previous instruction, repeating part of the algorithm. A repetition sequence is also called a loop.

reusable code—Software modules that are solutions to smaller problems and which can be applied elsewhere. Most of the software on a computer system is filled with layers of reusable code because computer programs contain many small tasks that need to be repeated, such as getting a user's name and password. Object-oriented programming and modular development encourage the use of reusable code.

RGB—A color model for computer graphics in which the color of a pixel is expressed in terms of its red, green, and blue light components.

root node—A node at the top of a tree, to which no pointers in the tree are directed.

scene—A part of a movie that takes place in a single location at a particular time. It is a collection of individual shots. A movie is a sequence of scenes, grouped into acts.

screenplay—The video equivalent of a play in a theatre. A screenplay unfolds over a series of scenes, and the plot determines the structure of the story. It could be fictional, or it could tell a true story. The word *screenplay* is also used to refer to the script for a screenplay.

script—A scene-by-scene description of a movie, with dialog and descriptions of the critical action. It is the primary design document for a movie.

selection sequence—An element of logical structure in an algorithm in which the path or flow of sequential logic splits into two or more paths.

sentinel loop—An element of logical structure in an algorithm in which a process is repeated until a condition or marker, called a sentinel, is encountered.

shot—A particular view of something from a specific camera, set up in a specific way. Each scene in a movie is a collection of shots.

shot list—A list of the shots needed for each scene in a movie, describing the kind of shot, the characters involved, roughly what happens in the shot, and the length of time the shot stays on the screen. Other details, such as lighting and special effects, could also be included.

side effect—An unintended result produced by running a method. Typically, side effects are caused by two events or methods that overlap each other.

slice-of-life vignette—A short movie showing an everyday event, such as a boy riding by on a bicycle, or a flock of geese flying overhead. Slice-of-life vignettes might tell a story, but they also might just be intended to show the subject in action, without really telling a story. They are often used to demonstrate that the moviemaker has mastered some new moviemaking techniques or technology.

software development cycle—An engineering process in which software developers (programmers and software engineers) design, code, test, and debug new software.

state of an object—The values stored in the properties of the object at any one time.

storyboard—A collection of rough sketches of particular shots showing both the visual flow of a movie from scene to scene and the progression of the movie's plot. They are called storyboards because the sketches for the shots in a single scene are usually pasted on a single large board so they can be viewed together. Storyboards can be an important tool in developing a movie.

structured language—Another term for pseudocode; structured programming languages are programming languages with built-in language for logical structures, like the WHILE command in Alice).

tessellation—A repeated pattern of an image on the surface of an object.

test for correctness—A test to determine whether or not a program performs correctly according to its original specifications. It is not concerned with the program's time or space efficiency, but simply its correctness.

testing shell—A short method created to simulate the environment in which a newly developed method will be run. This is especially important if the method being tested will be receiving values from other methods, or passing values on to other methods. The testing shell can be written to pass known values into the method being tested, and then the output can be captured and examined for correctness. A testing shell is also known as a testing hull.

text—The visual use of words (that is, the written language) in computer software.

thought bubble—A cloud-like box appearing in an Alice world showing words that are supposed to represent the thoughts of an object. Text created by the thought method appears in a thought bubble.

thread—A part of an algorithm that may be executed at the same time as other parts of an algorithm, or at the same time as another copy of itself.

tilt—To turn a camera up or down, similar to the way that you might turn your head up or down.

top-down design—A process in which a single concept or big idea representing a problem to be solved is broken down into smaller parts. If those parts can be further broken down, then the process continues. The end result is a collection of small solutions, called modules, which collectively contain the overall solution to the original problem. This process of decomposition is also known as a "divide and conquer" approach to problem solving.

typeface—A typeface is a design for a complete set of characters in a particular alphabet or character set. Although the term font is a more specific term than typeface, they are often used interchangeably. For example, Times New Roman is a typeface, whereas Times New Roman, 10 point, italics, bold is a complete specification for a font.

Unicode—A 16-bit code used to represent characters in a computer. It includes letters, numeric digits, and some "hidden" characters, such as the enter key and the escape key. Each character is given a numeric value, and the binary equivalents of those numeric values are used to store characters in a computer. It is beginning to replace ASCII, which is based on the English language. (ASCII is actually a subset of Unicode.)

unit test—A test of a single software method that checks to see if the method works as expected all by itself. Sometimes a testing shell is used in a unit test to provide the correct environment for testing a method, especially if the method has input or output parameters.

user-defined method—A method that is written by people who use Alice, and can be edited. A user-defined method is not encapsulated. Some of the objects in the Alice object galleries, such as the Penguin class of objects, have user-defined methods that were written by the people who created the object, in addition to the object's standard set of primitive methods.

variable—A memory location that temporarily stores a value while a method is running. Variables have names, data types, and values, just like properties do. However, properties are associated with an object, and their values are maintained as long as the object exists, whereas variables are associated with a particular method, and their values exist only inside the method.

vector—A one-dimensional array.

video game—A game played on a video screen, controlled electronically using computer software. It is an interactive combination of hardware and software that allows the user to play a game against another person or against a computer.

wipe—A transition that occurs when an image or another shot moves to cover the current shot like a curtain coming down. Wipes can occur from any direction. A curtain coming down would be a wipe from above.

zoom—To make objects appear larger or smaller in a camera's field of vision. Zooming in means the camera is moved in closer to get a tighter shot of something, so that it appears larger. Zooming out means the camera is moved out further to get a longer shot of something, so that it appears smaller. Most real cameras have a lens that will allow the photographer to zoom in and zoom out without moving the camera. In Alice, you zoom in and zoom out by actually moving the camera forward and backward.

Index

Please note that bolded numbers indicate where a key term is defined in the text.

N